Further praise for The Future of Investing

"The new regulatory framework is intended to facilitate significant change in the entire financial ecosystem of Europe."
—Steve Webb, Partner, Capco

"The implementation of MiFID raises significant issues for banks across Europe. There are few banks which are not buying or selling securities in some way or other and consequently all banks, whatever their precise business model, are likely to be affected by MiFID."
**—Michael McKee, Executive Director, British Bankers Association,
    Compliance Reporter Lobbyist of the Year for work on MiFID 2006**

"The Markets in Financial Instruments Directive has an impact on every firm that operates within the financial services industry, whether it is inside MiFID or whether superficially the Directive does not directly impact on that firm."
**—Angela Knight, Chief Executive Designate, British Bankers'
    Association (BBA)**

"MiFID represents a tough EU regulatory requirement which many banks and financial services firms have to deal with. Given the complexity of the regulation and the timeframe for implementation banks must allocate substantial numbers of skilled staff and significant monies around adoption of the rules.

This book provides an overall picture of both regulatory needs as well as drafting a picture of how the world of capital markets and investing might look like in the foreseeable future. A handsome guide for implementers and strategists inside financial services firms who want to understand the significance of that regulation in the emerging competitive landscape, where differentiation and a fine-tuned business model are key for survival."
—Michael Heinz, Banking Industry Expert, IBM

"Implementation of MiFID remains the major challenge for regulators and firms. In concert with the trade associations we have sought to raise industry awareness and to encourage firms to make early progress with their implementation plans. Through work in the Committee of European Securities Regulators, regulators across Europe, including the FSA, are well advanced in developing convergent application of key MiFID requirements. Against that background, I welcome the publication of this volume. It provides useful pointers to issues that firms should be considering in finalising their implementation plans in November 2007 and, on a broader canvas over a larger timescale, the contributions should be helpful input to the continuing debate about the longer-term opportunities and challenges that MiFID may bring."
**—Michael Folger, Director, Wholesale and Prudential Policy,
    Financial Services Authority**

The Future of Investing

The Future of Investing

In Europe's Markets after MiFID

Edited by

Chris Skinner

John Wiley & Sons, Ltd

Other Wiley Editorial Offices

John Wiley & Sons Inc., 111 River Street, Hoboken, NJ 07030, USA

Jossey-Bass, 989 Market Street, San Francisco, CA 94103-1741, USA

Wiley-VCH Verlag GmbH, Boschstr. 12, D-69469 Weinheim, Germany

John Wiley & Sons Australia Ltd, 42 McDougall Street, Milton, Queensland 4064, Australia

John Wiley & Sons (Asia) Pte Ltd, 2 Clementi Loop #02-01, Jin Xing Distripark, Singapore 129809

John Wiley & Sons Canada Ltd, 6045 Freemont Blvd, Mississauga, ONT, L5R 4J3, Canada

Wiley also publishes its books in a variety of electronic formats. Some content that appears in print may not be available in electronic books.

Anniversary Logo Design: Richard J. Pacifico

Library of Congress Cataloging in Publication Data

The future of investing : in Europe's markets after MiFID / edited by Chris Skinner.
     p.   cm. — (Wiley finance series)
   Includes bibliographical references and index.
   ISBN 978-0-470-51038-4 (cloth : alk. paper)
   1. Securities—European Union countries.   2. Investments—Law and legislation—European Union countries.   3. Banks and banking—Securities processing—European Union countries.
   I. Skinner, Chris.
   KJE2245.F88 2007
   346.24'092—dc22   2007013727

British Library Cataloguing in Publication Data

A catalogue record for this book is available from the British Library

ISBN 978-0-470-51038-4 (HB)

Typeset in 11/13pt Times by Integra Software Services Pvt. Ltd, Pondicherry, India
Printed and bound in Great Britain by TJ International Ltd, Padstow, Cornwall, UK
This book is printed on acid-free paper responsibly manufactured from sustainable forestry in which at least two trees are planted for each one used for paper production.

Contents

3 'Best Execution'   **31**
Anthony Kirby

About Chris Skinner

 Chris Skinner is the founder and Chief Executive of Balatro Ltd, an organisation dedicated to understanding the future of financial services. He is known for his regular columns in *Finextra* and *The Banker*, as well as other publications. He is Chairman of the Financial Services Club (www.fsclub.co.uk) and the Banker's Technology Awards, as well as being a Judge with the Asian Banker and Trade-Tech Awards programs. Chris has been a contributor to the World Economic Forum's scenarios for the future of financial services, and has worked closely with the financial markets research firm TowerGroup.

Chris Skinner is known as an exceptional speaker and is a regular keynote at the world's largest financial services conferences, including SWIFT's Sibos, the Bank Administration Institute (BAI) Conferences in the USA, IIR in Europe and the Middle East, and the Financial Times in Europe. Through these keynotes, he has shared the stage with leading world figures including Gary Hamel, Michael Eisner, Richard Branson, Lou Gerstner, Meg Whitman and Bill Gates.

Prior to founding Balatro, Chris was Vice President of Marketing and Strategy for Unisys Global Financial Services and Strategy Director with NCR Financial Services. These roles sparked Chris's specialization in the future of financial services after he created the Global Future Forum in Unisys and the Knowledge Lab in NCR.

He studied at Loughborough University in the UK, and holds a Bachelor of Science in Management Sciences alongside a Diploma in Industrial Studies. He is a Fellow of the Institute of Management Services, an Associate of the Chartered Insurance Institute and a Chartered Insurance Practitioner.

He can be contacted at info@balatroltd.com.

About the Contributors

Andrew Allwright

Andrew Allwright joined Reuters in March 2005 to shape the information vendor's response to the MiFiD. In this role, he has represented Reuters in discussions about MiFID implementation with clients, regulators and industry associations.

He was previously a Director within Credit Suisse First Boston's (CSFB) London-based Equity COO team. During his time at CSFB, Andrew was the representative on the LIBA Securities Trading Committee dealing with market infrastructure, competition and regulatory initiatives. He was also a driving force behind the consortium of sell-side firms, which established the Trade Ideas Warehouse for brokers to store the trade ideas they distribute internally and send to buy-side clients.

Anthony Belchambers

Anthony Belchambers is a barrister and currently Chief Executive of the Future and Options Association (FOA) and Chairman of MiFID Connect. MiFID Connect is a joint industry association project designed to simplify the UK implementation of the Markets in Financial Instruments Directive (MiFID).

Previously, Anthony served as General Counsel for the UK Joint Exchanges Committee (JEC) where his responsibilities included coordinating exchange activities and lobbying on behalf of the JEC in relation to international, EU and UK regulation and taxation issues and the role of futures and options generally.

Prior to joining the JEC, he held the position of Company Secretary and General Counsel to the Association of Futures Brokers and Dealers (AFBD), where he played a major role in securing the licensing of the first regulatory authority to cover derivatives and drafting the Self-Regulating Organisation's regulations for derivatives.

He is a member of the Court of the Guild of International Bankers (GIB) and a co-founder, in their original forms, of both the Alternative Investment Management Association (AIMA) and the European Parliamentary Financial Services Forum (EPFSF). He also sits on a number of financial service groups and committees.

Andrew Douglas

Andrew joined SWIFT's strategy division in 1999. Since 2004, he has been the leader of the team within SWIFT that is responsible for working on securities industry market reform initiatives. In this capacity, Andrew works closely with influential bodies such as the Giovannini Group, G30, the European Commission and international securities regulators to represent the interests of the cross-border financial community in specific reform initiatives.

From 1997 to 1999, he was a director of cross-product client services for investment banking at Deutsche Morgan Grenfell. Between 1988 and 1997, he held a number of positions in Citibank's world wide securities services division, including product development manager and senior account manager for global custody sales.

He has a BSc Hons in Engineering from Surrey University, England, and an MBA from Manchester Business School, England.

Bob Fuller

Bob Fuller is Chief Executive Officer of Equiduct, an organisation created to provide MiFID-compliant trading services and equity 'Best Execution' on its Belgian-regulated pan-European electronic exchange.

Bob Fuller joined Equiduct from his previous position as Director of IT Strategy at Dresdner Kleinwort, where he focused on infrastructure, exchange connectivity, SWIFT connectivity and centrally-cleared products including exchange-traded derivatives, equities and bonds. In addition to his work at Dresdner Klienwort, Bob was also co-chair of the IT sub-group for the MiFID Joint Working Group set up to evaluate MiFID legislation and its impact across Europe.

Michael Heinz

Michael Heinz is one of the leading banking industry experts in IBM Germany's Financial Services Software Group in Frankfurt. Michael originally joined Germany's Lotus Corporation in 1998, responsible for consultancy around banking solutions in EMEA and later worldwide. This role transitioned from Lotus to IBM in 2001, where he is now focussing on value-based offerings for banks and financial services firms. Before IBM, Michael specialised in the banking industry with various firms, including Software AG, Hogan Systems, the leading US applied research institute the 'Battelle Memorial Institute', and Dresdner Bank.

Alan Jenkins

Alan Jenkins joined BearingPoint in April 2005, and is BearingPoint's European lead for MiFID. He represents the firm at the MiFID Joint Working Group, where he founded and co-chairs the Cross Jurisdiction subject group.

Alan has substantial experience in global financial markets operations, risk and IT, including straight-through processing, Basel II, and ISO 15022/20022 as well as the EU's Markets in Financial Instruments Directive (MiFID). He is a frequent public speaker.

He has previously worked for participants in the financial markets including virt-x, Cedel and Morgan Grenfell. Alan rejoined the supply side with Hoskyns, where he spearheaded all of that firm's CREST initiatives between 1993 and 2000, before becoming the European lead in straight through processing for the group, latterly known as Cap Gemini Ernst & Young.

Dr. Anthony W. Kirby

Head of Regulation and Compliance, Accenture email:anthony.kirby@accenture.com. He is a Director responsible for Regulation and Compliance within the Capital Markets Division at **Accenture**. He is responsible for several initiatives in the Risk Management and Compliance space, including MiFID, Basel II, KYC/AML and RegNMS. He is also an active and well-known member of the financial community with 20 years of experience in the global marketplace in the business, operations and technology sectors of the business. He brings a unique perspective and enthusiasm in building awareness in areas such as Trading, Operations, Risk Management, Compliance and IT. Anthony was the founder of the **Securities Market Practice Group** in 1998, the **Reference Data User Group** (RDUG) in June 2002 and helped co-found the **MiFID Joint Working Group** (www.mifid.com) in April 2005.

Anthony has also been a member of FIX and ISSA since 1995, is an Executive Committee member of ISITC plus a member of the BSI Technical Standards Committee since 2004, and a participant within the FSA's Market Advisory Committee on MiFID since 2003. He gained vital knowledge and experience from working within the industry in senior client-facing roles **Merrill Lynch, S.W.I.F.T., Instinet, Deutsche Börse and Reuters**. Anthony is also a regular author of numerous articles on the subjects of Hedge Funds, Algorithmic Trading/DMA, Compliance/Risk Management, b2b/exchanges and Corporate Governance. He regularly addresses/chairs many industry events each year and is a visiting Fellow of the Promethee Think Tank in France. Additionally, he is also a Freeman of the City of London, and a member of both the Worshipful Companies of Information Technologists and the Bowyers. Anthony received his Phil. M.A. and PhD from the University of Cambridge, England in 1986.

Angela Knight

Angela Knight became Chief Executive of the British Bankers' Association (BBA) after several years as Chief Executive of the Association of Private Client Investment Managers and Stockbrokers (APCIMS). Angela was educated at Bristol University and was managing director of an engineering company in her early career. She gained early political experience serving on Sheffield City Council from 1987 to 1992, before moving into mainstream politics and becoming a Conservative MP for Erewash in 1992. Angela was PPS to the Minister for Industry (1993–94) and to the Chancellor of the Exchequer (1994–95) before becoming Economic Secretary to the Treasury (1995–97).

The British Bankers' Association (BBA) is the principal trade association for banks operating in the UK. It is a leading representative body in the financial services sector and has over 200 members, as well as many associate members, which fund its not-for-profit activities. Members of the BBA manage around 90 % of UK banking assets.

Steve Leggett

Steve Leggett is a Principal Consultant in Atos Consulting's Financial Services group and is responsible for MiFID activities. He has twenty-eight years' experience in the financial sector and in recent years has focused on regulation and the application of business and IT solutions to gain competitive advantage. Steve and his team have worked with organisations to analyse the detailed impact of MiFID, develop an implementation approach and establish the project structures. Throughout the last 18 months his team has also been involved with many European regulatory bodies and industry associations in discussions on the implementation of MiFID.

Ian Mason

Ian Mason joined Barlow Lyde & Gilbert as a partner in the Financial Services Regulatory Team in 2006. Ian's practice focuses on advising and representing firms and individuals facing FSA enforcement action, as well as also providing general compliance advice on FSA issues.

He was previously Head of the Wholesale Group in the UK FSA's Enforcement Division. Ian has extensive experience of managing complex FSA investigation and litigation relating to insurance, financial crime, banking, market abuse and other contraventions requiring enforcement action. Ian led the team that produced the original Enforcement manual part of the FSA Handbook, as well as developing the internal processes and procedures used by FSA staff in investigations.

Ian is identified as a leading practitioner in his field in both 'The Legal 500' and Chambers UK Guide to law firms.

Michael McKee

Michael McKee is an Executive Director of the British Bankers' Association and specialises in issues relating to UK and European regulation of financial services – particularly the wholesale markets. Michael is also the BBA MiFID co-ordinator and leads the UK financial services industry's MiFID Connect Secretariat. Mr McKee is a solicitor with considerable experience in the banking, financial services and regulatory field. He joined the BBA from Citigroup where he was a regulatory lawyer providing advice to the trading floor and across Europe.

He is a member of the Financial Markets Committee of the European Banking Federation and a Liveryman of the Guild of International Bankers. He has served on a number of pan-European Committees including the European Commission Post-Financial Services Action Plan Working Group on Capital Markets and CESR's Practitioner Group advising on the Market Abuse Directive. He has also given evidence to the European Parliament, the House of Lords and the EU Inter-institutional Monitoring Group on financial services issues. He is a frequent Chairman and speaker at conferences on banking, financial services and regulatory issues. He has published many articles in legal, academic and business journals on these issues and has been awarded Compliance Reporter's 2006 Lobbyist of the Year award.

Chris Pickles

Chris Pickles is Manager, Industry Relations for BT Radianz, and chair of the MiFID Joint Working Group. Chris is also Co-Chair of the Global Education

& Marketing Committee of FIX Protocol Ltd and a member of the Executive Committee of SIIA/FISD.

He has been involved in the financial technology industry as an international marketing manager for over thirty years. His previous jobs have included being secretary-general of the European Association of Securities Dealers in Brussels; Head of Exchange Products at Deutsche Börse in Frankfurt; and marketing with Reuters in London, Paris and Frankfurt.

John Ryan

Dr John Ryan is Associate Director for Executive Education at Cass Business School, City University and is a Professor at the Heilbronn Business School, Germany were he teaches Managerial Finance and International Economics. He formerly taught at the European Business School, New York University and EDHEC School of Management, Lille, France. He is a Visiting Scholar at the Centre for European Studies, Sciences Po and CRG Ecole Polytechnique. John has worked at PA Consulting as the Director of the Euro Centre of Excellence in Dublin. John appears in media programmes such as the BBC World Business Report speaking on issues such as the EU, French and German Economies, Financial Regulation and Transatlantic Economics relations. John has most recently published papers on Basel 2, MiFID, Chinese currency and Sarbanes Oxley.

Bernhard Schüller

Bernhard Schüller recently retired as a senior banker in charge of the securities business at BWS Bank in Germany. He has previously been a member of the board at Deutsche WertpapierService Bank AG; Managing Director of IT at the Deutsche Börse Group, Frankfurt; Head of IT at the insurance group, Aachener & Münchener Versicherungs; as well as the Head of IBM's Financial Services Business Unit for Germany.

David Smith

David Smith is a Principal Consultant in Atos Consulting's Financial Services group and is a MiFID specialist. He has twenty-five years' experience in the financial sector. Prior to joining Atos Consulting in 2005, David was Senior Vice President at Swiss Re where he structured credit risk portfolio transfers using derivative and insurance instruments. David is an FSA Approved Person in structuring and advising on investment instruments and has been a NASD

Registered Representative. He has an MBA in Finance and an Economics Honours B.A.

Richard Thornton

Richard Thornton is a Partner with SunGard Consulting Services, based in London, England, with specialisation in investment banking, asset management, process optimisation and risk management. He is a seasoned management consultant with in depth business and technology skills coupled with good teamworking. Richard joined SunGard in 2006 having previously been an executive consultant with Cap Gemini Ernst & Young.

Steve Webb

Steve Webb is a Partner in Capco's London office with responsibility for key client relationships and consulting project delivery in the UK. He has particular expertise in delivering transformational change to clients in the Securities Industry through the development of operational strategy and alignment of technical architecture.

Since joining Capco, Steve has worked with a number of European banks, developing and helping to implement pan-European operating models, driving rationalisation in response to changes in the European markets. He is a recognised subject matter expert in Custody and Securities Operations, and successfully helped a leading European bank and a Global Custodian to create a Securities Services joint venture.

Steve joined Capco from Intuitive Systems UK, where he was Project Delivery Director. Previously he spent fifteen years with Security Pacific Bank both in Europe and in California.

Laurence White

Laurence White is a member of the Securities Markets Unit in the European Commission's DG Internal Market. He is part of the team that has drafted and is overseeing the implementation of MiFID across the EU. Mr White joined the Commission in 2005 as a Seconded National Expert. Prior to this, he worked at the UK Financial Services Authority in London, where he specialised in MiFID-related issues, including conflicts of interest, investment research, and commodity derivatives. Born in the UK but Australian by upbringing, he has also worked as policy officer and as a solicitor in Australia. Mr White is the author of various articles and reports.

Nigel Woodward

Nigel Woodward was recruited by Intel from Sun Microsystems in 2006, in order to lead the chipmaker's financial services strategy. At Intel, Nigel occupies the retail and investment banking strategic lead in Europe. Operating out of the firm's London office, he is also responsible for managing the firm's worldwide financial services strategy.

Nigel started his career in 1979 in the international division of Midland Bank, working in a number of areas including correspondent banking, trade and corporate finance. After six years, Nigel moved across to the IT industry where he has held a number of European and Global roles associated with market development and strategic sales for the leading technology vendors, including GE, Reuters, Digital Equipment, and Informix before arriving at Sun Microsystems.

Nigel then spent many years as the public face of Sun Microsystems' Global Capital Markets Business. As the worldwide manager for Sun's capital markets and securities business, he helped shape Sun's strategy and positioning in the marketplace.

Acknowledgements

There are far too many acknowledgements for me to list here as it would include everyone in the markets involved in MiFID.

Even so, I do obviously have to extend a big vote of thanks to those who have contributed to this book. You really are Masters of the Universe or, at the very least, Masters of my Universe.

For those of you who were asked to contribute to this book but could not make the time, it would have been nice to include you. I wish you success and trust that 2007 onwards will make you millions.

For those of you I asked to contribute but you just could not be bothered, I trust the harbingers of doom prove to be true.

For all of the rest, may the force be with you and may you enjoy a little fortune. . .and a lot of luck, patience and tolerance.

Introduction

In late 2004, I heard someone mention MiFID, the Markets in Financial Instruments Directive. The conversation was in hushed tones in a corridor of a city bank. It was not a discussion of any significance and no-one took particular note of the term or its meaning. It was just, 'Oh yes, there's some new directive that folks are talking about. It's called MiFID. Nothing for us to worry about though'.

A year later, by the end of 2005, everyone was aware of and was talking about this Directive. During the course of that year, there was an explosion of interest, as the brokers in Europe's markets, the sell-side firms, began to worry that it would be their organisation's impacted by the combination of transparency and 'Best Execution' MiFID demanded. Equally, many of the technologists in Europe's investment banks had realised the major impact of the Directive's clauses upon operations and were concerned about the potential costs.

In late 2005, the conversation had moved onto something along the lines of, 'Ah yes, have you heard the news about MiFID? It's seriously worrying as it will apparently blow our business apart and cost us a fortune'.

The result was that several European centres, London in particular, formed working groups, committees and forums to lobby the regulators and implementers of the Directive to try to change it to something more manageable.

This lobbying succeeded to an extent, such that the final form of MiFID, being implemented this year, is fairly different to the original form. For example, when I first became involved in MiFID, I had thought that the major impact would be upon broker-dealers, whereas today I realise the impact is primarily upon national Exchanges.

So the conversation in late 2006 goes something like, 'Well yes, I remember all those discussions about MiFID. Can you believe all the hype? Nothing for us to worry about'.

Well, MiFID is neither hyped nor an explosion. It may have been over-exposed, but that is because it is a radical change to the way people will work in Europe's investment markets. For some people, this offers great opportunity; for others, it will revolutionise their business. For some people, it will have no impact at all; for a few, it will blow their business apart. So, through all of those conversations during the last three years, the fact is they were all right and they were all wrong.

It just depends where you sit.

I have been reviewing the implications for some time as an active participant of the MiFID Joint Working Group and commentator on the market which is why, in mid-2006, I was approached to produce a book about MiFID.

To be honest, my initial reaction was to ask why would there be a need for such a book? After all, by the time you read this, we should be nearing implementation of the Directive and everyone should know what it is and what it means.

Then I realised this was not the case.

Many people are still confused as to what MiFID is really all about, as evidenced by the overheard conversations of the last three years. Equally, few know what MiFID will really mean once it is implemented: how it will change Europe's markets and what firms really need to implement, consider or change as a result.

That is why this book has been produced.

It is not intended to be a guide to MiFID's workings or clauses.

To be honest, if you want to know that information, there are hundreds of publications available online that detail the in's and out's of the Directive, although my own recommendation is that you go to the source of all knowledge which, in this case, is the European Commission's website. At the weblink, http://ec.europa.eu/internal_market/securities/isd/index_en.htm, you should find all you need to know about Articles 21, 27, 28, 29 and any other specific areas you want to discover of the depths of MiFID.

Regardless of the good intentions though, there has to be some contextual detail so that you understand the basic of MiFID which is provided in the opening section. You will notice that in these, and later chapters, authors often refer to words in apostrophes, such as 'Best Execution', 'firms must take all reasonable steps to deliver the best possible result' and 'pre-trade block thresholds'. This is not because the authors are corporate wags who enjoy doing air bunnies – the raising of the index and middle finger of both hands – to represent apostrophes every time they throw in a catchphrase or buzz-word, but more because these phrases are directly attributable to MiFID's original text. The author is therefore using the terminology to refer directly to MiFID itself.

Equally, a fair few chapters extract paragraphs of original text from the Directive. This is not surprising considering this is a book about the MiFID and post-MiFID world and, where it is appropriate to do so, this text is kept in its full form.

The opening chapters provide a strong introduction to understanding MiFID, and cover the subject from different perspectives, although these opening chapters are **not** the reason why you should read this book.

What this book tries to provide instead, is a simplification and analysis of the critical areas of the Directive's aims and intents. The aim is to provide content that we hope can be digested by anyone interested in where Europe's investment markets are going, not just market specialists. The aim is to provide a review of what the world looks like **after** MiFID, which is why the book is titled, 'The Future of Investing after the Markets in Financial Instruments Directive (MiFID)'.

As well as the objective of trying to provide a vision of Europe's markets after MiFID's implementation, this book also tries to provide a summary of MiFID's true implications by the leading commentators and thinkers involved, rather than from just a single author's or company's viewpoint. That is why we have selected prestigious contributors from a wide range of sources, including:

- the creators of the Directive, the European Commission;
- those who represent the community affected by the Directive, such as MiFID Connect and the MiFID Joint Working Group;
- the associations which support these groups, including the Futures & Options Association, the Association of Private Client Investment Managers and Stockbrokers, and the British Bankers' Association;
- the organisations tasked by these institutions with the implementation of the Directive, including SWIFT, Reuters, Barlow Lyde & Gilbert, IBM, SunGard, Capco, BT Radianz, Intel, Atos, Bearing Point and Accenture; and
- those who seek to exploit opportunities from the Directive, such as the new pan-European Exchange, Equiduct.

The challenge of bringing together so many contributors was daunting.

After all, this is not a series of opinion pieces by people watching the markets, like myself. These are not professional writers or journalists, but practitioners and organisations engaged in implementing the Directive.

It would have been easier just to go out and interview these folks, but I wanted to capture their views in their words, rather than mine or someone else's interpretation. That is why these are all original essays in the words of their authors.

As a result, the real challenge for this book was to edit the contributions into something that flows and is digestible. That is why there is some overlap and duplication of words between each chapter. I do not apologise for this, as it would have taken away the essence of the author's ideas to remove much of this text. Equally, the principle of good presentation is 'say what you are going to say, say it and then say what you have said', and that is what happens during the course of your reading this book. Each contributor makes similar points using similar words and referring to similar text. Then you find what happens is that, although each author may make a point that you have heard before, they say it in a different way in a different context with a different interpretation and a different conclusion.

The result is a 360° review of MiFID in all its detail.

The result is a guide to understand how Europe's investment markets will operate and behave in the longer-term.

After MiFID's implementation.

Therefore, this is not a guide to what MiFID is all about, although it does achieve that in the process, but it is more of a guide to understanding Europe's investment markets over the next decade, once the Directive's vision is realised.

The only barrier to this process is that the essays were all written in late 2006, and so there will be things that have happened since they were written which will place these views into that time. Please make allowances for such transient issues, as the essence of the messages still remain the same: that MiFID aims to make Europe's capital markets as competitive and liquid as any marketplace anywhere else in the world. . .especially the USA. That is what the European Commission is trying to achieve through MiFID, and this is what we have tried to place in context through these pages.

I personally thank all of the contributors who provided their papers on the basis of enthusiasm to demonstrate understanding and share knowledge. We hope that by sharing this knowledge, you gain some insights into the challenges and opportunities for your own trading in Europe over the coming years.

Finally, I have two requests to make of you, the reader.

First, many of the contributors to this book have asked me to stress that the opinions expressed are purely the author's individual views, and are not necessarily consistent with the views of the organisations they represent.

Second, at the time of release, MiFID is still to be implemented as law across Europe's Member States. As the process of implementation takes place, I would personally be very interested in any views, anecdotes, ideas, examples or just notes that anyone affected by MiFID would care to share.

Please send such thoughts to me at cskinner@balatroltd.com.

Part 1
MiFID's Vision, Rules and Requirements: the Principles

'THE BENEFITS, OPPORTUNITIES AND CHALLENGES OF MiFID'
LAURENCE WHITE, DG INTERNAL MARKET AND SERVICES, EUROPEAN COMMISSION

The first chapter of any book about a European Directive should really be written by the European Commission, and so I thank Laurence White for his opening perspective. This chapter provides the vision of MiFID: what is the Commission really trying to achieve?

'AN OVERVIEW OF MiFID'
DR JOHN RYAN, PROFESSOR OF GLOBAL BANKING AND FINANCE AT THE EUROPEAN BUSINESS SCHOOL

Professor Ryan provided one of the most comprehensive reviews of the end-to-end of MiFID. What is it really all about? This chapter provides all you need to know.

'BEST EXECUTION'
ANTHONY KIRBY, HEAD OF RISK, REGULATION & COMPLIANCE, CAPITAL MARKETS, ACCENTURE, AND CO-CHAIR, MiFID JOINT WORKING GROUP

'Best Execution' principles are one of the most controversial areas in the MiFID rulings. Why? Because it has been hard to track down what it means, how it will be applied, who will be regulating what and so on. Tony Kirby, as co-Chair of the MiFID Joint Working Group alongside Brian Mitchell of Baring Asset Management, gives one of the best and most in-depth reviews of this subject I have seen to date.

'CLIENT CLASSIFICATION'
DAVID SMITH AND STEVE LEGGETT, PRINCIPAL
CONSULTANTS, ATOS CONSULTING

'Best Execution' principles are all wrapped up in MiFID's conduct of business rules. A specific area within this are the issues related to Client Classification, and how to handle the different forms of client: Retail, Professional and Eligible Counterparty. David Smith and Steve Leggett explore this subject and provides some key perspectives over and above those laid out in previous chapters.

'PASSPORTING'
ALAN JENKINS, DIRECTOR, BEARINGPOINT AND
CO-CHAIR, MiFID JOINT WORKING GROUP FOR
CROSS-BORDER JURISDICTION ISSUES

Another facet of MiFID's new rulings is passporting. This is the ability for investment firms to offer services into another European Member State, once they have registered their home state, as in headquarter operations. Alan Jenkins knows the subject intimately, as head of the MiFID Joint Working Group on Cross-Border Jurisdiction. Therefore, he provides valuable insights here into what passporting really allows.

1

The Benefits, Opportunities and Challenges of MiFID

Laurence White

The adoption of the Markets in Financial Instruments Directive[1] (**'MiFID'** or **'the Directive'**) Level 2 implementing measures[2] was the culmination of a lengthy European legislative process begun in November 2000.[3] Once the measures are fully transposed and implemented by the Member States, they will represent a step-change in the sophistication and flexibility of financial markets regulation in Europe, and will be the catalyst for significant and beneficial changes in market structure.

---

[1] Directive 2004/39/EC of the European Parliament and of the Council of 21 April 2004 on markets in financial instruments amending Council Directives 85/611/EEC and 93/6/EEC and Directive 2000/12/EC of the European Parliament and of the Council and repealing Council Directive 93/22/EEC [2004] OJ L145/1. As amended by Directive 2006/31/EC of the European Parliament and of the Council of 5 April 2006 amending directive 2004/39/EC on markets in financial instruments, as regards certain deadlines [2006] OJ L114/60. The latter Directive postponed the date on which the measures in MiFID would be applied to investment firms to 1 November 2007, but required Member States to have finalised transposition by 31 January 2007, thus giving firms a 9-month implementation period after finalisation of national measures.

[2] Commission Regulation (EC) No. 1287 of 10 August 2006 implementing Directive 2004/39/EC of the European Parliament and of the Council as regards record-keeping obligations for investment firms, transaction reporting, market transparency, admission of financial instruments to trading, and defined terms for the purposes of that Directive [2006] OJ L241/1 (**'the Implementing Regulation'**) and Commission Directive 2006/73/EC of 10 August 2006 implementing Directive 2004/39/EC of the European Parliament and of the Council as regards organisational requirements and operating conditions for investment firms, and defined terms for the purposes of that Directive [2006] OJ L241/2, p. 26 (**'the Implementing Directive'**). These are referred to as 'Level 2 measures' as they form Level of the 4-level 'Lamfalussy process'. See the *Final Report of the Committee of Wise Men on the Regulation of European Securities Markets* (2001), available at http://ec.Europa.eu/internal_market/securities/lamfalussy/index_en.htm for more details.

[3] European Commission, Communication COM(2000)729: 'Upgrading the Investment Services Directive'.

The Future of Investing in Europe's Markets after MiFID Edited by C. Skinner
© 2007 John Wiley & Sons, Ltd

MiFID as a whole is a ground-breaking package of measures and a cornerstone of the Financial Services Action Plan. It is intended to transform the landscape for the trading of securities and derivatives and to increase competition and efficiency throughout Europe's financial markets. It will both increase investors' level of protection and give them greater choice.

It is intended to drive down the cost of capital, generate growth and boost Europe's competitiveness,[4] thus contributing to the jobs and growth goals which form part of the Community's Lisbon Strategy.[5]

MiFID will remove obstacles to the use of the so-called 'single passport' by investment firms, foster competition and a level playing field between Europe's trading venues, and ensure a high level of protection for investors across Europe.

The rapid globalisation of financial markets is an opportunity which Europe cannot afford to miss. Europe is already emerging as a global leader in financial services and the MiFID measures will help Europe to stay competitive. In order to secure the full benefits of MiFID, the Member States must also cooperate by implementing the measures fully and on time.

1.1   ANTICIPATED BENEFITS OF MiFID

The main anticipated benefits of MiFID are increased competition, enhanced investor protection, greater transparency and more effective regulatory co-operation. There should also be significant deregulation as super-equivalent national measures are cut back and replaced by the simplified, principles-based approach of the rules contained in MiFID.

---

[4] The integration of EU equity and corporate bond markets holds out the prospect of significant reduction in trading costs and the cost of equity/corporate bond finance. Research conducted by London Economics in 2002 suggests that the static efficiency benefits of establishing integrated, deep and liquid equity and corporate bond markets alone are likely to be significant – involving a permanent reduction in the cost of equity capital by 0.5 %, triggering an increase in investment, employment (0.5 %) and GDP (1.1 %). See London Economics: 2002, *Quantification of the macro-economic impact of integration of EU financial markets*, at http://tinyurl.com/ewhum.

[5] The Lisbon Strategy was adopted in March 2000 and aims to make the EU the most dynamic and competitive economy by 2010. For more information see http://ec.Europa.eu/growthandjobs/index_en.htm.

1.1.1 Increased competition

MiFID is expected to significantly increase competition, both across borders and among trading venues and intermediaries.

Firstly, in relation to intermediaries, it will do this by substantially updating the 'single passport' for investment firms, allowing them to operate across Europe on the basis of an effective single authorisation, across a wider range of financial instruments and investment activities. For the first time, investment advice and commodity derivatives business will be covered by the passport, for example.

The 'single passport' will mean that a firm needs only to answer to one regulator for most of its compliance questions. Organisational requirements including, importantly, risk management and conflicts of interest, and all services provided on a cross-border basis will be subject to home state control. The host state regulator will have a limited role in supervising branches in its territory,[6] but that will be all.

This represents a significant advance on the Investment Services Directive,[7] where host state regulators retain significant potential regulatory authority over incoming services and branches.[8]

As a result of stimulating cross-border competition, intermediaries can be expected to come under pressure to match incoming firms' offers, cost structures and support services. This would diversify the range of products, services and markets that investors and issuers can access.

Secondly, and perhaps more profoundly, MiFID will lead to a step-change in competition between investment firms, stock Exchanges and other trading venues for the right to host transactions in shares.

Trading in shares will no longer be the prerogative of the local stock exchange as it is currently in a number of Member States.[9] Share trading will be able to be done on the stock exchange as before, but also on a Multilateral trading facility (**'MTF'**), a voice broker, a so-called 'systematic internaliser', or via a bilateral OTC transaction.

---

[6] Article 32(7) of MiFID.

[7] Council Directive 93/22/EEC of 10 May 1993 on investment services in the securities field [1993] OJ L141/27, as amended.

[8] See Article 11(2) in particular.

[9] See Article 14(3) of the Investment Services Directive. This enables Member States who chose to do so to impose the so-called 'concentration rule', requiring certain transactions in shares to be executed on a regulated market. This has the effect of limiting competition between other trading venues and the local bourse in a number of jurisdictions.

This should put significant pressure on Exchanges to improve their offering by reducing costs and offering a broader range of services. This in turn should lead to improved standards of service to investors, leading to more investors using capital markets, and therefore to deeper and more liquid markets. Where an exchange's market does become open to competition from another trading venue, spreads can be expected to narrow and the composite depth of the order books taken as a whole to be significantly enhanced. Ultimately, these effects should benefit issuers by lowering the cost of capital.

1.1.2   Enhanced investor protection

Existing investor protection rules vary widely within the wide latitude granted by the Investment Services Directive.[10] Under MiFID, investor protection rules will be harmonised at a high level, so that investors can feel confident in using the services of investment firms wherever they are in Europe and wherever the investment firms come from in Europe.

Clearly, there would never have been political agreement on a stronger passport without strong and consistent investor protection rules being agreed across the Community. This gives both investors and regulators the comfort that foreign firms will not be able to exploit vulnerable consumers.

For the first time, there will be consistent European rules covering the core investor protection topics: 'Best Execution', information to clients, order handling, suitability, investment advice, inducements and conflicts of interest.

While all these changes are equally worthy of mention, perhaps the most important, from the competition perspective, is the introduction of the 'Best Execution' rule. This rule will oblige intermediaries to direct orders to those execution venues offering the best overall result for their clients, according to a range of factors and criteria which will be set out in the intermediaries' own execution policies. (For retail orders, the Directive requires price to be given priority, in the absence of specific instruction otherwise.)[11] Brokers will be obliged to include, in the list of venues they make use of, all those venues which consistently offer the best overall result. In this way, the Directive

---

[10] See Article 11.
[11] Article 44(3) of the Implementing Directive.

aims to increase competition between trading venues, by effectively obliging brokers to seek out the best deals for their clients, even if they are not to be found on incumbent Exchanges.[12]

Another notable development is the articulation of a comprehensive framework for the identification, management and disclosure of conflicts of interest. Investment firms will need to have well-documented policies and procedures relating to conflicts of interest, and to disclose details of those procedures to their clients. There are special rules for the provision of investment research, which has been the focus of intensive regulatory action in recent years, but the general rules apply to conflicts of interest across the board.[13]

1.1.3 Increased transparency

Another significant change wrought by MiFID is increased levels of pre- and post-trade transparency for transactions in shares that are admitted to trading on regulated markets.

The Directive tackles the topic of transparency for such transactions in two broad ways:

- in relation to pre-trade transparency, regulated markets and MTF's are required to make information publicly available about orders and quotes on their systems, while firms that internalise customer orders on a systematic, organised and frequent basis (**'systematic internalisers'**) in relation to 'liquid shares' as defined are required to make publicly available quotes in those shares;
- in relation to post-trade transparency, regulated markets, MTF's and investment firms are required to make publicly available information about completed transactions. Large transactions are subject to a series of delays depending on the size of the transaction.

The elaboration of a uniform level of mandated transparency across different transaction venues was essential in reaching political agreement to abolish the 'concentration rule'. Otherwise, significant trading volumes might migrate from regulated markets to untransparent venues for reasons purely of regulatory arbitrage, leaving open, transparent markets unfairly exposed.

---

[12] Article 21 of MiFID and Chapter III, Section 5 of the Implementing Directive.
[13] Article 13(3) of MiFID and Chapter II, Section 4 of the Implementing Directive.

A second rationale for a high and uniform level of transparency is to prevent the fragmentation of liquidity into different liquidity pools, as a result of competition, from adversely affecting the price formation process. By requiring information about all comparable transactions to be made public by different actors in a form that 'facilitate[s] the consolidation of the data with similar data from other sources',[14] MiFID provides the building-blocks for market-led solutions to the problem of consolidating market data from a variety of trading venues.

Therefore, it can be expected that investors and their intermediaries will be able to subscribe to services which can display to them the share prices applicable across the whole market, not just those hosted on particular trading venues. This will enable investors to get better prices, and prices which more fairly reflect what is going on in the wider marketplace.

1.1.4   More effective regulatory co-operation

MiFID contains several technical innovations allowing for much more coherent supervision of pan-European financial markets. Transaction reports on a whole range of financial instruments will be channeled to the relevant supervisor of the overall market as well as to the local regulator of the trader.[15] Co-operation and information-sharing will likewise be enhanced across a range of topics.

1.1.5   Deregulation and the principles-based approach

Another significant MiFID impact will be deregulation. The rules that MiFID contains are for the most part principles-based. This means, for example, that they put the onus on firms to comply with high-level principles and only supplement those high-level principles with more detailed rules where absolutely necessary. For example, in relation to the obligation to act honestly, fairly and professionally laid down in Article 19 of MiFID,[16] more detail is prescribed but only on the topics of inducements[17] and the obligations of investment firms carrying

---

[14] Article 32(b) of the Implementing Regulation.
[15] Article 25(3) of MiFID.
[16] Article 19(1) of MiFID.
[17] Article 26 of the Implementing Directive.

out portfolio management and reception and transmission of orders,[18] analogous to 'Best Execution' obligations.

The principles-based approach means that much emphasis is placed on a firm's own policies on topics as diverse as risk management, internal audit, compliance, conflicts of interest, 'Best Execution', and order handling. MiFID does not prescribe in detail what these policies should contain, so long as these policies are appropriate to the firm's own circumstances and characteristics, and to the overarching objectives of the Directive.

As a consequence, the level of detail contained in the MiFID measures is in some areas significantly less than is contained in existing national rules. The so-called 'anti-gold-plating clause'[19] is aimed at stripping back layers of existing (and future) 'super-equivalent' regulation which go beyond the requirements of the Directive, unless they can be rigorously justified in terms of consumer protection or market integrity. Proper application of this clause can be expected to lead to significant deregulatory changes.

1.2   OPPORTUNITIES AND CHALLENGES

Market participants are faced with a choice: will they treat MiFID as just another compliance exercise, or will they think strategically about the new possibilities in the new competitive landscape?

There are first-mover advantages to those firms that are prepared to think about new business opportunities and not see MiFID simply as a matter for compliance professionals.

For firms, they will need to consider a range of business choices, including:

- whether to consider commencing or broadening their offering of services into other Member States;
- by what means and on what terms they will make available information about transactions they conclude; and
- whether to enter some of the competitive spaces opened up by MiFID, particularly competing with Exchanges and other trading venues for the provision of trading services.

---

[18] Article 45 of the Implementing Directive.
[19] Article 4 of the Implementing Directive.

For Exchanges, the changes will be profound. In those jurisdictions that currently have a concentration rule, they will face competition from other trading venues (including systematic internalisers), or will be able to compete with the incumbents, for the first time. Competition from other Member States will be ramped-up significantly. So both defensive and offensive options will need to be considered.

For the first time, MTF's have a clear, unambiguous passport with which to do business on a cross-border or branch basis throughout Europe. This is because the activity of operating an MTF has been made an investment activity for the first time.[20] For the first time, commodities exchange and MTF's will be able to provide their services in other Member States without encountering regulatory barriers.

Those firms that are currently or potentially operating as systematic internalisers will need to consider their competitive position vis-à-vis stock Exchanges and other trading venues. While there is significant upside for firms that are newly able to internalise orders that would otherwise go to incumbent Exchanges, this kind of business will also attract quoting obligations, which are part of the enhanced transparency measures mentioned above. So such firms will need to consider whether the risks of this business are worthwhile in light of the potential profits, and whether they can carry on similar business in a different way, such as on-exchange market makers or by providing execution facilities as MTF's.

1.3   CONCLUSION

MiFID has meant a lot of hard work for a lot of people.

High praise is particularly due to those stakeholders who responded with detailed and constructive comments to the numerous consultations during the legislative process. The process shows that industry and consumers, the European Parliament, European Commission regulators and Member States are able to work together in a sensible and pragmatic way in order to achieve the right result for Europe's financial markets and Europe's investors. As a result, Europe is the winner. And it shows that the Lamfalussy procedure – under which the two-level MiFID has been developed – works.

---

[20] Section A(8) of Annex I to MiFID.

The rapid globalisation of financial markets is an opportunity for Europe. MiFID means we are well placed to stay ahead. Our financial markets are in good shape. They are growing strongly and are set to grow even faster in future as the Union enlarges further, the middle classes expand in numbers, the population ages, and people increasingly take responsibility for their own pension provision. MiFID will be an important part of this ongoing story.

We in the Commission services have been pleasantly surprised by the range, depth and quality of guidance on MiFID available for market participants – in the form of briefing notes, conferences, podcasts[21] and even online television materials.[22] We expect that this book will uphold and even exceed those high standards.

---

[21] For example, The MiFID podcast at www.mifidpodcast.com.

[22] For example, TheBankingChannel at http://www.thebankingchannel.tv/cgi-bin/view.cgi.

2
An Overview of MiFID

Dr John Ryan

The Markets in Financial Instruments Directive (MiFID) is a set of rules that came into being in 2004 to replace the Investment Services Directive (ISD) which was adopted in 1993.

The ISD was created by the European Commission (EC) in order to force the concentration rules into the European equities markets, which meant all trading activity would pass through national Exchanges such as the London Stock exchange. However, these rules have not been working because brokers have been carrying out trades off the Exchange using their own book of business. This has caused a problem for the EC as this practice of internalisation is hidden within the trading firm, and not exposed to the regulator's touch. Thus, 'Best Execution' and transparency principles were created resulting in MiFID.

This transition from the ISD to MiFID is therefore a core element within the European Commission's Financial Services Action Plan (FSAP), in order to create a more integrated pan-European marketplace and removing the remaining existing barriers to trade. This directive will change the relationship between investment firms and their clients, as well as impacting most other parts of financial business, including IT, Operations, and Compliance.

MiFID will change and improve how investment firms operate and facilitate cross border trading, thus encouraging the integration of the European Union's (EU) capital markets. It will provide the ability for financial institutions to offer a number of services that can be passported to other EU Member States without additional local approvals. This is a very important extension of the rules, which will be outlined and discussed further on in this chapter, because it brings greater harmony into the governing of regulated markets.

The Future of Investing in Europe's Markets after MiFID   Edited by C. Skinner
© 2007 John Wiley & Sons, Ltd

Retail banks and smaller institutions, such as co-operative savings banks and building societies, will also fall under the scope of MiFID, but it is most likely to affect only specific parts of their business. Compliance here will be necessary with the Capital Requirements Directive (CRD), which positions the fundamentals for the regulatory capital a firm must hold.

MiFID is also known as the Lamfalussy Directive because it has been adopted using a legislative approach known as the Lamfalussy process.

2.1   THE LAMFALUSSY PROCESS[1]

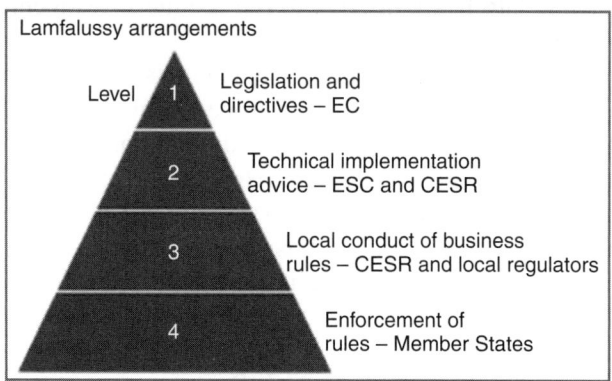

2.2   LAMFALUSSY LEVEL 1, LEGISLATION AND DIRECTIVES

This is the first stage of the process which involves a decision-making policy group representing the interests of the European Union in the subject matter concerned.

The framework principals of the directives and regulations are proposed by the Commission, and thereafter decided by the European Parliament (EP) alongside the Council. Under MiFID, this Level 1 directive eliminated the concentration rule, which meant that Member States' investment firms were no longer forced to transmit orders to their national stock Exchanges.

This also meant that Multilateral Trading Facilities (MTF's) will be as accountable for pre- and post-trade transparency and reporting

---

[1] http://www.virt-x.com/download/information/publications/mifid_guidel_0406.pdf.
Reproduced by permission of Virt-X, an SWX Group Company.

requirements as the Exchanges. This then provides a common ground between the new competitors and Exchanges by making all trading activity information accessible to the market.

Level 1 also revised the single passport for investment firms, originally introduced by the ISD. This enabled investment firms to accommodate services across Europe on the basis of a single authorisation from their 'home' Member State. Therefore, investor protection rules are modified and strengthened so that investors feel assured using the services provided by the investment firms.

2.3 LAMFALUSSY LEVEL 2, TECHNICAL IMPLEMENTATION AND ADVICE

The Level 1 measures were authorised by the European Commission after they were submitted to the members of the Ministries of Finance, known as the European Securities Committee (ESC). This also led to the creation of the Committee of European Securities Regulators (CESR), the securities regulators that advised the Commission on the technical aspects of the second stage legislation. The table below represents the instruments that are affected by the Level 2 measures.

2.4 INSTRUMENTS AFFECTED BY LEVEL 2 MEASURES[2]

Article	Name of Article	Instruments Affected	Level 2 Measure
21	Obligation to execute orders on terms most favourable to the client	All	Directive
22	Client order handling rules	Equities	Regulation
25	Transaction reporting	All	Regulation
27	Obligation for investment turns to make quotes public	Equities	Regulation
28, 30, 45	Post-trade disclosure	Equities	Regulation
29, 44	Pre-trade disclosure	Equities	Regulation

---

[2] http://uk.bea.com/solutions/fsi/mifid/index.jsp. Reproduced by permission of BEA Solutions.

Conduct of business requirements for firms relates to clients in different categories where firms assess whether products and services which they provide are suitable for their clients.

Organisational requirements for firms and markets relates to internal audit functions, risk management, and compliance that operate independently.

Transaction reporting covers the buying and selling of transactions in all financial instruments to the relevant authorities. All the instruments within transaction reporting are affected by the Level 2 measures.

Transparency requirements are required for the trading of shares such as the pre- and post-trade transparency for the regulated markets.

The Level 2 wordings of MiFID were agreed and signed off by the European Parliament in September 2006 leading to the Level 3 measures being implemented in February 2007.

2.5   LAMFALUSSY LEVEL 3, LOCAL CONDUCT OF BUSINESS RULES

Once the Level 2 wordings were in place, non-binding guidelines were adopted by CESR in order to facilitate the coherent implementation and application of the EU legislation. Common standards were also developed by CESR which are not covered by the EU legislation, taking into consideration that there has to be a compatibility of the standards between Level 1 and Level 2 stages.

2.6   LAMFALUSSY LEVEL 4, ENFORCEMENT OF RULES

This final stage looks at monitoring the correctness of the implementation of the European Union legislation into national legislation by the Commission and will come into effect in November 2007 when all Member States needed to have local rules implemented by their national financial regulatory authorities.

2.7   MiFID'S DETAILED PROVISIONS

The detailed provisions of MiFID fall into three main categories:

- Organisational Requirements;
- Conduct of Business Requirements; and
- Markets and Transparency Requirements.

Within these detailed provisions are the core essence of MiFID, in terms of 'Best Execution' requirements under the conduct of business rules, and systematic internaliser definitions under markets and transparency.

2.8   ORGANISATIONAL REQUIREMENTS

Firms face new requirements on a continual basis when they are endorsed under MiFID. These requirements are based upon a home state basis. In other words, for a firm authorised to trade investment services in France, the French authority will regulate their business whether that business is transacted from its French base, or on a cross border basis.

The requirements will play a key part in:

- maintenance and protection of money held by the firm and financial instruments of clients;
- management of conflicts of interest in order not to affect the interest of the clients;
- keeping records of transactions carried out by clients;
- important functions and investment services being outsourced;
- compliance arrangements such as governing personal transactions;
- internal controls and systems such as:

  - internal audit;
  - staff;
  - continuity of business;
  - IT systems and processing;
  - accounting and administrative procedures.

These requirements are mainly based on the Level 2 measures, and in order for these requirements to take effect, firms need to consider the following:

- Allocating the responsibility of senior management appropriately. Requirements of outsourcing also have to be satisfied and met as agreed in the Level 2 measure.
- Integrity of the firm's systems and controls, and the necessary provision has to be made for identifying conflicts of interest, and the resilience of the organisational arrangements to manage these. In addition to this, more focus is placed upon 'functional independence' of compliance and risk management controls. Therefore, firms have to pay special attention to their internal organization and the reporting lines.
- Preparation for risk and compliance management should also be carried out efficiently and effectively.

These requirements affect all investment firms within the scope of MiFID, and all credit establishments doing MiFID business. In addition to this, the Capital Requirements Directive (CRD) has high level requirements for systems and controls. Due to the overlap that firms have with MiFID and CRD, a common platform of system and control requirements needs to be developed, and regulatory authorities in many European states are combining their approach to regulating these two directives into a common platform approach.

2.9   CONDUCT OF BUSINESS REQUIREMENTS

Conduct of business rules focus upon all aspects of client dealings, and cover nine key areas of activity:

- Client classification;
- Marketing;
- Information about the firm and its services;
- Client agreements;
- Suitability and know your customer;
- Appropriateness and execution-only services;
- 'Best Execution';
- Client order handling;
- Reporting information to clients.

2.9.1   Client classification[3]

Client classification is regarded as the starting point of the 'conduct of business' rule changes that will affect firms. This basically means how firms' regulatory requirements for the business are conducted with each client category.

MiFID's rules categorise clients as 'retail client', 'professional client', and 'eligible counterparty'. This had a profound impact on some markets, such as the UK, as MiFID's rules are very different to the previous client classification rules. For example, the UK's Financial Services Authority (FSA) categories were 'private customer', 'intermediate customer', and 'market counterparty'.

Considerations in current client classifications therefore needed to be reviewed, with changes required for some firms' clients. Systems, processes and client documentation also needed alteration by firms, in relation to the business process systems of classification decisions.

In addition, under MiFID, both eligible counterparties and professional clients will be able to request regulatory protection either generally, on a trade-by-trade basis, or in relation to a 'particular investment service or transaction, or types of transaction or product'.

Finally, clients may fall into different categories in relation to the different products or services. MiFID contains transitional provisions which allow firms to continue treating professional clients in a certain manner, provided certain conditions are satisfied.

2.9.2   Marketing

There has been a great impact upon financial promotions based upon MiFID's provisions, which state that a firm is required to ensure all the information and marketing communications provided to clients is accurate and not misleading.

Financial promotions and marketing functions need to be reviewed thoroughly, paying special attention to whether or not the functions satisfy the expectations of the new regime. Furthermore, this change will involve high-level rules, which inevitably place more responsibility on senior management.

These requirements affect both MiFID and non-MiFID scope firms, with respect to firms that promote their investment products and

---

[3] See Chapter 4.

services to retail investors. For example, this includes both non-ISD investment firms and life insurance companies.

2.9.3   Information about the firm and its services

Information must be provided to retail or professional clients on the firm's products and services under MiFID. The following specific information should include:

- nature and detail of the information;
- when the information should be given and the type of form in which it should be provided; and
- when the information should be updated.

Consideration needs to be taken into account on the channels for capturing and developing the required information, in relation to the products and services offered by investment firms' to their clients. Furthermore, firms have to consider the process of updating the information to clients during the period of MiFID implementation. In addition to updating the information, delivering the information is also a key aspect for the firm's specific clients, and the circumstances the clients are in.

This affects all firms within the scope of business under MiFID. In addition to this, consideration needs to be taken regarding the extent to which the information requirements in the current rules for non-scope retail investment business should be adapted.

2.9.4   Client agreements

Under MiFID, firms are required to keep a detailed record of the documents that have been agreed with their clients covering the terms and conditions provided by the firm.

MiFID requires a number of specific information provisions, notification and consent requirements, deriving from both the Level 1 and the Level 2 provisions. Furthermore, for such provisions in client agreements, reviewing the agreements is necessary, in order to consider any adjustments that are needed.

All firms within the scope of MiFID are affected which will require adopting the MiFID standards for similar businesses, such as those carried out by non-scope firms with retail clients.

2.9.5   Suitability and know your customer[4]

Knowing your customer is also an important factor under MiFID. This will apply when a firm provides investment advice to both professional and retail clients. In order to know your customer, firms will have to pay special attention to the following;

- The extensiveness and adequacy of arrangements of information which relates to 'Know Your Client' rules and providing this information accurately to those who assist in making discretionary management decisions.
- Procedures for providing suitable guidance are given as well as investment management decisions taken with the addition for business with professional clients.

This affects all businesses providing advice to retail and professional clients within the scope of MiFID. It is important to review the effect of the suitability for retail client wordings within MiFID, as many non-MiFID firms will also need to be in line with the standards.

2.9.6   Appropriateness and execution-only services[5]

As well as investment products provided on an execution-only basis, the following products can also be provided on this basis under MiFID:

- 'Non-complex' instruments, such as the shares that are approved to trade on a regulated market, bonds, and money market instruments.
- Those that are only incorporated on execution or transmission of orders.
- Those where the client initiates the execution-only service, only when the firm has warned the client in terms of assessing suitability.

On the other hand, for investment products, information about the client's knowledge and experience has to be obtained first under the MiFID requirements. Thereafter, the information is assessed to see whether or not, the service is appropriate for that particular client. If it is inappropriate, the client should be warned that the information that they have provided is not sufficient to carry out the service.

---

[4] See Chapter 4.
[5] See Chapter 4.

Nevertheless, it is important to distinguish a clear difference between suitability and appropriateness:

- *Appropriateness* focuses only on the client's experience and knowledge.
- *Suitability* requires knowledge, experience, as well as the client's investment objectives and financial situation.

Services being offered by firms under the appropriateness test will need to:

- specify the systems being used for acquiring the information from clients and the operating controls over client activity;
- assess the appropriateness of these systems and controls, and carry forward the outcomes under MiFID by developing new systems and procedures where appropriate.

In addition, the 'execution-only services' that are offered by firms need to look at the quality of procedures for making the assessments, as well as specifying warnings whenever necessary.

Firms that provide 'execution-only' services on intricate financial instruments for retail clients are all affected by the appropriateness requirements. In addition to this, restrictions on certain forms of solicitation and disclosure requirements apply for firms that only provide business on an execution basis.

2.9.7 'Best Execution'[6]

Investment firms have to look at all ways to deliver the best possible results on behalf of their clients, taking into account the important factors such as price, time it takes to execute orders, and cost. All firms need to:

- develop effective procedures for 'Best Execution' by creating an execution order to obtain the best possible results for the clients;
- reveal accurate information to clients in relation to the procedures of the execution orders; and
- oversee the efficiency and effectiveness of the execution orders and constantly update them if necessary.

---

[6] See Chapter 3.

In order for these changes to occur, firms have to review their current policy or create a new execution policy. However, to carry this out, the consent of the client is required before any of the transactions are made. In addition to this, trading strategies by firms need to be taken into consideration whilst delivering these obligations. Furthermore, system impacts for some firms may occur, which in turn would initiate a broader scope of date relating to executions.

Dealers and brokers are particularly affected by these requirements, in relation to executing the orders to wholesale and retail markets, as well as all other MiFID financial instruments. These requirements also affect transmitters, order receivers and portfolio managers.

2.9.8   Client order handling

Investment firms are required to carry out client orders quickly and accurately under the MiFID directive. In addition to this, the Level 2 measures states that firms are required to:

- ensure that any orders that are executed from the client's assets in the form of settlements are required to be carried out quickly, and delivered efficiently to the account of each relevant client. In addition to this, under dominant market conditions client limit orders that are not immediately executed should be made public.
- investment firms should refrain from front running.

Considerations that are taken into account from the above requirements are similar to the 'conduct of business' rules. Nevertheless, it would be advisable to review the existing systems and processes, and firms have to consider the details of their contracts with clients, and the venues they use to make limit orders public.

All brokers and dealers are affected whilst executing orders within any MiFID financial instruments. Portfolio managers, as well as receivers and transmitters are also affected.

2.9.9   Reporting information to clients

Under the MiFID directive it is necessary for firms to provide accurate information to their clients, such as the correct details of the transactions that have been made on behalf of the clients. This will then provide an analysis to the clients on their investment portfolio.

According to the MiFID supplement, 'The main difference is that the flexibility under existing FSA rules for private customers to vary the content or frequency of contract notes for reporting on transactions and periodic information for portfolio management is not replicated in MiFID'.[7]

Changes to reporting systems are also required to those firms who use this flexibility to provide reports to their clients.

These requirements affect all businesses within the scope of MiFID, paying special attention to retail clients. These requirements are also similar to the conduct of business rules. Retail investment business retaining some flexibility under MiFID will also be looked upon.

2.10   MARKETS AND TRANSPARENCY

Markets and Transparency focus primarily upon all aspects of trade reporting, publishing and cross-border dealing, and cover five key areas of activity:

- Pre-trade transparency;
- Post-trade transparency;
- Transaction reporting;
- Cross-border business, branching, passporting;
- Use of tied agents.

2.10.1   Pre- and post-trade transparency

MiFID also introduces a complete detailed pre- and post-trade transparency for trading on shares on the following execution venues:

- Multilateral Trading Facilities (MTF) – this refers to alternative execution venues.
- Regulated Markets (RM) – this refers to Stock Exchanges such as the London Stock Exchange (LSE).
- Over the Counter (OTC) – this refers to firms that are trading shares outside the regulated market and Multilateral Trading Facility, including systematic internalisers.

---

[7] http://www.fsa.gov.uk/pubs/international/planning_mifid.pdf. Reproduced by permission of the Financial Services Authority.

2.10.2   Pre-trade transparency

RM's have trading systems and rules that implement transparency levels to accommodate the type of share being traded and the method of trading. Under MiFID, comprehensive pre-trade transparency requirements have been introduced for trades below specified size openings that take place outside the order book. In this area, the requirements for MTF's are the same as the RM's.

The new area here is that certain investment firms are being included under MiFID's transparency rules, and are required to publish prices in the same way as RM's and MTF's. The firms impacted are those defined as a 'systematic internaliser', 'an investment firm which – on an organized, frequent and systematic basis – deals on own accounts by executing client orders outside an RM or MTF'.[8]

Systematic internalisers must accommodate firm bids on liquid shares[9] on a continuous basis. However, systematic internalisers are not obliged to quote in all liquid shares, but can quote for a subset of liquid shares which, in time, can be changed.

Systematic internalisers are also allowed to execute orders from professional clients at prices other than the prices quoted, in some circumstances. The following activities are those which are not subject to quoting obligations:

- dealing with asset classes such as bonds;
- dealing in non-liquid shares, and the standard market size.

In order to comply with MiFID's requirements, RM's and MTF's have to highlight what modifications they need to make on their rules and trading systems. Requirements in relation to trading below the 'pre-trade block thresholds' also have to be looked upon, in order to guarantee the request for quote systems that fall within the new regulations.

Impact on their business models also needs to be taken into account by Exchanges and MTF members. Firms that are carrying out trades outside the RM's or MTF's have to make sure that whatever they

---

[8] http://www.fsa.gov.uk/pubs/international/planning_mifid.pdf. Reproduced by permission of the Financial Services Authority.

[9] Editor's Note: Liquid Shares are another critical component of MiFID as the Directive allows around 530 such shares to be defined across Europe; these are the most liquid European shares – similar to creating a European version of an S&P500. In other words, those equities defined as a liquid share under MiFID will immediately gain significant capitalisation and increased trading volumes over those that are not. This is a referred to extensively in future chapters, but particularly Chapter 14.

do fits the definition of 'systematic internalisers'. In addition to this, complying with the pre-trade rules may also involve creating new business models and changes in the current systems.

These requirements have the greatest effect on the RM's, MTF's, as well as firms that are systematic internalisers. For these firms, the impact is massive. These changes also have a direct impact on other firms meeting their execution obligations.

2.10.3   Post-trade transparency

The changes to the scope of post-trade transparency rules are going primarily to impact RM's and MTF's, as well as investment firms trading outside the RM's or MTF's. All these venues have to display the completed transactions in shares publicly, without any delays, and on a reasonable commercial basis.

According to the MiFID supplement, 'investment firms can choose the disclosure channel – RM, MTF, third-party or proprietary arrangements – through which they make the details of each transaction public'.[10]

The internal controls of investment firms, RM's, and MTF's, also need to be looked upon in order to apply the new trading provisions. For firms that are carrying out trades outside a RM or a MTF, emphasis will need to be taken into account for the method by which the firm publishes their trades, as well as reviewing the accuracy and correctness of the trades being published.

These requirements affect the RM's and MTF's. In addition to this, OTC trading is affected, as well as equity trade data disseminators.

2.10.4   Transaction reporting

Transaction reporting is viewed as post-trade reporting to regulators. Under MiFID the requirements for transaction reporting move from the competent authority of the regulated markets to the competent authority of the home, or state, of the firm. In particular, it is worth noting that even though MiFID does not require reporting of the following transactions, it is still necessary to review them:

---

[10] http://www.fsa.gov.uk/pubs/international/planning_mifid.pdf. Reproduced by permission of the Financial Services Authority.

- reporting of transactions traded on prescribed markets that are not regulated markets;
- reporting of transactions in OTC instruments that are endorsed to instruments on prescribed markets.

Furthermore, no matter where the firms provide investments, it is necessary for them to report the transactions that are traded. However, it is a possibility for a firm not to report the transactions that are only quoted on Exchanges that are outside the European Union.

With MiFID, consideration will need to be taken regarding the impact it has on commodity firms, which now have to report all the trades on those commodities Exchanges that are regulated markets. Nevertheless, if these transactions are not compliant with the MiFID requirements, then alternative measures can be taken in order to receive the reports of the transactions traded.

On the other hand, authorised firms that present transaction reports to non-EU Exchanges need to look at the key aspect of how to report the transactions. In addition to this, the MiFID Supplement states 'that trades on non-EU Exchanges will still need to be transaction reported by firms if the subject instrument is also traded on a regulated market in the EU. For example, a transaction in IBM common stock on the NYSE will still need to be reported to us as the instrument also has a London quote. It is unlikely that UK firms will have to report transactions in instruments that are not admitted to trading on any exchange within the EU.'[11]

The requirements affect almost all firms, depending on the nature of the business. To illustrate this point, UK-based firms that only operate in UK traded instruments are not affected much. However, all UK-based firms do now have to make sure that the current transaction reporting they carry out covers all the instruments accurately, and that it is received by the correct authority. In the case of UK-based firms, this would be the FSA.

2.10.5   Cross-border business, branching, passporting[12]

The MiFID supplement states that 'firms that are authorized in one Member State can provide ISD services in other Member States either

---

[11] http://www.fsa.gov.uk/pubs/international/planning_mifid.pdf. Reproduced by permission of the Financial Services Authority.
[12] See Chapter 5.

cross-border or through a branch without having to be authorized separately in each Member State in which they wish to do business – this is known as the 'passport'. MiFID extends the range of activities and instruments that are covered by the passport, and clarifies the home/host supervision of passported firm's.[13]

Under MiFID, this means firms need to:

- define that running an MTF is covered by the passport, and the scope of the passport is upgraded to cover financial contracts, credit and commodity derivatives for any differences; and
- extend advice to a core investment service that involves personal advice, which can then be passported on a stand alone basis.

Under MiFID, supervising the responsibility for organisation and conduct of business requirements, are passported by a firm's home state regulator. However, there are exceptions where the right host state regulator takes the responsibility for conduct of business requirements. Therefore, home and host state requirements can apply when a firm provides services on a cross border basis. For example, establishing a branch in another state will mean the firm has to comply with the home state requirements with respect to the organisational requirements, under MiFID. Activities within a host state area will also require host state requirements on the conduct of business. Home state requirements should only apply when a passported branch provides services outside the area of it host state.

2.10.6 Use of tied agents

MiFID introduces an open tied agent rule, which sets out rules for the investment firms should they choose to make use of the tied agents. Although this is similar to the current rules, cross border activities of tied agents developing branches in other Member States is now covered under the passporting principles. Reviewing the conduct of business, how the business is laid out, and arrangements for changes to be made if necessary, needs to be taken into consideration throughout the EU.

These requirements affect all regulated firms within the scope of MiFID. In addition to this, firms that make use of the passport

---

[13] http://www.fsa.gov.uk/pubs/international/planning_mifid.pdf. Reproduced by permission of the Financial Services Authority.

to conduct business throughout Europe, including tied agents, are affected.

2.11 CONCLUSIONS

Overall, I believe MiFID is the correct way forward for the financial industry throughout the UK and Europe.

MiFID reduces the barriers to cross-border trading of shares and cross-border provision of investment services. It ends the traditional monopoly on the trading of securities which Stock Exchanges have had, thus creating opportunities for consumers, companies, and markets. Cross border trading provides a strong platform to benefit the overall European economy. Productivity and efficiency will increase from the levels of competition between investment companies, which will lower the costs for investors accessing the capital markets, allowing them to maximise their returns. Inevitably, this enables all businesses to invest more, in order for them to grow and develop more job prospects and wealth.

---

* Use of FSA material does not indicate any endorsement by the FSA of this publication, or the material or views contained within it.

3

'Best Execution'

Anthony Kirby

The delivery and evidencing of 'the most reasonable result for the client' has taken on a whole new meaning under the banner of fulfilling 'Best Execution' and the shape of the measures could result in serious tensions and conflicts across the EU, unless competent authorities take steps to manage their differences.

Without action we might have a future scenario where it becomes apparent that fulfilling 'Best Execution' is the topic that challenges investment firms the most when it comes to MiFID compliance. Evidencing 'Best Execution' under MiFID becomes no longer merely a question of best price, but depends upon taking all reasonable steps to obtain the best possible result, taking a range of factors into account.

This grants the investor the flexibility they need.

Meanwhile, a number of large investment houses decide to classify themselves into categories where they receive the most generous protections per their own interests. Less sophisticated clients are ignorant of MiFID's measures and gain no benefit. And regulators find themselves unable to agree common market practices.

This leads to the media querying why some investors are enjoying substantially better benefits than others across the various EU and EEA territories, and just how did the European markets get themselves into this mess in the first place?

Let's imagine that this is futuristic scenario is one that no one wishes to see happen.

It is the exact reverse of what the European Commission's Lisbon process is trying to achieve. It is a scenario which would dampen investor confidence, and thus the appetite for firms to raise capital cross-border. After all, confidence in cross-border investing is what MiFID is meant to be all about and, given the vast amounts of

The Future of Investing in Europe's Markets after MiFID   Edited by C. Skinner
© 2007 John Wiley & Sons, Ltd

intellectual capacity and management time dedicated to crafting MiFID through its various forms, most firms would wish for the competent authorities to collaborate more and compete less.

However, without action to manage the uncertainties surrounding differential client categorisation and 'Best Execution', MiFID's intentions will come to nought.

3.1   THE INVESTMENT SERVICES DIRECTIVE (ISD)

Before we look at this future state, we must first take a couple of steps back to see where we have come from. The Investment Services Directive or ISD, the precursor to MiFID, proposed a common passport so that firms could transact cross-border under home state authorisation. Besides the idea of a common passport, the ISD also formalised a market state called the concentration rule, whereby liquidity was directed formally towards a central execution venue within a residual six EU Member States, in order to forestall internalisation abuses in some of them.

By 2004, it was clear that the ISD needed an urgent overhaul. Not only were there eleven new accession countries within the EU to cover, but there were also new:

- firms, including hedge funds and private wealth management;
- execution venues, including electronic markets and bank liquidity pools; and
- instruments, including exchange- and OTC-traded derivatives, exchange traded funds, UCITS and money market instruments.

What did this have to do with 'Best Execution'?

Well, around 1993 when the ISD was enacted, early computer-driven trading was implemented by desks facilitating electronic conveyance, crossing and program trading from lists tracking the indices. These lists operated for own account and also on behalf of customers. At the time, a head trader on the buy-side told me that 'if anyone was brave enough to think about achieving such a thing as "Best Execution", you might as well forget calling a broker, dealing in size, entering the market near the open or close, dealing when large program trades were known to kick in', and so on. Back then, I focused upon quantitative trading techniques and measuring trading costs, so this hardly came as a big surprise; but it taught me the lesson that 'good' and 'best' may well lie on different roads. 'Best Execution' did not automatically imply achievability in practice or expediency and, even then, its definition came loaded with connotations and interpretations across the various Member States.

In addition, the paucity of key information was a significant impediment to tracking trading costs on a consistent basis during the 1990's. Both market and client record information was not always recorded or immediately accessible to external agents. There were breaks in the order handling process and proprietary communications, bearing in mind that this was all pre-FIX. Nevertheless, some cross-border spreads used to be wider than a barn door. Meaningful trading cost analysis was simply impossible. The necessary data was often not recorded and computing power was limited.

However, more recently, the increased accessibility to quality structured data, combined with a greater awareness of transaction cost analysis methods, contributed towards greater market transparency and, some might argue, falling margins.

This means that the micromanagement of securities trading had become increasingly automated by the year 2000, as a result of some serious advances in technology.

Exchanges started delivering on their promise of better cost-effectiveness, liquidity management, direct market access and market transparency, becoming more electronic and order-book driven. Broker/dealers, increasingly invested in the use of technology, such as order management systems (OMS's), to improve their execution quality, manage their collateral inventories and reduce their latency, particularly with regard to volume sensitivity for high-margin instruments. Technology also enabled buy-side traders to join in the fun, by quantifying market impact and opportunity costs more efficiently, in order to enhance portfolio alpha and justify 'Best Execution' to end investors.

3.2 'BEST EXECUTION' AND ASSET MANAGERS

These innovations have brought asset managers ever closer to the price formation process and the point of sale. So a practical but empirical way to view 'Best Execution' is to view it from the perspective of how the client is best served.

The client of the broker/dealer is the asset manager, for example, and if the asset managers receive poor-quality execution from their brokers, they are unlikely to come back for more. Lindsay Tomlinson, former Chairman of the IMA, put it this way, ' "Best Execution"? You know it when you see it'.

With sophisticated metrics such as the use of Transaction Cost Analysis (TCA) methodologies among buy-side firms increasing by the day, it becomes an area where market forces apply in the form of positive or negative reinforcement. The feedback is such that firms consistently offering their clients a recognisably poor quality of execution are likely to lose business as a result, especially given the growing trend towards the unbundling of research and soft commissions.

The question for the buy-side is whether asset managers have got what it takes to stay the long course? As my colleague, Brian Mitchell who is Head of Dealing and Portfolio Control at Baring Asset Management and Co-chair of the MiFID JWG 'Best Execution' Subject Group, elaborates:

> These days, most buy-side firms also look at one or two-day pre-trade momentum, passed on from fund managers along with detailed post-trade market impact. Here, we also look at thirty-day and quarter-end net returns, which are what clients actually want and are paying for.

So the current definitions of 'Best Execution' already grace many a marketing pitch, tender and vendor offering, but the fifteen year or more search for 'Best Execution' has proved highly elusive, despite the many assurances otherwise. The trade-off for equities, for example, is whether obtaining the best possible price is more important than achieving immediacy, defined as speed, coupled with certainty of execution, or even the best possible result in a client's trading portfolio.

Firms preparing themselves for MiFID compliance are therefore asking themselves whether the scope should merely cover market prices as such, or should it be more expansive and cover overall end-to-end transaction execution, extending into consideration of trading, clearing and settlement costs. For example, from the point of view of the buy-side's trading desk, 'Best Execution' could be defined in two subtly different ways representing as either a value or a cost play. The *Value Play* involves placing trades via a broker/dealer or automated trading system in order to realise the maximum value of the firm's investment decisions; whilst the *Cost Play* entails placing trades with the intent of minimising transactional implementation costs.

How might end-investors influence which route the market professionals and intermediaries take on their behalf and would trustees of pension funds, for example, understand or even care?

The FSA and the other competent authorities, such as the AMF, have done a good job situating 'Best Execution' within a principles context of achieving 'the most reasonable result for the client' under Article 21 of MiFID. However, important questions remained as to whether these measures could easily apply in dealer-led markets.

For example, Article 21(1) of the MiFID Level 1 text stated that:

> Member States shall require that investment firms take all reasonable steps to obtain, when executing orders, the best possible result for their clients taking into account price, costs, speed, likelihood of execution and settlement, size, nature or any other consideration relevant to the execution of the order.

There were new obligations to tell clients on which venue or venues a firm would execute the trade and obtain the best result for its customer, per the firm's order execution policy.

The 'Best Execution' obligation under MiFID accrues 'to the firm that has the contractual or agency obligations to the client', regardless of whether the order is executed directly or indirectly. For the provisions to be effective, they must address the challenge that 'Best Execution' can be viewed differently depending on whether you happen to be the final buy-side, for example as a pension fund; the intermediate buy-side, for example as an asset manager or a hedge fund; or the sell-side. Each view is refracted by the transparency of processes and the availability of underlying information to support each process. The problems with achieving 'Best Execution' therefore cannot be separated from the existing economics of trading systems, and the appetite of traders to change the way they approach the trading as applied to portfolio trading versus benchmarks, such as Volume Weighted Average Price (VWAP), Time Weighted Average Price (TWAP) and trading with 'Actual or Expected volume'.

'Best Execution' is therefore not synonymous with measuring and minimising trading costs, but about having an implementation process which is consistent with the underlying management style, and about measuring the process and gathering feedback to make changes.

An asset manager might enquire, however, what 'the most reasonable result for the client' might look like in a fragmented liquidity environment post-MiFID. This might consist of an explosion of regulated Exchanges, multilateral trading facilities, such as automated trading systems including crossing networks and ATS's, internalised matching by systematic internalisers, and multiple order management systems (OMS's).

Would a sell-side firm offering the price discovery function have the interests of the buy-side client at heart? Or might proprietary trading considerations get in the way, particularly as sell-side firms typically commit capital to provide immediacy of execution?

Lastly, if there is to be a notion of 'Best Execution', might the thinking evolve to enable buy-side firms to begin to think about 'best settlement' and 'best asset servicing' over time? Should they care?

3.3 'BEST EXECUTION' – PROCESSES, POLICIES AND PRACTICES

A part of the answer to demonstrating and evidencing 'Best Execution' lies in having the process to measure it.

Article 21 of MiFID currently leaves it to each firm to make reasonable judgements about the relative significance of explicit and implicit costs for its trading processes (see Figure 3.1).

- The iceberg of trading costs is thawing under global warming!
- MiFID introduces a new dimension – assessing the cost of clearing & settlement in basis points

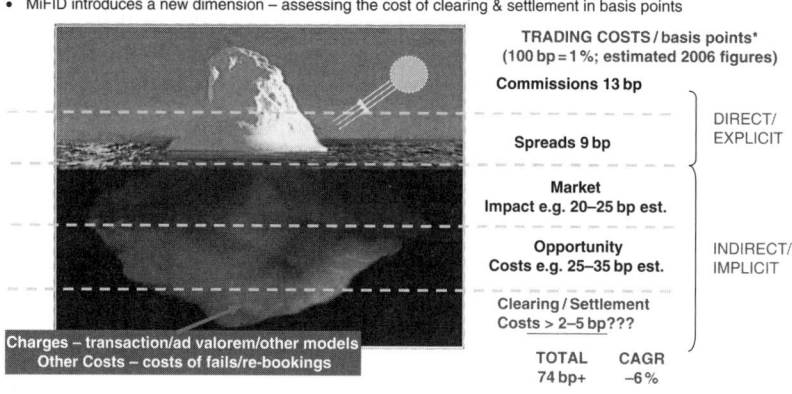

Figure 3.1 Illustration of Explicit and Implicit Trading Costs 2006
Source: © Accenture Research 2006. Adapted from a figure by Accenture.

Explicit costs include spreads, taxes and bundled commissions which are evident to both dealer and client. Implicit costs include elements such as opportunity costs and market impact costs, and firms must make judgement calls about how best to address these costs within their client agreements.

Article 21(5) states that:

Member States shall require investment firms to be able to demonstrate to their clients, at their request, that they have executed their orders in accordance with the firm's execution policy.

As a process argument, 'Best Execution' is difficult to define given the different prices quoted for different types of order, different needs for immediacy, different portfolio weightings, etc. One size won't fit all.

MiFID approaches the challenge by suggesting that 'Best Execution' be addressed as a best practice by market participants, rather than centrally. Investment firms must establish and implement effective arrangements for complying with the requirement to deliver 'Best Execution'.

'Best Execution' means that, when firms execute client orders, they must take all reasonable steps to deliver the best possible result for their clients taking into account price, costs, speed, likelihood of execution and settlement, size, nature or any other consideration relevant to the execution of the order.

For retail clients, 'best possible' means the most favourable result in terms of the total consideration payable. This approach sidesteps the question of whether 'Best Execution' should be the responsibility of market centres and regulators versus the responsibility of each firm.

Next, investment firms must establish and implement a formal and codified order execution policy to allow them to obtain the best possible result.[1] This execution policy is the firm's key instrument in achieving 'Best Execution', and must be reviewed every 12 months. The policy should differentiate between different types of client – retail, professional or eligible counterparty.[2] Information must be recorded sufficient to evidence 'Best Execution' compliance with a firm's policy for every asset class in scope and made available to the client or regulator on request. Service levels must be applied to trades in all asset classes in scope, including portfolio trades and investment funds. The duty of 'Best Execution' accrues to all clients, with the exception of clients categorised as eligible counterparties, and the obligation should apply to the firm which owes contractual or agency obligations to the client. Firms have to obtain prior consent from their clients as regards their execution policy.[3] An individual client may agree to the policy or

---

[1] MiFID Lamfalussy Level 1 text, Article 21, Paragraph 2.
[2] MiFID, Article 21, Paragraph 3.
[3] MiFID, Article 21, Paragraph 3.

can decide to issue specific instructions, for example, to execute only at a single venue of choice. These instructions always prevail over what is in the policy.

3.4   THE TRADING VENUE

The selection of execution venues is a critical consideration when crafting the 'Best Execution' policy.

An investment firm's 'Best Execution' policy must at least include, in respect of each class of instruments, information on the different venues where the firm executes its client orders and the factors affecting the choice of execution venue.

The European Commission's Frequently Asked Questions[4] document identifies the fact that the policy has to be dynamic, and must include those venues that enable the investment firm to obtain, on a consistent basis, the best possible result for the execution of client orders. The investment firm's policy may have to be amended to take account of the emergence of new venues, particularly for equities. The elimination of the monopoly of directing liquidity onto a central exchange – the Concentration Rule – means that Order Routing systems may need to identify and manage the existing Exchanges as well as anything up to twenty to forty new execution venues, including investment firms internalising orders on a systematic basis. The challenge and opportunity for the asset manager is that this trend is occurring against a backdrop of electronic trading systems, such as DMA and algorithmic trading,[5] and the unbundling of research and execution-commissions.

A firm must, of course, have access to at least the venues cited in its execution policy. This can be achieved by gaining access to these venues directly by becoming a member of an exchange, for example, or via an intermediary or intermediaries. Firms will have to monitor and regularly review their execution policy and decide which option – direct access versus intermediated access – is likely to secure the

---

[4] Frequently Asked Question on MiFID: Draft Implementing 'Level 2' measures, Reference: MEMO/06/57, Published by the European Commission on 6 February 2006.

[5] Algorithmic trading refers to portfolio managers or dealers on the buy-side conveying requests for bid, orders and allocations (splits) to their brokers and/or trading counterparts via the FIX protocol. Instead of the orders for single stocks or portfolio trades needing to be executed manually (often by highly-compensated dealers on the desk), a trading engine is used to slice and price the order intelligently using a selected set of rules of algorithms pre-defined between the trading counterparties.

lowest execution costs for their clients. Supervisors will have to decide whether the decisions taken by firms are reasonable. In doing so, they will take into account a number of factors including the size and cost structure of the firm concerned.

Clearly, the cost of direct access to a multitude of venues may be high. In many cases, therefore, an indirect access through an intermediary may be the best solution. For example, TCA data will eventually evolve and further push some less technology and algorithmically focused buy-side houses into going electronic.

When these TCA providers start reflecting median execution and research costs separately, they will become powerful tools. In the interim, however, the commissions paid by asset managers to intermediaries providing access to execution venues can mount up over time, and it may become clear that gaining direct access is more economical and efficient than going through intermediaries (see Figure 3.2).

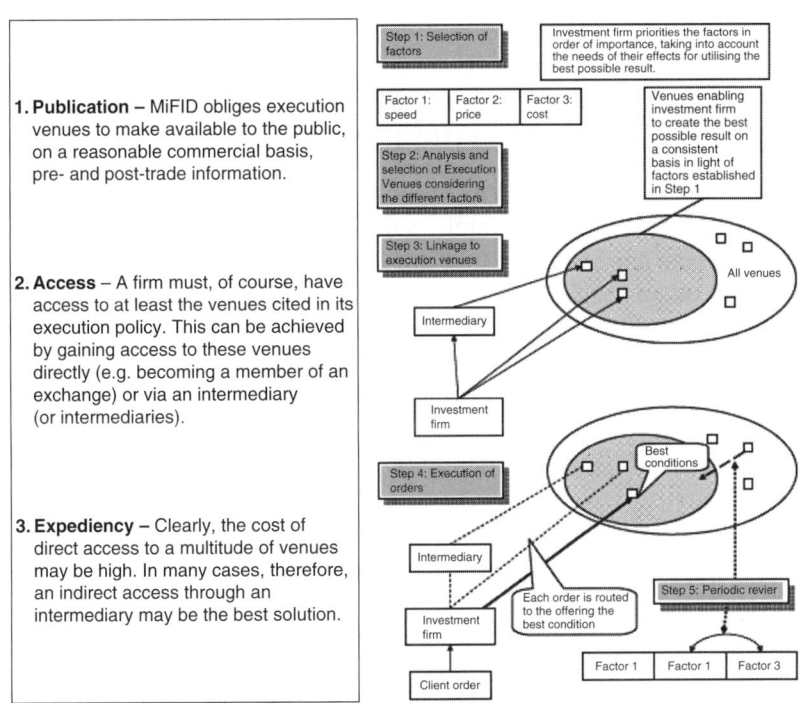

Figure 3.2   The Expediency argument in relation to accessing various Execution Venues

Source: MiFID Draft L2 Implementing Measures – Directive – Background Notes Feb 2006. Reproduced by permission of the European Commission.

The issue of cost comes to the fore here, because implicit costs are clearly dependent on the quality of execution venues, and that dealers have the tools at their disposal to differentiate between the relative importance of factors such as price, speed, size, costs, and probabilities of execution and settlement in the heat of making a trade.

It is clear that under MiFID, the need to devise, populate and update metrics will grow exponentially and to benchmark every area will require a relatively high degree of sophistication and data maintenance, not to mention solid business process and data management. The challenge will be how to maintain order out of data chaos, and how to employ transaction cost analysis as an effective benchmark.

The draft Level 2 MiFID text[6] rightfully does not mandate investment firms to access venues where it would not be commercially viable to do so. So without consistent benchmarks for market quality, as a function of price delivery, much less price discovery, some have questioned whether 'Best Execution' could ever be a viable candidate for regulatory oversight alone.

3.5 THE SOLUTION FOR 'BEST EXECUTION' COMPLIANCE?

What is missing in the trading space is a best practice surrounding the frequency of monitoring, and the solution to the trade-off between the need for best price versus expediency may lie in the monitoring. If, for example, asset managers are able to demonstrate best use of trading rules encompassing investment vehicles and execution options to the regulators, this could result in a significant shift in market behaviour post-MiFID and offer a massive boost to direct market access (DMA) and algorithmic trading.

'The research and execution costs are central to this debate', notes Brian Mitchell.[7]

'Automation and algorithmic trading usage accounts for 4–5 basis points[8] (bps), but a lot of buy-side firms already outsource the technology. They may pay up to 7 bps for "full service execution" to

---

[6] MiFID Articles 44–46, and recitals 66–76, which have legal force.

[7] Head of Dealing and Portfolio Control at Baring Asset Management and Co-Chair of the MiFID JWG 'Best Execution' Subject Group.

[8] Editor's note: a basis point measures the percentage change in the value of a financial instrument, and is usually associated with changes in interest rates and bond yields. One basis point is 0.0001.

intermediaries in the UK, and this extra 2 bps which the sell-side are getting is primarily for advice and services but, to my mind, also for the provision and facilitation of the intermediaries' algorithmic technology', adds Mitchell.

The obligations for dealers on the desk are expected to increase sharply as a result of the continued growth in DMA and algorithmic trading (see Figure 3.3).

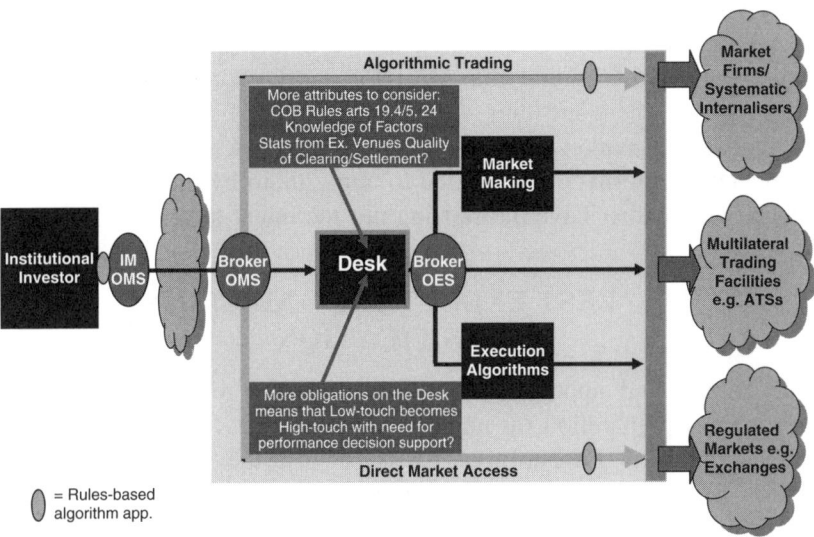

Figure 3.3 Greater obligations of MiFID will turn the desk into a 'high-touch' zone and catalyse the pace of Algorithmic Trading

Source: MiFID JWG BESG Mar 2006. Reproduced by permission of the MiFID JWG Best Execution Subject Group May 2006.

Exposing costly or inefficient practices as well as the technological advances in electronic trading, have improved execution speed, execution certainty and business transparency. It has also dramatically reduced margins and prompted a rush into algorithmic, hedge fund and derivative trading.

If algorithmic trading is one possible vision for MiFID, this will presuppose that a critical mass of asset managers will invest in the necessary technology. The price-performance argument is a critical one as it persuades more asset managers of the case to make the switch towards algorithmic trading. This is supported by the incessant scrutiny of transaction costs, a natural result of activism on the side of the asset managers and end investors, and the widespread innovations in technology impacting overall securities trading.

Buy-side traders have mobilised to suggest changes to the market structure and regulatory reforms, such as the Myners Review,[9] that have transformed the market from a sell-side dominated structure to one that better serves the needs of both sophisticated institutional buyers and individual investors. Therefore, the casting of 'Best Execution', client classification and conduct of business rules would afford most clients greater scope for flexibility, which is a positive signal. However the 'spirit' of realising and evidencing 'Best Execution' and client classification within MiFID is tightly-worded and relatively prescriptive. There are thus doubts how some of the measures will be realised in market practice. There is a significant risk that some competent authorities may decide to apply them by the letter, versus others who neither have the staffing nor the intent to do so.

3.6   'BEST EXECUTION' AND CLIENT CLASSIFICATION

The correct and appropriate classification of a firm's clients is a key area of preparation for undertaking the process of delivering and evidencing 'Best Execution'. This is because the status of a firm's client, depending on their knowledge and experience, has a direct bearing on the level of duty of care which must be applied.

For example, if we look at clients as being on a ladder of knowledge, the experienced investors as a rule tend to be more knowledgeable when compared with many retail clients, and will therefore be placed higher up the ladder as generally the experience investor has the experience and wherewithal to support their strategies. As things stand under MiFID, each party on the ladder owes a duty of responsibility to deliver and evidence 'Best Execution' to the previous party down the ladder.

In addition, a minimum, legally-codified, 'Best Execution' policy may differ from policies which firms might operate in practice. For example, net consideration for clients classified as 'retail', could well include the costs of clearing and settlement as a relevant factor. It is

---

[9] Editor's note: In March 2000, UK Chancellor Gordon Brown commissioned a review of institutional investment in the UK to be led by Paul Myners, the then Chairman of Gartmore Investment Management.

far from clear how a dealing desk might source this information. It is also unclear as to how 'dynamic' policies will need to be in practice. For example, how far are firms obliged to connect to every execution venue, which is implied as the requirement for the principle that 'firms must take all reasonable steps to deliver the best possible result'. The question is what is 'reasonable'?

MiFID is structured to enable the maximum degree of client protection, and the truly revolutionary aspect to MiFID is the way that the measures link client classification with 'Best Execution' and order handling.

Client Classification requirements applies to all clients an investment firm deals with in relation to products and services under the scope of MiFID, and are categorised into different levels of experience and expertise per three categories of client – retail, professional and eligible counterparties (see Figure 3.4).

1. **Client Categorisation** – Client Classification requirements will apply to all clients an investment firm deals with in relation to products and services under the scope of MiFID.

2. **Dynamic Classification** – MiFID provides the flexibility for clients to move between categories provided conditions are met. Rules allow clients to change their initial classification on request, and clients can move between categories on request (the same client can have different classifications).

3. **KYC / COB** – Firms must notify clients if they are to be treated as professional before providing services, and clients must state in writing (contractually) that they wish to be treated as professional (and that they are aware of the consequences of losing their protections).

4. **Grandfathering / Repapering** – Some clients may need to be re-papered with updated agreements.

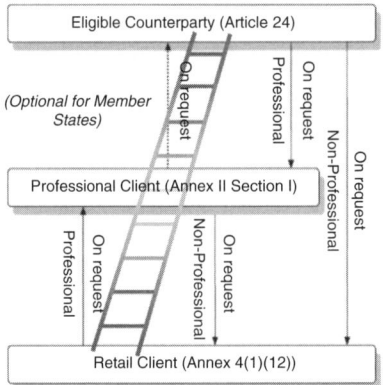

Figure 3.4   The Importance of Client Categorisation as the precursor to 'Best Execution' evidencing

Source: MiFID Draft L2 Implementing Measures – Directive – Background notes Feb 2006. Reproduced by permission of the European Commission.

MiFID provides the flexibility for clients to move between categories, provided certain conditions are met. The rules also allow clients to change their initial classification upon request, and clients can move between categories upon request. In fact, you can get the situation where the same client can have different classifications.

For the sell-side investment firms, the duty is that they must notify their clients of their right to change their classification, and they must keep records of the client's confirmation of their classification. Although there are some issues here, as this principle is subject to interpretation by the relevant competent authority in each Member State, so how do you avoid a differential interpretation?

'Retail Clients'[10] are typically less-sophisticated investors, who warrant the greatest degree of regulatory protection. It is expected that more clients will wish to receive the regulatory protections afforded them as retail clients, and that many retail and some intermediate customers will wish to fall into this category.

'Professional Clients'[11] are clients who possess the experience, knowledge and expertise to make their own investment decisions, and properly assess the risks that those decisions incur. Even so, these clients can request non-professional treatment.[12]

'Eligible Counterparties' are the most sophisticated investment client or participant. They can request to be treated as a professional or retail client generally, or on a trade-by-trade basis. In principle, this covers investment firms, credit institutions, insurance companies, UCITS and their management companies, pension funds and their management companies. For each transaction, adequate risk warnings must be given and the transaction must be 'at the initiative of the client' as well as meeting certain conditions, for example this applies only for the trading of non-complex financial instruments.

The classification of clients according to their knowledge and experience is the result of two tests which the investment firm must conduct.

Firstly, the 'Suitability Test'[13] applies to entities providing investment advice or portfolio management. The investment firm must obtain the necessary information regarding the client's, or potential client's, knowledge and experience in the investment field relevant to the specific type of product or service, their financial situation and their investment objectives, so as to enable the firm to recommend the investment services and financial instruments that are suitable for them.

Secondly, the 'Appropriateness Test'[14] requires that investment firms providing investment services[15] ask the client or potential client to provide information regarding their knowledge and experience in the

---

[10] MiFID Lamfalussy Level 1 text, Article 4, Paragraph 1.12.
[11] MiFID Lamfalussy Level 1 text, Annex II.
[12] MiFID Lamfalussy Level 1 text, Article 24, Paragraph 2.
[13] MiFID Lamfalussy Level 1 text, Article 19, Paragraph 4. See Chapter 4.
[14] MiFID Lamfalussy Level 1 text, Article 19, Paragraph 5. See Chapter 4.
[15] Other than those itemised in MiFID Lamfalussy Level 1 text, Article 19, Paragraph 4.

investment field relevant to the specific type of product or service offered or demanded, so as to enable the investment firm to assess whether the investment service or product envisaged is appropriate for the client.

To conclude, the 'Common Provisions'[16] stipulate that European Member States are to ensure that the information regarding a client's or potential client's knowledge and experience in the investment field includes the following:

(a) the types of service, transaction and financial instrument with which the client is familiar;
(b) the nature, volume, and frequency of the client's transactions in financial instruments, and the period over which they have been carried out;
(c) the level of education, and profession or relevant former profession of the client or potential client.

MiFID creates an implicit relationship between client classification and 'Best Execution'. As clients are allowed to opt-up as well as down for lower versus greater levels of 'Best Execution' protection, how do dealing desks adapt to this? Considerable behavioural change has to occur on the trading desk as dealers need to be versed in conduct of business rules and need to pre-select factors in execution of the orders, such as the statistics relating to number of execution venues.

3.7 THE MiFID JOINT WORKING GROUP (JWG), 'BEST EXECUTION' SUBJECT GROUP

The MiFID Joint Working Group (JWG) was formed in April 2005 as a not-for-profit, international grouping of individuals. The MiFID JWG then established a number of specialist subject groups to address the issues the Directive raised in different areas, namely:

- 'Best Execution';
- Reference Data;
- Cross-Border Jurisdiction;
- Real-Time Market Data;
- Standard Protocols;
- Technology in general.

---

[16] MiFID, Article 37, Paragraph 1.

The objective of the MiFID JWG 'Best Execution' Subject Group (BESG) was to agree market practice guidelines, with regard to the timeliness, commonality, availability, storage and retrieval of market and reference data, relevant to firms wishing to demonstrate or evidence 'Best Execution' processes under the MiFID. Rather than reinventing the wheel, the BESG gathered input from documents and discussions from experts in as many asset classes impacted by MiFID as possible and hosted a number of lively debates as to where clarification was needed.

The specific focus was around the issues of where the obligations of 'Best Execution' are placed, and whether 'Best Execution' should be applied in a rigid, rules-based manner. This is a relatively convenient approach if the aim is the harmonisation of all asset-class processes in Europe, but one which is not likely to be popular with the business. By contrast, enforcement of 'Best Execution' practices through principles-based regulation is seen to be an important consideration if the aim is to encourage both innovation and market liquidity.

In either outcome, the BESG concluded that FIX-based[17] electronic trading will have a big role to play, irrespective of whether 'Best Execution' is driven by direct regulation or through policies, procedures and practices.

The BESG also debated how the measures might apply to quote-driven markets, to evidence 'Best Execution' processes in fixed income, derivatives or structured products, where a provider might be the only market professional entity making a price and where the credit worthiness of the client could be an important factor in pricing.

It was argued that the duty of a firm to demonstrate that they had executed their orders in accordance with the firm's execution policy could prove challenging under volatile trading conditions in fragmented markets, and that firms may struggle to explain 'Best Execution' processes to their clients equally for all asset classes in these circumstances.

Finally, in the post-MiFID world, the BESG anticipates a three- to four-fold expansion of transaction volumes and believes that the amount of data required to demonstrate 'Best Execution' will prove to

---

[17] Editor's note: FIX is the Financial Information eXchange Protocol, controlled by the FIX Protocol Limited organisation, a not-for-profit group that manages its release and structure. FIX Protocol is a standard that was created in the mid-1990's by Fidelity and Salomon in the USA, to enable ease of processing using technology in the pre-trade environment, and is now widely used and mandated by buy-side firms in their dealings with the sell-side.

be prohibitively expensive for many, unless there are sensible boundaries established by way of scope and expectation.

There were other areas of controversy within the measures debated between the BESG and MiFID-Connect[18] such as:

- delivering and evidencing 'Best Execution' in fixed income and other dealer-led or quote-driven markets would be challenging, for what is the definition of an 'order';
- the option for the fund manager to pass the 'Best Execution' obligation back to the broker is precluded, although there is nothing to stop the broker-dealer from providing the data;
- the terminology such as 'take all reasonable steps to ensure' is open-ended, and it is clear that the legal test should form the bottom line;
- does a fund manager reaching out to three separate dealers and specifying size really obtain 'the best result'?;
- surely 'Best Execution' is a contradiction in terms, as it has to be 'best' in relation to other forms of execution;
- how would this work for OTC markets if there is only one market-maker for an illiquid structured product?; and
- if the 'Best Execution' principle is implemented as a Directive subject to interpretation per competent authority in each Member State, might firms take advantage of what is described in common parlance as 'regulatory arbitrage'?

To help answer these questions, the practitioners within the BESG took part in a survey during the summer of 2006 to try and identify some of the roadblocks and dependencies in evidencing 'Best Execution' for their clients. The survey was completed by dealing and compliance professionals on both the buy- and sell-side from over twenty-five firms of various sizes and investment styles. For asset classes where a duty of 'Best Execution' was required, firms were asked to indicate the range of difficulty in delivering and having the data to evidence that the most reasonable result for the client was fulfilled.

Firms were asked to record their responses in colour ranges, consisting of:

---

[18] Editor's note: MiFID-Connect represent the majority of London Market Associations. For a full listing, see the Glossary.

- green for 'unlikely to be a challenge';
- lime-green indicating 'an occasional challenge', for example, large sizes;
- yellow indicating 'periodic challenges', for example, the lack of price benchmarks or illiquid securities;
- orange indicating 'regular and significant challenges', for example, where there are no benchmarks, relative intransparency, or custom-tailored instruments; and
- red signifying 'unlikely to be possible'.

The results of the survey are shown in Figure 3.5.

There are some interesting conclusions to be drawn.

Firstly, most practitioners did not foresee significant problems in evidencing 'Best Execution' for most order-driven markets, such as cash equities, except under specific conditions, for example when working with a significantly large order.

Secondly, although some dealer-led markets showed similar characteristics, there were significant difficulties for some segments, such as, corporate bonds, emerging market bonds, asset-backed securities, and structured products such as swaptions, credit derivatives or CFD's.[19]

Thirdly, the evidence of information asymmetry was not a consistent feature in this survey and, in some asset classes, the sell-side fared worse than the buy-side. This is due to the fact that professional investors are at least as well informed as, and often better informed than, dealers as each dealer only knows what they are quoting to a client, while a client dealing with multiple dealers has a broader view.

Finally, the survey indicated that it would be good for the competent authorities across the EU to agree what lies in and out of scope as there is widespread confusion over FX forwards and securities money market instruments, for example.

The UK's FSA then published their 'Best Execution' discussion paper in May 2006, clarifying their intentions with regards to implementation. This was closely followed by France's AMF, whose paper on 'Best Execution' was released in July 2006.

---

[19] Editor's note: these are all forms of more complex financial instruments. A swaption is a financial instrument granting the owner an option to enter into an interest rate swap. Credit derivatives transfer the risk of a credit asset's returns falling below an agreed level, without transfer the underlying asset itself. CFD is a Contract for Difference; a product traded on margin which allows the investor to gain the returns of a share's performance (price, dividends, etc.) without the stamp duty costs.

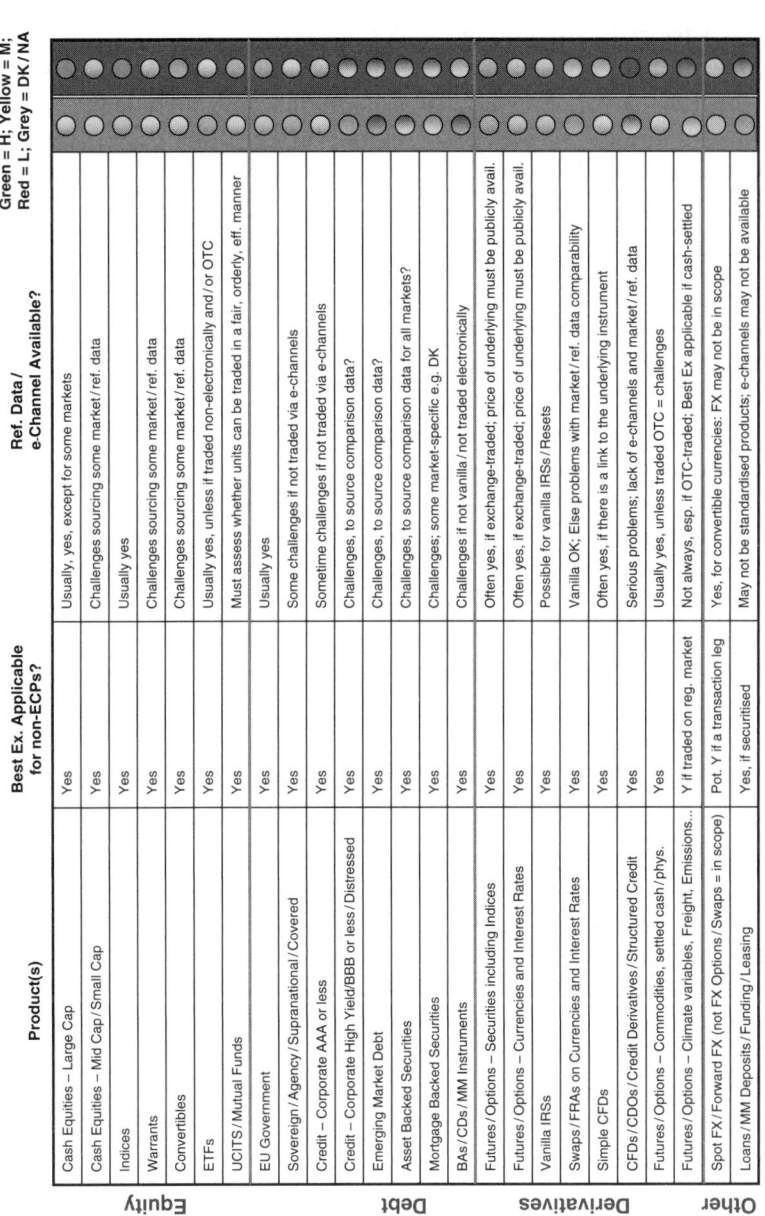

P(Ability to Evidence)?
Green = H; Yellow = M;
Red = L; Grey = DK/NA

	Product(s)	Best Ex. Applicable for non-ECPs?	Ref. Data / e-Channel Available?
Equity	Cash Equities – Large Cap	Yes	Usually, yes, except for some markets
	Cash Equities – Mid Cap/Small Cap	Yes	Challenges sourcing some market/ref. data
	Indices	Yes	Usually yes
	Warrants	Yes	Challenges sourcing some market/ref. data
	Convertibles	Yes	Challenges sourcing some market/ref. data
	ETFs	Yes	Usually yes, unless if traded non-electronically and/or OTC
	UCITS/Mutual Funds	Yes	Must assess whether units can be traded in a fair, orderly, eff. manner
Debt	EU Government	Yes	Usually yes
	Sovereign/Agency/Supranational/Covered	Yes	Some challenges if not traded via e-channels
	Credit – Corporate AAA or less	Yes	Sometime challenges if not traded via e-channels
	Credit – Corporate High Yield/BBB or less/Distressed	Yes	Challenges, to source comparison data?
	Emerging Market Debt	Yes	Challenges, to source comparison data?
	Asset Backed Securities	Yes	Challenges, to source comparison data for all markets?
	Mortgage Backed Securities	Yes	Challenges; some market-specific e.g. DK
	BAs/CDs/MM Instruments	Yes	Challenges if not vanilla/not traded electronically
Derivatives	Futures/Options – Securities including Indices	Yes	Often yes, if exchange-traded; price of underlying must be publicly avail.
	Futures/Options – Currencies and Interest Rates	Yes	Often yes, if exchange-traded; price of underlying must be publicly avail.
	Vanilla IRSs	Yes	Possible for vanilla IRSs/Resets
	Swaps/FRAs on Currencies and Interest Rates	Yes	Vanilla OK; Else problems with market/ref. data comparability
	Simple CFDs	Yes	Often yes, if there is a link to the underlying instrument
	CFDs/CDOs/Credit Derivatives/Structured Credit	Yes	Serious problems; lack of e-channels and market/ref. data
	Futures/Options – Commodities, settled cash/phys.	Yes	Usually yes, unless traded OTC = challenges
Other	Futures/Options – Climate variables, Freight, Emissions...	Y if traded on reg. market	Not always, esp. If OTC-traded; Best Ex applicable if cash-settled
	Spot FX/Forward FX (not FX Options/Swaps = in scope)	Pot. Y if a transaction leg	Yes, for convertible currencies: FX may not be in scope
	Loans/MM Deposits/Funding/Leasing	Yes, if securitised	May not be standardised products; e-channels may not be available

Figure 3.5 Summary results of BESG Survey illustrating the Likelihood of evidencing 'Best Execution' – Heat map for further Validation

Source: © MiFID JWG BESG and Accenture May 2006. Reproduced by permission of the MiFID JWG Best Execution Subject Group May 2006.

The FSA's paper focused on the dealer markets specifically, with a hugely controversial approach based upon the management of conflicts through the use of benchmarks. This direction came as a surprise to the industry and the broader issue as to whether other competent authorities in the EU/EEA would follow suit.

Here is a selection of reasons why the course of action proved hugely controversial:

(1) The concrete case for consistent market failures in price transparency, abuses and conflicts of interest were not made for the dealer-led markets. Any arrangements for benchmarking were therefore too early, as there was a due-diligence exercise being conducted by the European Commission around pre- and post-trade transparency. The markets were not given the opportunity to evaluate any measures arising from the latter for the dealer-led markets. Although there may have been a link between evidencing 'Best Execution' and pre- and post-trade transparency for all asset classes, this was only just moving onto the regulatory agenda. Therefore, applying the measures to non-equity markets in 2007 was felt to be inconsistent from the point of view of timing.

(2) The assumption of automatic information asymmetry between buy-side and sell-side[20] failed to recognise two facts: first, the buy-side was not homogenised by virtue of investment style; and second, the buy-side was not homogenised by virtue of purchasing power. Some buy-side firms such as hedge funds could hold large positions and could have access to information and prices, giving them a better liquidity picture than certain sell-side firms. This was borne out of the study performed by the MiFID JWG BESG for certain products.

(3) Measures which would benefit the final buy-side entities – pension funds, local authority funds, corporates and retail – might actually differ from arrangements which the buy-side intermediaries – fund managers, hedge funds, private banks, fund supermarkets – enter into. Adding an extra laying of monitoring and extra due diligence for the buy-side intermediaries could represent extra costs, and that would be a far from popular measure if buy-side intermediaries

---

[20] Information asymmetry in this context assumes that the buy-side is consistently disadvantaged by a lack of information which the sell-side has access to.

need to invest in the systems and monitoring, in order to check every order directed at the sell-side.

(4) Many dealer-led markets already functioned as liquidity providers in making firm prices, as in they are not liquidity takers from the market. It was not in their primary interest to make false prices if they are competing for the buy-side's business on the basis of best price, best size handling, best market timing, or similar. The system worked through a negative feedback loop where firms that make bad prices do not get the buyers coming back for more. Besides, by having to disclose proprietary information, dealers would also be exposing themselves to the distorting effects of gaming, particularly by hedge fund clients. These players could have access to a full spectrum of information, and would not run their risk that dealers would face in committing capital.

(5) Many dealer-led markets are managed over-the-counter (OTC) by definition. The spreads were wider because sell-side firms committed capital in support of immediacy – getting the order done – but many studies had indicated that the market functions at efficiency, and there is little extra that can be drawn from the spread. The cost of risk capital differed per firm because some sell-side firms are part of banking groups. Transparency might be a benefit for the buy-side, but if that deterred sell-side firms from making prices in the first place, competition could thin and paradoxically, the spreads could actually widen. Therefore, the opposite effect could be achieved from the intended.

(6) Benchmarking for products, such as illiquid instruments or highly tailored structured products, was unworkable from several perspectives. There were confidentiality arrangements in place, including Chinese walls which prevented open disclosure for commercial reasons. There were existing internal valuation systems in place which were proprietary with a strong differentiation between firms. There was also informal evidence that data vendors were unlikely to support such measures by offering to carry the data, especially if it meant expensive adaptations or liability arrangements to consider.

There are other questions which arose from the debates.

• If 'Best Execution' is regarded as a process, not a hard and fast result, would it not be extremely unwise for 'Best Execution' to be cast as a rigid regulation or even a tightly drafted legal policy with the same boundary conditions under each trading circumstance?

- What about common market data standards for pricing and instruments?
- Will this be available in time, and what are the Intellectual Property Rights (IPR) issues? Is this question answered as a function of time?
- How complex would the processes need to be, and are we talking about any more paperwork that must be translated, applied and affirmed into a form which clients can read, understand and apply correctly, particularly concerning OTC derivatives?
- Do all European Member States have the core competences to apply this measure in a consistent manner?

Finally, there was an extensive debate around the best approach to dealing with 'Best Execution' with several perspectives in play, namely:

- Benchmarking;
- Proactive Process Management;
- Laissez Faire.

Each Member State appears to be adopting one of these three approaches in their implementation of MiFID's 'Best Execution' requirements.

3.8 APPROACHES TO 'BEST EXECUTION' NO. 1: BENCHMARKING

Benchmarking as a concept is not new, and asset managers have been active supporters of the concept over the last fifteen years, at least as applied to areas such as modern portfolio theory, portfolio modelling, and rebalancing. The sell-side are also big supporters of benchmarking as applied to client connectivity, algorithmic trading and straight-through processing. This means that it is fair to say that, in principle, the industry is familiar with employing benchmarks provided the processes allow for meaningful comparisons and that the benchmarks are robust, with verifiable external data available to hand.

If the quality of execution is to be benchmarked to assess 'Best Execution', then the critical issue for benchmarks is that they must be robust. They should yield a demonstrable quantitative result and be industry-neutral if they are to win widespread acceptability.

The Investment Managers Association (IMA) response to the FSA's proposals were published in August 2006 and stated that for benchmarking to offer a form of safe harbour to firms, in terms of price achieved for trades, then it should be based on real-time executable or executed trade data, preferably in markets with high-frequency trading and execution processes which are comparative in a qualitative, not quantitative, fashion. This means that there is little chance of externally evidencing 'Best Execution' in markets that either are decentralized and/or lack any realistic form of post-trade transparency in a quantitative manner.

The FSA defined the ideal benchmark as one that needs to be 'robust'[21] for the purposes of achieving 'Best Execution'. The key determinants of 'robust' stated that the benchmark must 'be an accurate reflection of real prices for the relevant instrument' and 'drawn directly from a relevant pool of liquidity'.

The IMA's response also noted that the quality of a benchmark of that kind is based on the following four factors:

- the number of dealers making markets;
- the frequency of price updates (which can vary by firm and/or by instrument);
- the firmness of the price; and
- the size for which the price is firm.

There are signs that the industry across the EU is moving beyond the notion that benchmarking has to be applied to prices only. This is because there needs to be continuously executable prices available from a predominant source of liquidity, and there needs to be appropriate standards to allow comparability to occur. This is far from the case in dealer-led or OTC-traded markets for high-yield corporate debt, distressed debt, some emerging market and asset backed instruments, and especially non-vanilla IRS's and CFD's, as the research shown earlier in Figure 3.5 makes only too clear.

Given the strong views expressed by the various associations and firms against imposing prescriptive benchmarking for dealer-led markets, there were strong signals that such an approach would not win acceptability with buy-side firms. Equally, it was felt that such an approach would offer no protection to the end investors, especially if

---

[21] FSA Discussion Paper 06/03, 'Implementing MiFID's "Best Execution" Requirements', Paragraphs 3.24/3.25.

the sell-side felt inclined to withdraw liquidity across the market as a whole.

3.9   APPROACHES TO 'BEST EXECUTION' NO. 2: PROACTIVE PROCESS MANAGEMENT[22]

Some industry observers believe that the best option for implementing the 'Best Execution' obligation would be to adopt a principles-based approach. Regulators should strive to provide valuable additional guidance to reinforce the principles that apply to dealers when executing client orders.

The UK's FSA, for example, is praised for its approach to the processes for systems and controls[23] required under the Capital Requirements Directive (CRD) and MiFID. This is an excellent principles-based approach based on intelligent copy-out of MiFID which saves firms a great deal of time and effort. The paper proposed a common approach and platform for firms wishing to address CRD compliance at the same time as MiFID in a convergent manner.

An example of such an inclusive (and iterative approach) for the buy-side featuring the principles of KYC, portfolio modelling, plus IOI, order and execution management is shown in Figure 3.6, and I have called this approach 'Proactive Process Management'.

There is plenty of scope for firms to mix and match components provided that some basic rules are adhered to. For example, applying KYC to both new and existing clients could be linked with AML measures and to the quality of 'Best Execution', should the client demand flexibility in classification.

Admittedly, the possibility of dynamic client classification is bound to be more of a problem for the sell-side rather than the buy-side, but it is posited that the correct client qualification, consent and categorisation, drives the duty of care and no doubt the price points that will be applied to the same. This is far preferable to introducing measures to create 'two-tier' 'Best Execution' measures, which would otherwise be highly ambiguous to implement in practice.

There is even scope for proactive process management to apply benchmarks in their proper context, for example to oversee the

---

[22] This term is copyrighted.

[23] CP06/9 – Organisational systems and controls http://www.fsa.gov.uk/pages/Library/Policy/CP/2006/06_09.shtml.

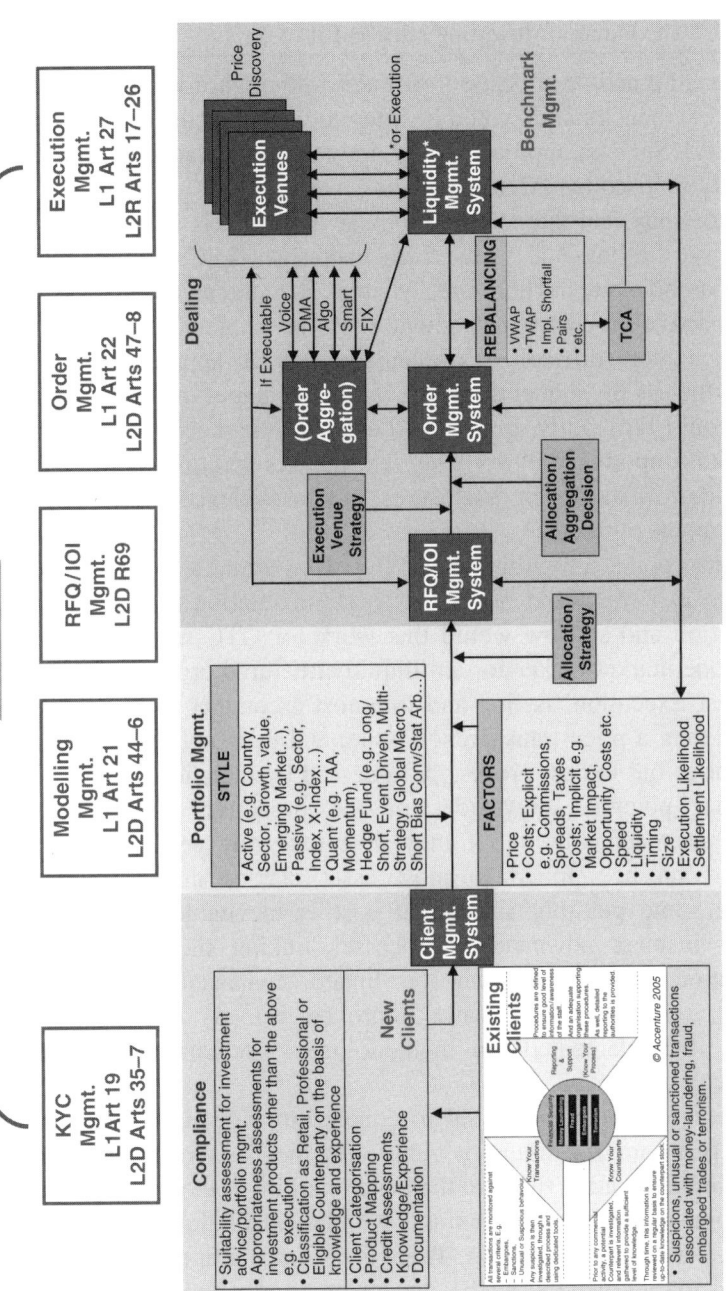

Figure 3.6 'Best Execution' Schematic – Pro-active Process Management© for the Buy-side (Illustrative)

Source: © Anthony Kirby Oct 2006

rebalancing and/or allocation of trades, although it should be stressed that these benchmarks would be internal to each firm and certainly not imposed. Such an approach could draw upon the valuable innovations already realised by TCA providers.

Some may feel that such a modular approach is idealised as many firms on the buy-side suffer from makeshift KYC, AML, OMS and EMS architectures. Therefore, whereas it looks as though the model of proactive process management could be implemented in theory, it is much more difficult to implement such an approach in practice. Nevertheless the model carries several advantages over benchmarking and could be readily applied to dealer-led markets, as it recognises the vital importance of voice-driven markets and does not require the sell-side to make open disclosures, nor to evidence 'Best Execution' at the point of quote.

At this point, it highlights that 'Best Execution' is actually a contradiction in terms, as it has to be 'best' in relation to other forms of execution and so how would this work for OTC markets if there is only one market-maker for an illiquid structured product?

'Best Execution' is first and foremost a conduct of business issue, rather than a price transparency issue, and does not merely equate to best price but to best process, as assessed by the client.

Other potential downsides of the proactive process management approach are that it may cost to create seamless processes which can be applied to most asset classes in the short term. While some possibly substantial cost is inevitable, the model has some business advantages. Processes linking the IOI, order and execution management can be linked, managed and thus optimised, resulting in a greatly improved velocity of trading, especially if implemented via methodologies such as the FIX FAST protocol.

There is also the potential to enable buy-side firms to compile a steadily improving liquidity picture on the basis of greater trust of their brokers, rather than via the benchmarking route which could lead to more legalistic outcomes and withdrawal of liquidity from some markets as mentioned above. There is thus a benefit to both investment intermediaries which can be passed on to the end investors, which might not be the case in 'laissez faire' methods and will not be the case if dealer-led markets are benchmarked. Moreover, the investment managers are not excluded from participating in particular liquidity opportunities.

Another issue is subtler and concerns any approach which unleashes further liquidity onto the markets, for example by accelerating trading opportunities or creating more ability to provide cross-asset class or derivative trading, has to be welcome. Approaches such as the one outline here for proactive process management, offer flexibility to recognise the judgement calls that take place every day and yet provide better opportunities for product differentiation, scale solutions and deeper investor participation.

Liquidity, rather than price, is one of the principal factors in pricing OTC-products in the fixed income, derivative and structured product sectors. Dealers will apply trade-offs to hedge their risks and commit capital effectively, if they are allowed to participate freely in liquidity opportunities in the free market while expressly under the duty to deliver the right result for their clients. Any model which allows the dealers to apply their judgement skills in quoting the appropriate price by client and channel, recognises the reality that quality dealing is more art than science. The rumour of the demise of the dealer is premature.

3.10   APPROACHES TO 'BEST EXECUTION' NO. 3: 'LAISSEZ-FAIRE'

There is a school of thought that argues that MiFID is far too much stick and not enough carrot as the costs of implementation of its measures far outweigh any benefits to be gleaned. The eventual costs to the industry and market users of the client classification, 'Best Execution', order handling and record-keeping aspects of MiFID, it is argued, resulted in costs in the range of $ 30–50 million for a typical European universal bank, and a tenth of that amount for a money manager or private bank.

Taking account of these factors, dealers would pass on to their clients the increase in their costs via a commission-based structure or via wider spreads for some asset classes, if the measures represent a significant departure from current market practices. Dynamic client categorisation is an excellent example of this. This school of thought might argue that, as a result, the imposition of 'Best Execution' would actually cost investors more before.

A survey of more than 100 firms by Accenture during the summer of 2006, for example, identified fewer than 14 % of firms who were inclined to view MiFID as either strategic or transformational. This means that too many firms were still of the mindset of 'wait and see until the process is finished', and even then, their mood can probably be described as 'comply-only'.

Many respondents from the world of investment banking, asset management, private banking and especially retail, expressed the view that the costs of introducing extra compliance fees and systems, along with new processes and workflows, would be passed onto clients with no counter benefits in terms of market efficiency and investor protection. It is noticeable how many in the supplier community are remaining restrained in trying not to hype the demand, given the benefits are likely to accrue to the few first movers, and not the late arrivals.

Since 'Best Execution' is likely to be an area where firms will seek to differentiate themselves on a competitive basis, it is important that any regulator avoid being overly prescriptive in specifying how firms should meet their 'Best Execution' obligations, regardless of client wishes.

'Laissez-faire' schemes, whereby firms do little to bring their systems in line with their more developed competitors, will be a significant reality for many firms unable or unwilling to commit compliance or system resources to keep up with MiFID. A large percentage of these firms rely on a relaxed approach to implementation on the part of their competent authorities not having the headcount or processes to monitor everything that happens.

In many Member States, for example, many client classification schemes differentiate only retail from professional, and there is a modicum of 'Best Execution' evidencing with a sole focus on price. The Italian market for example already enjoys reasonably low execution costs and practitioners there see some risks in liquidity fragmentation for the retail investors. With over 800 banks and over 300 bilateral and organised Alternative Trading Systems, known as SSO's, the general view seems to be that such retail investors will need to turn more to financial advisors or portfolio managers in the more complex MiFID world. Given this existing legal and institutional context, MiFID could present a significant headache, with its focus on the investment required for real-time market quotes for 'Best Execution' comparisons between the bilateral ATS's.

Other markets such as Germany already have some measure of 'Best Execution' in place, although this does not apply to all products traded OTC. In Germany, as in France, there might be somewhat less focus on competition and much more focus upon avoiding fragmentation of liquidity and avoiding information leakage.

Privacy is preferable in certain other Member States, and firms use various tools to ensure they stay in line with market prices. For example, the CSSF in Luxembourg[24] devised a pre-law to help investors in this area.

However, this still leaves the fact that Member States took different approaches to the subjects of client classification and 'Best Execution'. In addition, it is clear that the 'laissez-faire' approach comes loaded with obvious disadvantages, such as the likelihood of some form of sanction by the European Commission or even the threat of legal action from some firms who are exposed to the costs of poor quality. Investment firms who are inclined to follow this course of action and implement minimal changes may find that they are disadvantaged in the longer term.

It is clear that the competent authorities will need to work hard to adopt approaches which are market-friendly, under the principle that MiFID is evolutionary not revolutionary.

3.11   SUMMARY OF APPROACHES TO 'BEST EXECUTION'

The three forms of approach to evidencing 'Best Execution' – benchmarking, pro-active process management and 'laissez-faire' are not the only likely avenues. Indeed, hybrids may be contemplated depending on the asset class. Each approach has merits and, perhaps more importantly, demerits which are noted in Figure 3.7. Both pro-active process management and 'laissez-faire' are likely to be popular with buy- and sell-side firms alike, who do not wish to invest large amounts behind benchmarking. Benchmarking will not be popular with the dealer-led markets for the reasons highlighted above although, to be fair, it is not benchmarking per se that attracts the criticism but its loading with prescription and disclosure obligations.

In the longer term, investor protection is likely to be best achieved through pro-active process management, on account of greater efficiencies and optimisations in trading practices, although more work is needed on market quality and evidentiary issues in dealer-led markets, especially where it is not possible to prove the case for forms of market abuse or manipulation.

---

[24] Commission de Surveillance du Secteur Financier (CSSF), the Luxembourg regulator.

	Prescriptive Benchmarking	Pro-Active Process Management (PPM)©	Laissez-faire 'Self Regulation'
Approach to Best Execution evidencing	*Directive, rules-based*	*Intelligent copy-out*	*Principles-based*
Likely Acceptability to Buy-side Firms?	Medium	High	High
Likely Acceptability to Sell-side Firms?	Low	High	High
Likely Protection to the End Investor?	Medium	High	Medium
Likely Evidenceability for Dealer-led Markets	Low	Medium	High
Likely Acceptability to Regulators?	High – Low	High – Medium	High – Low
Supports DKYC (Dynamic KYC) / e-Consent?	Low	High	Low
Supports Best Execution Policies / Processes?	Medium	High	High
Supports Versatility (e.g. IOI engines / Alloc.)?	High	High	Medium
Ease of Implementation by Nov 07?	Low	Low	High
Cost / Benefit of Implementation for OTC?	Low	Medium	High

Key: ● High   ◍ Medium   ❖ Low

Figure 3.7 Trade-offs between approaches to evidencing 'Best Execution' (Qualitative)
Source: © Anthony Kirby Oct 2006

'Laissez-faire' is likely to be acceptable to some regulators and completely unacceptable to others, such as the FSA. The pro-active process management approach goes out of its way to try and link KYC and AML whilst evidencing 'Best Execution', which the other approaches do not. It can be argued that raising the game through benchmarking or pro-active process management will support more versatile forms of trading, such as faster equity trading. Finally 'laissez-faire' carries the obvious advantage that it can be easily implemented, with the least degree of costs passed on to other participants.

In summary, the case for pro-active process management is just ahead of 'laissez-faire', and will be further ahead by the end of the decade. It is also clear that the case for benchmarking was made and not taken up. If the results had been judged on equities and exchange-traded derivatives, rather than dealer-led markets, the approach would have had a great deal to commend it however, as it is very complementary with pro-active process management for example.

As suppliers of order flow to any 'Best Execution' process, the views of the buy-side are critical to success in any endeavour to deliver and evidence a quality such as 'Best Execution'.

3.12   CONCLUSIONS

There are a number of conclusions and affirmations made in this chapter.

Firstly, 'Best Execution' policy must set out a rationale for a particular selection of broker or execution venue if there is direct access, including detail of whether any orders will be executed outside a regulated market. The policy should cover the relative importance of the following factors in fulfilling the portfolio management policy: price, costs, speed, likelihood of execution and settlement, size, nature, and any other relevant considerations. The policy should also take into account the fund classification, nature of order, characteristics of financial instruments and characteristics of execution venues, and other factors such as liquidity, timing or curves for other asset classes such as fixed income.

Secondly, the asset manager needs to ensure that all intermediaries have a proper 'Best Execution' policy. This 'Best Execution' policy should be reviewed at least annually and always when there is a material change in the relationship to correct any deficiencies. The 'devil is in the detail' as well, with regard to client agreements, particularly if there are multiple client classifications involved. The asset manager must ensure that they deliver the appropriate information regarding their 'Best Execution' policy to enable the fund to track their performance against agreed benchmarks. They must also obtain the necessary prior consents, with regard to treating the fund as a professional client or executing outside a regulated market.

Thirdly, the asset manager needs to maintain metrics in respect of each class of instrument against the different venues where the executing firm executes client orders, including transmission methods to those venues. The asset manager must pay attention to market practices within dealer-led markets, particularly in cases where there are liquidity or market timing challenges, such as corporate debt trading, or where price benchmarks are not feasible, for example in OTC-traded derivatives.

Fourthly, the asset manager will need to assess whether intermediaries or execution venues offer the best possible result for the fund, on the basis of transaction cost analysis, other metrics or overall performance, as in portfolio alpha. The asset manager also needs to keep track of execution quality from the various regulated markets, MTF's and Systematic Internaliser execution venues. In doing so, they will need to pay attention to their liquidity maps and the likely trade-offs, in terms of their routes to execution. They need to pay particular attention to the potential for fragmentation in the price discovery process, executable prices and market timing, for example.

Lastly, the asset manager should seriously consider investing in the appropriate automation and decision support tools required to fulfil the portfolio management process to completion, if they have not already done so. This consists of Order Management Systems and Direct Market Access capabilities. The asset manager will also need to verify that they have the right database and reporting infrastructure to provide an audit trail, and extract the relevant market and reference data when called to do so. These records should be adapted to the type of business and the range of investment services and activities performed by the investment firm.

The asset manager will need to check the applicability of this auditing and storage, and the scope of any co-dependence with other participants, particularly any outsourcing parties. They will also need to avoid distractions; for example, a call for net consideration to be included in the factors means that the costs of clearing and settlement must be drawn as a relevant factor.

However, it is not clear at the time of writing how dealing desks might source this information or how 'dynamic' the policies need to be in practice, especially if firms are not obliged to connect to every execution venue to be consistent with the principle that 'firms must take all reasonable steps to deliver the best possible result'. What is 'reasonable' in this context?

To close, the thinking is that 'Best Execution' will be translated as a process, not monitored trade-by-trade in a prescriptive fashion. Both investment banks and asset managers will need the underlying data in order to evidence 'Best Execution' practices when called to evidence the same. Expediency and common sense judgement calls are not going out of fashion as prices, sizes, timings, and so on all have to relate to executable transactions. This means completed according to the size and other conditions stipulated by the client.

Both investment banks and asset managers will also likely need to draw up policies to demonstrate the reasonable steps to be carried out, especially for illiquid, fixed income and OTC-traded instruments. For these structured products, the recording of the circumstances to the trade could be seen as advantageous. Logically and legally, if a firm's quality of execution is likely to be open to doubt or challenge, then making a note of the circumstances and building in the relevance of the factors at the time will help mitigate disciplinary action. However, so much of this is likely to emanate from whether a client understands 'Best Execution' policies and has the necessary systems, processes and practices in place to benchmark the same. It also depends on the degree of regulatory arbitrage which could well occur if different Member States implement MiFID's policies with different approaches. If the risks of the latter are greater than 50:50, it will take us right back to the scenario which was posited at the beginning of this chapter as the future regulatory hell and the functioning of markets in the EU will be all the poorer for it.

4
Client Classification

David Smith and Steve Leggett

The Markets in Financial Instruments Directive (MiFID) is a key element of the European Union's Financial Services Action Plan (FSAP), and encompasses an unprecedented level of detail, especially in the area of client classification and protection.

MiFID prescribes a proportional approach to client protection centred on the classification of clients. Retail clients, presumed to have the least experience and knowledge of capital market products, are afforded the greatest level of protection, while regulated investment firms and other Eligible Counterparties receive limited protection.

This is driven by rapid advances in information technology and a trend toward financial disintermediation, affording private individuals access to vast amounts of financial market data. Across the European Union, comprising twenty-five Member States in 2006, fast internet access measured by broadband penetration rates – the percentage of total population accessing the Internet through broadband connections – exceeded 14% in March 2006, narrowing the gap with both the American and Japanese markets.[1] Online shopping activities are increasing with online banking, in particular, achieving usage rates of up to 50% in some EU countries.

However, fragmented national markets and institutional practices have impeded broad-based individual participation in European capital markets. The percentage of share ownership of European listed companies by individuals was 16% at the end of 2003. This is well below American levels, where half the population hold shares of some form.

---

[1] The European Competitive Telecommunications Association (ECTA), Quarterly Scorecard, March 2006.

The Future of Investing in Europe's Markets after MiFID   Edited by C. Skinner
© 2007 John Wiley & Sons, Ltd

The FSAP aims to reduce barriers to the single European market and to increase cross-border retail financial activity. It is estimated that a working European retail market for financial services contributes between 0.5 % and 0.7 % to incremental GDP, depending on the country concerned, as a result of a variety of factors:

- an increase in product choice, particularly in small countries;
- lower prices for retail financial services;
- lower interest rates; and
- a reduction in the 'home bias' in private investors' portfolios.[2]

4.1   WHY THE DETAILED FOCUS ON CLIENT CLASSIFICATION?

In formulating regulations that are proportional to the needs of a wide range of clients, the European Commission – with input from Member State securities regulators through CESR – focused on the need to provide both clients and regulators '. . . the necessary tools to be able to discern and punish inefficiency and unprincipled conduct by firms'.[3]

Retail clients, in particular, depend upon the firms with which they have account agreements to provide market information on the types of products, prices and trading venues; investment advice and transaction execution services. Unlike retail banking, where there is increasing disclosure and the ability to compare prices on products such as annual percentage rates on loans, retail clients of investment firms or insurance companies offering investment products are typically unable to compare the appropriateness of advice they are receiving. Nor are they able to gauge the efficiency of trade execution. They are unable to detect if firms have conflicts of interest or if they are receiving inducements to execute trades in a way which might not provide the best value to the client.

Regulation is viewed by the EC as essential to create a balance between greater **transparency** – disclosing more information to clients who then take responsibility for analysing and evaluating information supplied by investment firms – and more stringent **fiduciary controls on firms**, which are obliged to provide 'Best Execution' and carry out suitability and appropriateness checks based on the nature of the product or service,

---

[2] 'The EU Financial Services Action Plan: A Guide', prepared by HM Treasury, the Financial Services Authority and the Bank of England, 31 July 2003, p. 3.

[3] European Commission, Background Note to Implementing Directive 2004/39/EC, 2006, Section 7.1, p. 16.

and the experience and capability of clients. The fundamental asymmetry of information available for informed decision-making, bearing in mind that retail clients are wholly reliant on firms to disclose and advise, has led to the drafting of MiFID protections based on the type of client to whom the service or product is being offered.

In order to avoid over-regulating advice and services between expert institutional clients and investment firms, MiFID client classification is structured to apply regulation inversely proportional to the experience and financial resources of the client.

This is summarised in Box 4.1 below:

Box 4.1   MiFID Client Classification

All clients, and, in particular, all legal entities within each client group, must be separately classified according to new categories introduced by MiFID. There are three categories of clients:

- **Retail Clients** – private individuals and corporate entities not meeting two of the three financial criteria listed below:
  - net turnover of €40 million
  - total assets of €20 million
  - and own funds of €2 million

- **Professional Clients** – 'per se' (specifically listed in the Directive) financial firms, some hedge funds and larger corporate firms which meet two of the three financial criteria listed above.
- **Eligible Counterparties** – regulated financial institutions and central government public bodies. This category is a subset of Professional Clients – all Eligible Counterparties are also Professional Clients.

MiFID Level 1 text, as in the original Directive adopted by the EU parliament in 2004, introduced fixed financial criteria – such as balance sheet, own funds and turnover – to differentiate between professional and retail clients.

The criteria apply to all Member States and are not subject to interpretation during national transposition which means that all Member States need to implement identical criteria. Clients not achieving two of the three criteria listed above, and not falling into one of the 'per se' professional categories, are classified as retail clients.

4.2 CLIENT CLASSIFICATION DRIVES CLIENT PROTECTION REQUIREMENTS

The MiFID Lamfalussy Level 1 text,[4] as well as the more detailed Level 2 implementation text, contains detailed provisions for the testing of clients. The EC could have taken a high-level principles-based approach but was concerned that, absent detailed regulation, prevailing practice would weaken the quality of fiduciary protection to clients.

Two tests have been introduced to cover the range of investment products and services within the scope of MiFID:

• Suitability tests, mainly related to investment advice and advised products (see Box 4.2 below); and
• Appropriateness tests, intended for non-advised products and ancillary services such as corporate finance advice (see Box 4.3 below).

In general, full tests need to be carried out for all retail clients, with limited testing required for professional clients, reflecting their ability and experience in investment services. Clients classified as eligible counterparties for specific products and services do not require testing. MiFID conduct of business provisions are waived for eligible counterparties. This is because eligible counterparties are deemed to have the required experience and ability to make judgments on products and services as they see fit.

Box 4.2   Suitability Testing

Investment firms must conduct a suitability test with each client, subject to exemptions following, for **advised services**, including investment advice or entering into a transaction in the course of portfolio management.

The obligation of the firm in this test is to obtain, not merely to request, the necessary information from clients or potential clients, in order that the firm is able to understand the essential facts about the client. These facts must provide evidence that there

---

[4] See Commission Staff Working Document, 'The Application of the Lamfalussy Process to EU Securities Markets Legislation', Commission of the European Communities, Brussels, 15 November 2004.

Box 4.2   (Continued)

is a reasonable basis for believing, giving due consideration to the nature and extent of the service being provided, that the specific transaction being recommended, or entered into in the course of portfolio management services, satisfies the following criteria:

- Meets the investment objectives of the client;
- The client is financially able to bear any related investment risks consistent with its investment objectives;
- The client has the experience and knowledge to understand the risks;
- (Note: depending on the circumstances, several of the bullet points above can be assumed in relation to advisory/portfolio management services for which clients are classified as professional clients);
- Firms are not obliged to comply with MiFID Article 19 requirements (Conduct of Business, generally) when bringing about or entering into transactions with clients which can be classified as Eligible Counterparties for the subject transaction;
- If a firm does not obtain information that it considers necessary to assess suitability, it must not recommend an investment service or transaction to that client.

Box 4.3   Appropriateness Testing

For services other than investment advice and portfolio management, which are generally referred to as **non-advised services**, MiFID requires firms to assess whether an investment service or transaction is appropriate for the client. This is based on whether the client, or potential client, has the necessary knowledge and experience in the investment field relevant to the specific type of product or service offered or demanded, in order to understand the risks involved. Unlike the suitability test, a firm can provide services even if it cannot determine appropriateness, so long as it provides a warning to the client.

Box 4.3　(Continued)

Professional clients can be assumed to possess the necessary experience and knowledge in order to understand the risks involved in investment services or transactions so that, in the case of professional clients, the only remaining assessment is a basic appropriateness test. This test is to ensure that if the client does not know something, it would not lead to a situation where it could be reasonably construed to indicate inappropriateness.

Suitability tests are also relevant for the provision of Investment Advice (see Box 4.4). The MiFID definition of investment advice is focused on recommendations that are tailored for a specific client regarding a specific action involving specific financial instruments.

Box 4.4　Investment Advice

Investment advice is defined under MiFID as the provision of personal recommendations to a client, either upon its request or at the initiative of the investment firm, in respect of one or more of the actions listed below:

- to buy, sell, subscribe for, exchange, redeem, hold or underwrite a particular financial instrument;
- to exercise or not to exercise any right conferred by a particular financial instrument to buy, sell, subscribe for, exchange, or redeem a financial instrument. A recommendation is not a personal recommendation if it is issued exclusively through distribution channels or to the public;
- The investment advice provided must be presented as suitable for the client, or must be based on a consideration of the circumstances of the client. This is established by undertaking Suitability tests (see Box 4.2);
- As investment advice is considered an investment service under MiFID, it is subject to a licensing requirement in some jurisdictions within the EEA where licensing was not required prior to MiFID. Therefore any firm providing investment advice must be licensed to do so.

Client classification is also relevant for the provision of Investment Advice, which is a newly-regulated activity in a number of EU Member States.

4.3 FLEXIBLE REGIME

Mandating fixed financial criteria (as described in Box 4.1) to distinguish between client types is a 'top down' approach to regulation, which could be counterproductive for individual or corporate clients with circumstances not fitting the standard classifications. For instance, an experienced private individual employed in the financial sector could have expert knowledge of complex products and could have amassed a significant portfolio through active trading in such products. That individual may want the flexibility to trade with investment firms without the requirement for suitability tests and warnings.

Special purpose financing subsidiaries of large industrial groups, such as an automobile finance company securitisation conduit, may hold small amounts of 'own funds' and may not meet one of the other financial criteria tests to qualify as a professional client (Box 4.1). Yet such subsidiaries could be major participants in securitisation markets, launching several multi-billion Euro securitisations each year.

Box 4.5   Client Re-Classification 'Opting Up' or 'Opting Down'

MiFID introduces considerable flexibility for clients to request a re-classification to a different category depending on certain criteria. For instance, an 'Eligible Counterparty' could request to be treated as a 'Professional' or 'Retail' client (in both cases 'opting down') generally, on a product-by-product basis or on a trade-by-trade basis.

Why would a client request to 'opt down'? One reason would be to gain protection when purchasing an unfamiliar investment product. For instance, a clothing retailer seeking to protect its revenues in the event of a decline in sales activity during periods of stormy weather might seek to 'opt down' to benefit from additional protection afforded to retail clients when considering complex protection products, such as weather derivatives.

Retail clients may request investment firms to re-classify them as professionals ('opting up') to enable trading in complex products.

> **Box 4.5** (Continued)
>
> Such re-classification requests are subject to tests applied to the number of client transactions in each of the most recent four quarters, the size of the client's portfolio (minimum €500,000) and professional expertise.

In these circumstances, MiFID provides flexibility for clients to request re-classification – to 'opt up' or 'opt down' – on a general basis, for specific products or even on individual trades. The Directive does not address the role of firms in driving a re-classification, but there are clear business reasons for firms to do so.

Apart from a client's investment experience or objectives in requesting re-classification, firms may themselves seek to promote re-classification, in order to reduce administrative complexity of handling retail clients in the implementation and monitoring of MiFID. For instance, a firm with mainly professional clients and eligible counterparties may take a decision to either re-classify any private individuals or firms failing the financial criteria tests to professional clients, if such clients meet MiFID's 'opting up' requirements, or to migrate the client relationship to another part of the firm, such as a private bank, or even to end the relationship.

4.4   IMPLICATIONS FOR FIRMS

The classification and client testing requirements create both opportunities and challenges for investment firms, insurers and financial advisors with activities in the scope of MiFID.

4.4.1   MiFID drives firms to truly know their clients

Client take-on processes and systems need to move beyond a focus on identity checks and criminal activity. The suitability and appropriateness tests require firms to collect further information about client investment objectives, transaction experience in a range of products, and the financial capability of clients to absorb risks. This is not just a compliance expense, but an opportunity for firms which choose to feed richer client data into client relationship management systems to strengthen their cross-selling capabilities.

4.4.2 Firms need to pay close attention to client-facing staff training

Staff should be aware of information received from clients which has a material impact on client classification. For instance, a merger of two small manufacturing firms, which are each individually classified as retail clients, could create a combined firm large enough to qualify as a professional client. But is financial size alone a reason to promote the firm to professional status if client investment objectives have not changed? There is a need to balance the letter of the regulation against individual client needs and experience in MiFID-scope products and services.

4.4.3 Data storage requirements are significant

Firms need to document the classification of clients, and inform new clients going forward of their classification status. The results of suitability and appropriateness tests need to be recorded. If professional clients are permitted to opt down to retail status, firms need to re-run suitability and appropriateness tests required for retail clients. Firms need to record when they are giving Investment Advice and to document suitability tests required for giving such advice.

4.5   CONCLUSION

From the adoption of the FSAP in Lisbon in 2000 to 'go live' MiFID implementation in 2007, a substantial amount of consultation and negotiation has brought into force a highly-principled and detailed body of law and regulation, centred around the varying needs of clients in European capital markets.

Investment firms, and other financial services providers with in-scope instruments and activities, are obliged to provide a level of information and duty-of-care which has never before been regulated on such a vast scale across national boundaries. Private individuals, as well as major institutional investors, now have the opportunity to invest across Europe without legal and institutional restrictions. Clients with the computing power to increasingly access and assess financial data benefit from MiFID as a catalyst for a continuing increase in transparency and competition among investment firms. The winning firms are exploiting their enhanced client take-on and client relationship management systems to better anticipate client needs and to increasingly cross-sell new products and services.

5

Passporting

Alan Jenkins

Passporting is the right to offer investment services to clients anywhere in Europe. It is one of the key simplification rules being introduced by the Markets in Financial Instruments Directive (MiFID). What difference will this make to the European landscape long-term?

Previously known as 'ISD2', MiFID replaces the original EU Investment Services Directive (ISD) of 1993, with effect from 1 November 2007.

The new rules will apply throughout the European Economic Area (EEA), which includes Norway, Iceland and Liechtenstein, as well as the twenty-five EU Member States and the EU accession countries (Bulgaria and Romania).

Despite the adoption of a 'Principles based approach', many aspects of MiFID are more prescriptive than existing regulations for many of these countries, bearing in mind MiFID's objective of creating a single, harmonised financial market for the whole of Europe.

But where cross-border services are concerned, MiFID abolishes any intervention by regulators in the investor's country. If an investor is willing to do business with an investment firm anywhere in the EEA then they can do so based on the firm's 'home' state authorisation and investor protection regime. With a more level playing field, this becomes more likely,

5.1 NOT QUITE SO SIMPLE

In case this all sounds too simple, there are a couple of exceptions. If an investment firm chooses to operate with branches in other EEA countries, or to use tied agents, some 'local' rules will still apply.

The Future of Investing in Europe's Markets after MiFID   Edited by C. Skinner
© 2007 John Wiley & Sons, Ltd

Here lies one of the open questions: MiFID makes it easier for firms to set up branches in other countries, but also makes it easier for investors to deal 'direct'. So, it remains to be seen whether there will be an increase, or a decrease, in the number of branches.

The answer must lie with the perceptions of the investors: the firms' clients.

Some will no doubt be comfortable using the internet, say, supported by local advertising and mailboxes. Others will prefer to maintain a face-to-face relationship with their advisers. The critical factor is that it is no longer legally necessary for those advisers to be based in a branch in the client's country.

My own prediction is that there will be a polarisation of investment services between the 'advice boutiques', which cater exclusively for high net worth investors, and the consolidated 'execution only' style firms, which includes savings, credit cards, mortgages, and insurance firms, as well as distributors such as Tesco and Carrefour.

5.2   WHAT SHOULD AN APPROVED FIRM DO?

In order to provide investment services anywhere in the EEA, all that an approved firm has to do under MiFID is to notify its 'home' regulator of its intentions, as regulators in other countries are prohibited from imposing any local requirements.

If a firm chooses to operate branches, the 'host' regulator does have supervisory and enforcement powers. The biggest change to current rules for firms with Branches is the introduction of local 'transaction reporting' for instruments admitted to trading on any EEA regulated market. There are also other requirements relating to six of the 'Articles' in the new Directive.[1] These are:

- Article 19: Conduct of Business;
- Article 21: 'Best Execution';
- Article 22: Client Order Handling;
- Article 25: Transaction Reporting and Record Keeping;
- Article 27: Pre-Trade Transparency;
- Article 28: Post-Trade Transparency.

---

[1] Editor's note: although this book does not define or detail the articles of MiFID, they can be found by downloading the full MiFID text from http://ec.europa.eu/internal_market/securities/isd/index_en.htm.

The last two of these apply only to 'over the counter' (OTC) transactions in shares, and therefore only affect investment firms that choose to engage in such business.

MiFID also imposes changes for regulators, who are newly required to forward transaction reports to other EEA regulators in either of two circumstances:

• transactions reported by Branches; and
• transactions in shares where the most liquid market is in another country.

Thereby, both the regulator in a firm's 'host' country, and the regulator in the country of the most liquid market, will achieve complete pictures of market activity in their spheres of interest.

5.3   WHAT'S NEXT FOR INVESTMENT FIRMS?

Once firms have obtained authorisation, the two key questions that any investment firm needs to consider are:

• What services are you providing?
• Where are you providing them?

What services you provide are important, because MiFID defines the following investment services and activities as 'core':

• Reception and transmission of orders, in relation to one or more financial instruments;
• Execution of orders on behalf of clients;
• Dealing on own account;
• Portfolio Management;
• Investment Advice;
• Underwriting and placings;
• Operation of a Multilateral Trading Facility (MTF).

together with a range of 'ancillary services' including custody, foreign exchange and investment research.

Your authorisation may be for one or for several of the 'core' services. In addition, your authorisation may be for none, one or several of the Ancillary Services. The scope of your 'passporting' rights then follow directly from your 'home' authorisation, as this is automatically valid for the entire EEA Community, either directly, or through the establishment of branches.

5.4   HOW ABOUT SUITABILITY AND APPROPRIATENESS?[2]

If you choose to provide the services of Portfolio Management and/or Investment Advice, you then need to also take into account the highest level of investor protection in MiFID. This is known as 'suitability', and you are prohibited from providing these services unless, and until, you have received sufficient information from your client to make this assessment.

For almost all other services, you need to assess 'appropriateness', particularly for retail investors, or alternatively to issue 'risk warnings'.

The least onerous rules apply to execution-only business in non-complex instruments, which may be provided without any client assessment. However, these can only be provided at the client's request and are also subject to specific warnings.

In addition, firms have a general responsibility under MiFID to obtain the best possible result for their client, the 'Best Execution' responsibilities. For the purposes of passporting, however, firms need to distinguish between the two alternative services of 'reception and transmission' of client orders versus 'execution'.

5.5   THE LEAST COST OPTION – RECEPTION AND TRANSMISSION OF ORDERS

Using passporting services, firms can then choose to delegate their responsibility for 'Best Execution' to a related entity or to their branch in another country or to another investment firm. Although they may make this delegation, they still remain responsible to their clients. This means they must periodically review the counterparties they are using, to ensure they are obtaining the best possible result for their clients.

Such firms also continue to have other obligations including:

- Organisational requirements;
- Conflicts of Interest obligations;

---

[2] See Chapter 4.

- Prompt, fair and expeditious[3] execution;
- Record keeping, and retention for five years.

Another open question is to what extent firms operating in 'reception and transmission' mode can continue to justify their fees and charges in the new regime of greater transparency and a more level playing field.

My prediction is that this will again lead to further polarisation. Niche players will survive by offering tailored services, including nationally based wrap products to those local customers willing to pay for them, such as the selling of ISA's in the UK. More cost-conscious investors will deal directly with the consolidated superstores either directly or through other 'white labelled' services.

5.6 SO WHAT EXACTLY IS INVOLVED IN PROVIDING 'BEST EXECUTION'?

Firms that take responsibility for 'Best Execution' are required to determine their Order Execution Policy, which is published to clients, and the potential trading venues they use in each of the three MiFID categories of execution venue:

- Regulated Markets (RM's);
- Multilateral Trading Facilities (MTF's);
- Systematic Internalisers (SI's).

In addition, they must review and ensure that the venues they decide to select are continuing to provide the best possible result for their clients.

For retail clients, the definition of 'Best Execution' is biased towards total costs including clearing and settlement costs, but not including custody fees; for professional clients, a wider variety of factors have to be taken into account.

Firms taking responsibility for 'Best Execution' are also then responsible for:

---

[3] Editor's note: this means sequential execution, as in you cannot prioritise a favoured client's order over one already received but must process orders in the chronology they are received.

- Post-trade disclosure, which includes publication of trade details in real time, analogous to the classic Stock Exchange ticker data, either through an RM, an MTF, a data vendor or independently; and
- Transaction reporting to their local Competent Authority by the close of the following working day, again either through an RM, an MTF, an approved system or independently.

The investment needed to comply with 'Best Execution' is clearly greater than that involved in order reception and transmission, but the potential returns are also greater. This means that a firm's Order Execution Policy is actually going to be their competitive differentiator.

5.7 IS THAT ALL?

Not quite.

The third level of sophistication that a firm can consider is to become a Systematic Internaliser in liquid shares, or to set up or participate directly in an MTF. This option requires the highest level of investment by a market participant, and offers the greatest potential economies of scale.

Systematic Internalisers are required to continuously publish their prices, and may not offer any price improvement to retail clients. These obligations are effectively the price that major investment firms must pay, under MiFID, for the abolition of the national concentration rule in a number of European countries. Such firms can make corresponding savings in exchange fees and spreads, and potentially also in clearing and settlement fees.

Firms providing cross-border services should also note that MiFID rules for client classification are client-centric. Each country can define its own variations to the classification regime for so-called 'eligible counterparties', the most sophisticated and least protected investors. EEA-based clients can then assert their classification, based upon those national variations in their own country.

The final open question in this context concerns regulatory arbitrage.

It is still a matter for debate what extent firms may choose to relocate all their operations, or any part of their operations such as execution, either to other EEA countries with lower costs, lower taxes and lighter touch, or offshore.

Clients' perceptions will be all important here. In any event, the firm's offices within each EEA country will still have a number of obligations under MiFID.

5.8   WILL MiFID REALLY MAKE A DIFFERENCE?

You may think this is all too much to contemplate, but firms that do not rise to the challenge of passporting will find themselves at a competitive disadvantage, as significant rationalisation and consolidation is likely among Exchanges, brokers and investment managers. The upshot is reduced margins, resulting from greater transparency and the elimination of national barriers throughout the EEA.

The European Commission, amongst others, has asserted that there will be a first-mover advantage for those firms that are best prepared for the changes under MiFID.

The much improved and more level playing field will also facilitate cross-border investment services, on the assumption that clients and potential clients will be willing to do business with firms in other EEA jurisdictions.

As a result, passporting is both an opportunity and a threat to investment firms.

I would recommend that you gear up to attract more cross-border business, including the ever-growing expatriate business, by providing services via the Internet for example. The question then is how many languages you replicate your website into.

The alternative is to be an ostrich, and moan about the increased competition from other firms which are now both domestic and pan-European.

5.9   I DON'T BELIEVE IT

In the 1990's BBC situation comedy 'One Foot in the Grave' the lead character, Victor Meldrew, has a catchphrase 'I don't believe it'. Similarly, I don't believe that MiFID will create a radically altered competitive landscape in the near-term – the first few weeks after 1 November 2007. Initiatives such as Tradepoint (now virt-x) and Jiway have shown that liquidity is sticky, and traditional markets have continued to thrive.

Having said that, continental European Exchanges cannot be complacent. For example, twenty years ago, they had to fight hard, heavily investing to win back their national liquidity from London's innovative Stock Exchange Automated Quotation (SEAQ) International system.

Will those same Exchanges continue to dominate the landscape?

That is not the intention of the European Commission, nor is it the expectation of those major investment firms that are gearing up to internalise more and more business. I also do not think it is the case.

Investment firms that fail to invest in passporting, and smart order routing to embrace new alternative execution venues, will find themselves losing clients, losing money, and having to consolidate by 2009–10.

One foot in the grave? Indeed so!

Part 2
MiFID's Regulatory Regime: Will it Work?

'PRINCIPLES-BASED REGULATION –
WILL IT WORK?'
BY IAN MASON, PARTNER, BARLOW LYDE &
GILBERT

This chapter reviews the differences in approach under MiFID at the European level, and the FSA at the UK level. The UK's FSA is viewed as a leading regulator in Europe, and one of the first to interpret and consult upon the implementation of MiFID. This chapter highlights the issues MiFID raised for the UK national regulatory implementation, and the conflicts between European and national approaches. After all, if the UK's FSA struggled then how would other EU Member State regulators cope?

'REGULATORS: CONSISTENT OR CONFUSED?'
BY ANDREW ALLWRIGHT, HEAD OF MARKETING,
EXCHANGE TRADED INSTRUMENTS, REUTERS

Continuing the theme of consistency, or the lack of consistency, of the interpretation and implementation of MiFID, Andrew Allwright of Reuters takes a look at the issues this causes the markets practically and, specifically, the challenge for market data.

'REGULATORY CONVERGENCE: THE PROSPECT
FOR A EUROPEAN SEC'
BY ANTHONY BELCHAMBERS, CHIEF EXECUTIVE,
THE FUTURES & OPTIONS ASSOCIATION AND
CHAIRMAN, MiFID CONNECT

This chapter naturally follows Andrew's, and reviews the idea that if you have inconsistency at European Member-State level of MiFID implementation then the regulations do not work. What is needed is a harmonised European regulatory regime with a central regulator, just like the USA.

'DO WE NEED A PAN-EUROPEAN REGULATOR?' BY CHRIS SKINNER, CHIEF EXECUTIVE, BALATRO

Anthony's chapter relates strongly to an EU summit which debated this subject and I include this as a continuation of the last two chapters' themes. Do we need a pan-European regulator? The answer is that the industry wants a pan-European regulator but governments and regulators do not see this as being practical in the current political climate.

'MiFID AND RegNMS: CHANGING THE DNA OF THE CAPITAL MARKETS' BY MICHAEL HEINZ, BANKING INDUSTRY EXPERT, IBM AND BERNHARD SCHÜLLER, RETIRED SENIOR BANKER IN CHARGE OF THE SECURITIES BUSINESS AT BWS BANK

Another area key to MiFID's implementation is to make Europe's capital markets as competitive as America's. In this context, the USA is also implementing regulation, RegNMS, to avoid trade-through operations – 'the execution of an order in its market at a price that is inferior to a price displayed in another market'. There are similarities and learning from this regulation for Europe, as this chapter highlights.

6
Principles-based Regulation – Will it Work?

Ian Mason

The intentions behind MiFID are entirely laudable.

The current regime, under the Investment Services Directive 1993, does not work well enough. Although there is a passporting regime, the scope of the passport is not broad, and barriers still exist to the cross-border provision of financial services in the EU. In addition, although there is strong investor protection in some European states, such as the UK, it is weaker in other states. The regime of investor protection needs to be updated to attract retail investors to capital markets. In some EU states, the Exchanges have a virtual monopoly on the trading of securities, so there is a need to increase competition between trading venues.

The European Commission believes MiFID will address these concerns.

MiFID will broaden the scope of the passport. Investment firms and Exchanges are now able to provide services in Europe's twenty-seven Member States, and the three members of the EEA, on the basis of their home country licence. This is the passport.

New services such as investment advice, and financial instruments such as derivatives, are covered. Investor protection in the EU is strengthened, particularly in areas such as 'Best Execution' and conflicts of interest. Competition in EU capital markets increases, as the existing exchange monopolies are abolished and new categories of trading venue become available, such as Multilateral Trading Facilities (MTF's) and Systematic Internalisers (SI's).

A further critical point is that the European Commission has stated that MiFID is intended to introduce principles-based regulation

The Future of Investing in Europe's Markets after MiFID Edited by C. Skinner
© 2007 John Wiley & Sons, Ltd

throughout Europe, so as to increase deregulation and reduce bureaucracy.

So surely MiFID is a good thing, and everyone should be happy? Unfortunately this has not proved to be the case.

From some perspectives, MiFID is seen as another in the series of unpopular diktats emanating from Brussels, joining the Insurance Mediation Directive, Market Abuse Directive, Transparency Directive and Capital Requirements Directive, to name but a few. Firms have to comply with MiFID, but the benefits are not clear.

Another difficulty is that the economic rationale for MiFID has not been made. The Commission has admitted that it did not undertake a cost-benefit analysis, the *sine qua non*[1] of any new piece of regulation, before deciding to introduce MiFID. The costs of complying with MiFID are not insignificant. For example the FSA has estimated that the industry may spend from £20 million to £40 million in aggregate one-off costs, and £8 million to £20 million in aggregate ongoing costs, just to comply with MiFID's pre-trade transparency regulations.

6.1   PRINCIPLES-BASED REGULATION, THE UK EXPERIENCE

In the UK, the FSA is also strongly championing principles-based regulation.

In September 2006, the FSA's CEO, John Tiner, asked himself the question 'Are we heading towards over-regulation?' and replied 'My simple answer is yes'.[2]

The FSA's rulebook has grown to in excess of 5000 pages, as its regulatory responsibilities have increased. The FSA has been required to respond to initiatives such as the Better Regulation Task Force, and the current UK government imperative to cut red tape. As part of its 2010 vision, the FSA has therefore stated that it will move increasingly towards regulation by principles. It will be, and will expect firms to be, focused on outcomes. In other words, the FSA will be focused on the end, rather than the means. The FSA considers this less prescriptive

---

[1] Editor's note: '*sine qua non*' is a Latin legal term which means 'without which it could not be', meaning an essential action for the regulation to work.

[2] Speech by John Tiner, Chief Executive, FSA, Rendez Vous de Septembre, Monte Carlo, 12 September 2006, available at http://www.fsa.gov.uk/pages/Library/Communication/Speeches/2006/0912_jt.shtml.

approach should empower senior management, and give them greater flexibility to order their businesses to comply with FSA rules.

In fact, regulation by principles is nothing new in the UK. The FSA's predecessor, the Securities and Investments Board, also had a high level set of principles. The FSA has also brought a number of enforcement cases previously based upon breaches of the FSA Principles alone, such as the Citigroup case, 2005.[3]

What is different is the FSA's commitment and pace of change towards principles-based regulation. For example, the FSA has already removed sections of its rulebook, such as the Money Laundering Sourcebook, and other sections of the rulebook have also been identified for abolition.

However, the move towards a more principles-based approach has not been universally welcomed by the industry. Detailed rules and guidance provide greater certainty of compliance and, as these are reduced, uncertainty increases.

This concern is seen at its highest level in the enforcement context, where the worry is that the FSA will bring action against firms and individuals under increasingly unpredictable principles. The FSA has attempted to assuage these concerns by stating that it will not use hindsight to judge standards of misconduct so that, for example, misconduct which occurred three years ago will be judged by the standards at that time, not today's standards. In addition, the FSA has stated that enforcement action based on the principles alone, rather than the principles combined with more detailed rules, will only be brought in cases where it would have been reasonably predictable that the behaviour in question would breach the relevant principles.

This provides some comfort, and a degree of objectivity, but still leaves an element of subjective discretion to the FSA. Given that the European Commission is implementing MiFID as principles-based, and that the FSA wants to be a more principles-based regulator, one would expect implementation to be straight-forward? In fact the position is considerably more complicated than it may at first appear.

---

[3] Editor's note: the FSA fined Citigroup Global Markets Limited (CGML) £ 13.9 million, € 20.9 million, in June 2005 for breaching FSA Principles 2 and 3 which related to failing to conduct its business with due skill, care and diligence and failing to control its business effectively. The action was taken after Citigroup executed a trading strategy on the European government bond markets on 2 August 2004, which involved the firm building up and then rapidly exiting from very substantial long positions in European government bonds over a period of an hour.

The FSA has stated that it is adopting an approach of 'intelligent copy-out' to the directive, as the new FSA rules are generally based on copied-out directive text without further amendment to avoid placing unintended additional obligations on firms. The FSA has also stated that it will impose rules that go beyond the Directive's requirements only when justified in their own right, including through use of appropriate market-failure analysis and cost-benefit analysis, and where consistent with directive provisions. Furthermore, Article 4 of the Level 2 Directive further constrains national regulators from imposing additional rules in those matters covered by it such that additional requirements can be imposed, or retained, only in 'those exceptional cases where such requirements are objectively justified and proportionate so as to address specific risks to investor protection or to market integrity that are not adequately addressed by this Directive', and then further conditions must be met. The European Commission also wants to strongly deter gold-plating of the Directive. As Commissioner Charlie McCreevy has said, 'the gold-platers, in short, should go back to the jewellery shop'.[4]

In fact the FSA stated that it is seeking to impose a number of additional obligations on firms, and has notifyed the Commission accordingly under Article 4.

One example relates to the depolarisation regime, where the current FSA disclosure documents include a Menu and Additional Disclosure Documents sent to clients. This is unlikely to be popular with firms, which would prefer the FSA to stick to its 'intelligent copy-out' approach, and remove these additional requirements.

6.2   CONFLICTS OF INTEREST

Implementation is complicated further by the fact that MiFID is more prescriptive or adopts a conceptually different approach to the pre-MiFID FSA provisions in a number of key areas. For example, on conflicts of interest, FSA Principle 8 states that 'A firm must manage conflicts of interest fairly, both between itself and its customers, and between a customer and another client'.

---

[4] Editor's note: Charlie McCreevy, European Commissioner for Internal Market and Services Speech to the Finance Foundation Conference, 'A European or Transatlantic Global Capital Market?', Brussels, 3 October 2006.

This is a relatively high-level principle, and the FSA has avoided being too prescriptive, giving firms the freedom to decide how best to comply. For example, the FSA's conduct of business rules require firms to take reasonable steps to ensure fair treatment for customers, and four alternatives for managing conflicts:

- disclosing the interest to the customer;
- relying on a policy of independence;
- establishing internal arrangements, such as Chinese walls; or
- declining to act for a customer.

In practice, many firms have relied on disclosure as their principal means of dealing with conflicts.

In contrast, MiFID is significantly more prescriptive on conflicts of interest than the current provisions. It requires firms to identify potential conflicts of interest and document them with a specific written policy for dealing with conflicts. In addition, the written policy must cover all organisations within a group, even those that would be otherwise out of scope. This means it could include any conflicts that arise as a result of the group's structure, or the activities of others within the group.

Another new MiFID requirement is that firms must consider conflicts in relation to all categories of client, including eligible counterparties. Given that these are, by definition, experienced professionals who have a full understanding of the way in which the market works and the risks and rewards involved, one wonders if this is proportionate.

MiFID also places a different emphasis on disclosure, in fact viewing it as a last resort, so that disclosure is permitted only where a firm cannot be confident that all other conflict management measures will prevent damage to client interests. The likely outcome is not that firms will be unable to use disclosure as a tool, but clearly they will need to be satisfied that disclosure is an appropriate tool to use compared with other methods.

As a result of MiFID's provisions on conflicts, firms will need to spend a considerable amount of time rewriting their conflict of interest policies or, in some cases, writing them for the first time. They will need to undertake an extensive exercise of identifying conflicts, mapping them against business lines, customer base, affiliated entities and persons within the group, and whether they relate to MiFID activities within scope or outside scope. They will then need to document the conflicts, develop procedures and apply the policies.

There will no doubt be some difficult judgement calls when considering disclosure.

The eventual result may be a long-term higher level of protection for customers in this area, although this is certainly not beyond doubt, and one has to question whether this truly represents a principles-based approach to regulation.

6.3 'BEST EXECUTION'

Another area where MiFID is more prescriptive is 'Best Execution'.

Under the pre-MiFID FSA conduct of business (COB) rules, a firm must take reasonable care to ascertain the best available price for the customer order, for transactions of the size and kind concerned, in the relevant market at the time. The firm must then execute the order at a price that is no less advantageous to the customer. The only exception is if the firm has taken 'reasonable' steps to ensure that it would not be in the customer's interests to do so. Reasonable care in this context has been defined to exclude the necessity of having access to competing Exchanges, or even to all or a minimum number of price sources.

Article 21 of MiFID changes this substantially. It provides that a firm must take all reasonable steps to obtain the best possible result, taking into account a number of prescribed factors: price, costs, speed, likelihood of execution and settlement, size, nature, or any other consideration relevant to the order.

Managers are also required to have effective arrangements in place to comply with this, including having an execution policy in place and informing clients about the policy; assessing execution venues at least annually and giving consideration to other venues; and showing that an order has been executed in line with the firm's final 'Best Execution' policy.

The FSA's attempts to implement the new MiFID provisions on 'Best Execution' in the UK have already demonstrated some of the pitfalls of working out how this works in practice. In an early Discussion Paper 06/03, the FSA suggested the introduction of price benchmarks.[5] This proved highly controversial, and a number of industry trade bodies pointed out to the FSA that whilst price benchmarks could work in highly liquid equity markets, they could not work in some dealer markets with sophisticated financial instruments that were much

---

[5] Chapter 3 on 'Best Execution' discusses this in depth.

less liquid. Consequently, the FSA has backed off from this proposal, which it emphasised was put forward for discussion rather than as a firm proposal.

Overall, the retail investor may end up with a better deal on 'Best Execution' under MiFID, but it may be an arduous route for firms to achieve this.

6.4   TREATING CUSTOMERS FAIRLY (TCF)

The FSA's treating customers fairly initiative is a central part of its work in the retail market to protect consumers. FSA Principle 6 states: 'A firm must pay due regard to the interests of its customers and treat them fairly'.

Given that one of the main objectives of MiFID is also to increase the level of protection for retail consumers, one would expect to see a good deal of overlap and cross-referencing between the two. Yet this is far from the case. For example in the FSA report published in July 2006 on 'Treating Customers Fairly – Towards fair outcomes for consumers', there is no reference to MiFID. Similarly the TCF phrase is not used expressly in the MiFID legislation. The image is of two parallel initiatives, running alongside each other, but without interacting.

In fact this is not so surprising.

TCF is very much part of the FSA's move towards principles-based regulation. The FSA has deliberately refrained from defining more precisely what MiFID means. Instead, the FSA has identified six improved outcomes for retail consumers that it wants firms to achieve, and has provided a considerable volume of further material on good and bad practices in dealings with consumers on its website and in speeches.

In addition, there is a strong emphasis on disclosure. For example, the FSA's desired outcomes include consumers receiving clear information and being kept suitably informed before, during and after the point of sale, as well as receiving suitable advice which takes into account their circumstances. In contrast, although the Commission's intention is that MiFID is principles-based, in practice it is highly prescriptive in a number of areas such as conflict of interest and 'Best Execution'. In addition, MiFID does not place such reliance on disclosure, in fact it distrusts disclosure as a tool, and regards it as a last resort.

The result appears to be that firms are faced with a two pronged attack: a high-level principles-based approach from the FSA's TCF initiative and a more prescriptive approach, under the guise of a principles-based approach, from MiFID.

How should firms respond to this?

The key objective for firms and their senior management should be to avoid enforcement action. The FSA has stated that it is less likely to take enforcement action for breach of Principle 6, where the firm has at least made an attempt to implement TCF. It will therefore be important to be able to demonstrate that a firm's senior management has carefully considered the implications of TCF for their business, has developed a programme of action, and has implemented it. This will need to be fully documented.

In addition, firms will need to have documented and implemented their MiFID-compliant conflicts and 'Best Execution' policies, amongst others. A holistic and integrated approach is required, since such policies are of course part of the broader picture of demonstrating that a firm treats its customers fairly. Firms should not therefore view the MiFID requirements as an additional 'bolt-on' to their existing compliance position, but as part of an overall integrated compliance culture.

6.5 CONCLUSION

Although MiFID purports to bring a more principles-based focus to regulation, it is very different from how principles-based regulation has been understood in the UK. This is well demonstrated by the development of the FSA's Treating Customers Fairly initiative.

Firms will need to attend to the particular and prescriptive requirements of MiFID, the remaining FSA rules for UK-based firms, as well as the more high level compliance culture aspects that principles-based regulation requires. However, if firms adopt an integrated approach to responding to these issues and the FSA continues to adopt a risk-based approach in dealing with breaches, using enforcement tools only where serious contraventions have required, then the future for firms may be brighter than it otherwise appears.

It is to be hoped, at least, that consumers will benefit from the higher standards of protection and greater competition that MiFID encourages, although consumers also require a higher level of financial capability so that they have more ability to protect themselves.

7

Regulators: Consistent or Confused?

Andrew Allwright

It is the most far-reaching piece of legislation to ever hit Europe's financial markets, and yet preparation for the implementation of the Markets in Financial Instruments Directive (MiFID) on 31 October 2007 appeared random and rather confused. To some extent this confusion can be attributed to lack of information available from most financial regulators, and conflicting interpretations from those who have shown their hand.

Ironically, much of this confusion should have dissipated by late 2006, when the European Securities Committee of the European Commission published the final wording of the implementing measures, the final Lamfalussy Level 2 text. The Committee separated the measures into elements to be applied as Regulations transposed verbatim into national law, and Directives which allow for some local interpretation.

However, this local 'discretion' caused other issues to arise, for example it prompted eleven UK trade bodies – known as MiFID Connect – to express concern that the Financial Services Authority (FSA) may 'gold plate' the Directive. Gold-plating is where a domestic regulator adds extra provisions, which go beyond the basic requirements, or alternatively follow an overly prescriptive interpretation.

The impact of implementing the various elements of Regulation, including record keeping, transaction reporting and pre- and post-trade transparency should have been clear, but to make such an assumption was erroneous.

Equally, the FSA was the first regulator affected by MiFID among the twenty-seven European states, plus Norway, Iceland and

The Future of Investing in Europe's Markets after MiFID   Edited by C. Skinner
© 2007 John Wiley & Sons, Ltd

Lichtenstein, to indicate its preferences. Its Consultation Paper,[1] published in July 2006, recommended that UK investment firms publish their Over The Counter (OTC) trades via a Trade Data Monitor (TDM), which would have to receive accreditation from the FSA. However, no such scheme was envisaged by the Committee of European Securities Regulators (CESR) in its consultation paper on Market Transparency, published in October 2006. It is this paper that was supposed to provide the framework for a consistent approach in this area across all European regulators.

The FSA also went beyond the scope of the Directive, and stated that its transaction reporting regime would include derivatives that are priced with reference to exchange traded instruments. It is not clear if all other regulators would follow suit. Indeed, considerable uncertainty remains over the mechanism that will be used by regulators to share transaction-reporting data, and how this may impact measures then imposed on the firms reporting to them.

If there was confusion over the elements to be implemented as Regulation, there was even greater uncertainty over the elements to be applied as Directive. These include conflicts of interest, conduct of business rules, client order handling rules, investment advice and 'Best Execution'.

The most contentious of these is 'Best Execution' and in particular how this was implemented in the OTC markets, where there is less transparency than in the Exchange traded markets. For example, the FSA caused major concern amongst UK firms with the publication of its 'Best Execution' Discussion Paper[2] in May 2006, in which it suggested that benchmarking be imposed across all OTC traded markets. It argued that it would be insufficient for a firm to rely upon a Request For Quote (RFQ) process, whereby an executing broker seeks quotes from multiple market makers and trades against the most competitive.

By contrast, in June 2006, the French regulator Autorité des Marchés Financiers (AMF), in one of its few pronouncements on MiFID, dismissed benchmarking as impractical and produced a paper that appears more supportive of the Request for Quote model.

---

[1] The FSA's Consultation paper 06/14 entitled 'Implementing MiFID for Firms and Markets' was published in July 2006 with consultation ending on 31 October 2006.

[2] FSA Discussion Paper DP 06/03 – 'Implementing MiFID's "Best Execution" Requirements.'

It is clear the regulators must agree on similar responses to avoid the prospect of firms pursuing 'regulatory arbitrage',[3] an outcome completely at odds with the stated objectives of MiFID.

UK firms had to wait until the FSA published its proposed revision of its Conduct of Business rules at the end of October 2006 to gain greater certainty in this area. Contained within the 350 page document was a section that set out the FSA's conclusions on 'Best Execution' which were much more accepting of the status quo, and largely addressed the concerns raised by both buy- and sell-side. The paper reaffirmed the FSA policy of principles-based regulation and did not set out specific measures for firms to adopt to deliver or validate execution. Instead the FSA stated that it expected the markets to identify the appropriate level of response, although this meant that there was a broad range of interpretation and responses as to what was sufficient and cost justified.

One key question was to what extent firms needed to retain a record of full order book data for up to five years if they were required to produce and evidence, for any given trade, that the execution was on the 'best possible terms for the client'?

There is nothing in the implementation measures that specifically requires this, and the cost of creating and maintaining such a database would be prohibitive for all but the largest firms with member feeds from all venues. There were also definitely cheaper and more pragmatic solutions, but with no clear guidance as to whether these were sufficient. In the meantime it was difficult for individual firms or vendors to justify the investment in a complete historical TIC database, when it was unclear as to who would be prepared to pay for its use and at what price.

Such confusion, lack of information and disharmony among financial regulators led to speculation that the dates for implementation of MiFID would be pushed back. Against this uncertain backdrop, investment firms had to plan their responses to MiFID.

The leading institutions had project teams in place through 2006, while some of the smaller firms were gearing up their efforts for 2007, perhaps alarmed by the looming deadlines and media reports about the cost of implementation. It was no longer dismissed as just a compliance problem!

---

[3] Taking advantage of one Member State's regulatory regime at the expense of another.

The initial efforts of the impacted firms concentrated on studying various draft documents and lobbying regulators on certain points, but more recently they have been trying to establish the potential impact on their trading operations. They are also considering ways in which they might gain commercial advantage from the changes that occur from the implementation of MiFID. Such advantages may range from reducing fees paid to Exchanges, to repositioning the services offered to customers, to differentiating their execution capabilities from those of competitors.

Those firms that have acted proactively have been reluctant to indicate their planned response, taking the view that there is competitive advantage in not revealing their hand too soon. As one investment banker said: 'The early bird may catch the worm, but the second mouse catches the cheese.'

That may be true but it does make it difficult for system providers to assess how to help firms achieve MiFID's objectives as a result, because the challenge is to anticipate the various potential impacts of MiFID in order to offer solutions that meet the requirements of affected firms.[4]

In October 2006, the announcement by a consortium of nine of the largest sell-side firms of their intention to create a mutually owned publication venue for their pre- and post-trade data, Project Boat, came as a surprise to few people. These firms have been trying to get the Exchanges to reduce the cost of trading, publication and data feeds for a number of years. Through the creation of their own venue for publication, they are looking to force the London Stock Exchange (LSE) – which is estimated to generate up to 40% of its revenues from the provision and selling of information – to reduce its charges for collecting and publishing data. The open question is whether the consortium can really deliver on its plans, or whether it is just seeking exchange fee reductions.

MiFID requires that such a system ensures that published information is both reliable and accurate, and able to facilitate the consolidation of data with similar data from other sources. The information must also be made available to all parties on a non-discriminatory commercial basis at a reasonable cost. Although, by acting together the firms possess a degree of pricing power, which they may wish to exploit,

---

[4] Editor's note: without knowing what the firms anticipate those requirements to be in many instances.

their customers on the buy-side may be less enthusiastic about paying for this data.

The desire of investment firms to drive down the costs of exchange trading has already led to the emergence of new trade venues. One such entrant, Chi-X, claims to be cheaper and faster than most European Exchanges, and could succeed in capturing liquidity in European equities where virt-x and the LSE's EuroSetts failed. The most recent entrant, Equiduct, has been launched specifically to try and tap into the need for a guarantee of 'Best Execution'. However, it is unclear whether these initiatives or others will make the fragmentation of liquidity in Europe a reality.

The challenge for Reuters will be to carry the additional feeds from these new venues, and to consolidate this fragmented information in a way that is appropriate and affordable for different customers with various needs and agendas.

Reuters provides one of the biggest delivery mechanisms for market data, either directly to the users' desktop or increasingly to systems within their trading infrastructure, as well as solutions across the trading workflow. Consequently, we have taken a close interest in MiFID's development, recognising its potential to impose changes to these workflows, and find increasingly that firms across Europe are keen to know where solutions are being provided for issues created by the implementation of MiFID.

The range of their concerns is broad:

- How to manage the fragmentation of sources in trade and quote data, and still present it in a way their sales force, traders and customers can use?
- How to manage the potential increase of price and quote data?
- How to internalise order flow in equities, and meet transparency and 'Best Execution' obligations?
- What are the most cost effective mechanisms to publish OTC trades and Systematic Internaliser (SI) quotes?
- What order routing solutions support compliance with the execution policy for that asset class to meet 'Best Execution'?
- What kind of analytics and market data is available to validate both execution quality, choice of venues in equities and other asset classes?
- If Multilateral Trading Facilities and SI's emerge to compete with Exchanges, how can firms determine which venues offer 'Best

Execution', taking into account settlement costs, latency, cost of connection and likelihood of execution?

- How can firms report transactions across all relevant asset classes to their home regulator without massive cost implications?
- What process is necessary to classify customers in a way which is compliant with MiFID, and are standard tools available?

At the time of writing, the answers to all of these issues were not fully resolved, but we do not see 31 October 2007 as the finishing line in a race for firms to adapt to the post MiFID world. It is just the start.

8

Regulatory Convergence: The Prospect for a European SEC

Anthony Belchambers

There are some who believe that the emergence of the more formalised Committee of European Securities Regulators (CESR) has laid the foundations for a European equivalent of the American Securities and Exchange Commission (SEC). This is largely due to its Charter and a more defined role within the EU's multi-tiered legislative structure, as opposed to its predecessor body, the more informally structured Forum of European Securities Commissions (FESCO). The same might also be said of CESR's growing role in the Commission's programme to deepen intra-EU regulatory convergence, and ensure even-handed implementation of EU measures by EU Member States.

There is no doubt that progressive European regulatory and market convergence, and the need to contain regulatory cost, adds lustre to the argument for bundling the bulk of Europe's financial regulators into a single body. In fact, many believe this to be the case because the UK's FSA which is a working example of the advantages of unifying regulation within one organisation. However, the FSA's blueprint of a single regulated body was largely achievable because the UK operates in a single jurisdiction under a unified set of overarching laws. Moreover, notwithstanding that there was a significant degree of rules' convergence between the original five UK Self-Regulating Organisations (SRO's), it was not necessary to reconcile different regulatory cultures, practices and procedures or enforcement policies. These were all already held in common between them. That is clearly not the case in the EU.

The Future of Investing in Europe's Markets after MiFID   Edited by C. Skinner
© 2007 John Wiley & Sons, Ltd

Even the most cursory look at the EU's fifty-five or so regulatory authorities, depending upon how you define them, uncovers significant differences in terms of the range of their powers, their regulatory policies, and even in the kinds of financial services regulated by them: wholesale versus retail and large firms versus small firms.

This puts the EU case in a totally different context.

For example, some regulators adopt a very authoritarian approach towards their regulated firms, whereas others look to regulate more by consensus than by dictat. Others yet are heavily politicised and are little more than the agents of their ministries of finance. Some are driven by a strong 'protectionist' approach, whereas others place significant reliance on the role of market forces. Others yet, despite the Lamfalussy principles, have a fairly begrudging approach towards transparent and consensual rule-making, whereas others have to meet extensive open rule-making and consultation procedures.

Moreover, structural regulatory convergence on a pan-EU basis is made even more complex and difficult to the extent that a number of Member States have not yet delivered internal convergence within their own jurisdictions amongst their own sectoral regulatory authorities (and others have shown no particular desire to pursue that unified model).

These significant variables in regulatory culture, procedure and structure point to the fact that, even if it could be achieved, the establishment of a single European SEC would only serve to internalise these divisions and attitudes, rather than cure them. This means, in turn, that there can be no realistic expectation that pan-European structural convergence at this time would be able to deliver on any of the arguments that are most often deployed in support of a single EU SEC namely, greater regulatory efficiency and coherence, cost-effectiveness, proportionality and transparency.

There is one other argument that needs to be given consideration.

That is whether the fierce competition that exists among Europe's financial centres, in promoting their jurisdictions as a location of choice for global market players to base their European operations, will generate a new wave of regulatory competitiveness and arbitrage. There is no doubt that the vast majority of surveys which review the criteria that is taken into account by financial institutions have listed, on a consistent basis, regulatory pragmatism in the top criteria. The other critical factor is the availability of large pools of skilled labour operating under flexible employment laws.

Of course, there is a limit to which public policy will allow standards of regulation to be used as a means of attracting financial institutions to a particular location. Nevertheless, the continuance of individual jurisdictional regulatory authorities will significantly increase, and add to, the national propensity to use regulation as a means of location promotion. Obviously, this is permissible only within the constraints of the Commission's drive for pan-European implementation of EU regulation.

This, however, also suggests that the continuance of individual authorities, even though they are working to common standards and principles, would preserve a valued element of competitiveness in the development of regulatory policy; and would help to ensure that those regulators who do have an open, consensus-building approach to regulation do not become subordinated to a more protectionist, monopolistic approach. Indeed, while regulatory arbitrage may be frowned upon, in terms of encouraging unhelpful regulatory differentiation and adding to the cost and confusion of all those engaged in cross-border financial services business, it also incentives regulators to pay meaningful attention to the principles of good regulation.

In the current climate, the development and observance of pan-European principles of better regulation will be an infinitely more efficient driver for cost efficient, practical and market sensitive rules, than the structural convergence of all of Europe's regulators into a single financial services body. This will no doubt change if the continuing trend towards deeper constitutional and legal Member States integration, and the progressive migration of regulatory authority into CESR, is successful.

However, that time is not yet.

Until that does happen, and for all the reasons set out above, the most efficient framework for regulating the EU financial services sector must be the continuance of independent regulatory authorities, working in close cooperation and, increasingly, to common regulatory standards.

Perhaps the bottom line of the argument is that, until the case for better regulation is held in common and regulatory pragmatism has demonstrably won the day over protectionism, it would be dangerous to give any one regulatory authority the 'key to the door'.

9

Do We Need a Pan-European Regulator?

Chris Skinner

At a recent debate between the European Commission and the Banking and Insurance Community, the question was asked: 'Do we need a pan-European regulator?'

The debate comprised a panel of some stature. In the financial services corner were Rolf Breuer, former chairman of Deutsche Bank, and Henri de Castries, chief executive and chairman of AXA Group. In the politician's corner was Alexander Schaub who recently retired as one of Charlie McCreevy's troops in the European Commission's grand plan for European Financial regulations, and Ieke van den Burg, a member of the European Parliament (MEP). On the regulator's side was Fabrice DeMarigny, secretary general of the Committee for European Securities Regulators (CESR), which drew up MiFID. The referee was Antonio Borges, vice chairman of Goldman Sachs International.

A little bit like the boxing match in Frankie Goes to Hollywood's 1980s hit, *Two Tribes*, where the chorus goes: 'When Two Tribes go to war, a point is all you can score', these two tribes did try to score some points.

9.1 ROUND ONE

The match opened with Rolf Breuer of Deutsche Bank addressing the question, 'Do we need a pan-European regulator?' by saying something to the effect of:

The Future of Investing in Europe's Markets after MiFID   Edited by C. Skinner
© 2007 John Wiley & Sons, Ltd

There are three issues in financial markets supervision – effectiveness, efficiency and accountability. The effectiveness of financial markets supervision is concerned with key decisions being taken at the group level, not the subsidiary level, because we need to look at group-wide rather than national supervision. The efficiency of supervision is that highly educated resources are needed, which are scarce and costly. The duplication of resources is a waste and creates a non-level playing field where competition can get distorted and unnecessary supervisory burdens create unnecessary costs. The accountability structure is also unclear.

This makes sense and scores a point – bankers 1, politicians 0.

Breuer followed up with another scrunching blow to the stomach:

For the near term, there should be a lead supervisor for firms such as ABN Amro, BNP and Deutsche. These firms should only have one point of contact in their home country for all operations across Europe. For banks that are only national players, the national supervisor should be their contact point and regulator. In the long-term, there should be transparent, stable and consistent EU supervision. The result would be a pan-European range of supervisors comparable to the Eurosystem for Central Banks. A Euro-FSA in other words. The Euro-FSA would then resolve national regulatory conflicts and release rule-sets such that Member States work to a common set of rules, with national regulators purely supervising national banks and applying those rule-sets.

Another good point – bankers 2, politicians 0.

9.2   END OF ROUND ONE

A good opening salvo for the bankers which made me think about Fabrice DeMarigny's CESR Committee, who I suspect had sparked up the whole debate, about whether there should be a pan-European regulator.

The debate has been fuelled by CESR's A-bomb piece of regulation called MiFID. MiFID is intended to make Europe's pre-trade operations as competitive as the US's through 'Best Execution' and price transparency. The only problem is that the directive is being implemented across Europe by Member States that have their own discretion as to how they implement it.

As one banker recently said to me:

> I went to the Committee of European Securities Regulators (CESR) and asked them to define the phrase 'facilitates consolidation', a term used in the wordings of MiFID. The response was, 'it will be up to your competent authority'. I asked whether 'competent authority' was my home regulator, my host regulator or the regulator of the most liquid market of the stock that I'm consolidating?' I had a standard politician's answer, which was to ignore that question.

Considering the question he asked, I would have probably said: 'I don't know what the question means'. Because it gets far too complicated. In fact, how politicians, regulators, bankers and corporates get to talk through this stuff at all, in a common language, amazes me. Maybe that is the problem, there is no common language; and no common language means no common rules.

Hence, the argument over national versus regional versus global regulation. By way of example, another banker recently said to me:

> Charlie McCreevy has said that the Financial Services Action Plan is the last regulatory development in Europe but then we also hear people saying 'we may have got this wrong'. We, as bankers, should be asking Europe for a single regulator operating under a single series of controlling rules, regulations and procedures.

This banker's concern was that the countries around Europe can define their own rule-sets. This is also the concern of Rolf Breuer and most other bankers.

Huh?

9.3 ROUND TWO

Round Two began with Fabrice DeMarigny, Secretary General of CESR. Fabrice, surely we need a pan-European regulator?

> CESR will force supervisory convergence. A precondition for this to work is that all supervisors should be networked with equal powers. . .where two national regulators disagree on passporting, they can talk to a group of peers to gain a decision.

Urmmmm. . .

In other words, if two regulators disagree, go and get a decision from your friends and, if you don't like their views, then what do you do?

Sorry, can't give you a point for that one.

But it turns out M. DeMarigny had other priorities:

> CESR will go through a metamorphosis by focusing on operational areas and creating common working methods and prioritising where these can be integrated. Our priorities for supervisory convergence are based upon risk, EU-wide impacts and the ability for CESR to manage these. Therefore, the areas we shall focus upon will include a moratorium on home-host issues; developments of IT data sharing of cases and data management overall; the implementation of MiFID; the consistency of IFRS implementation and asset management; the corporate governance directive; and cross-border bank activities with a view toward opportunities for self-regulation.

OK, he has enough on his plate but still nil-point. What do you think European Commissioner for the Internal Markets, Mr Alexander Schaub?

> A single EU supervisor has gone away as a term because it takes us back to the idea of single structures and single EU markets. That is too simplistic. In some circumstances, harmonisation is the right answer. In others, it is only part of the answer. In others, it is completely the wrong answer.

I think you are hedging your bets. Come on Alex, what do you really think?

> What we need to develop is a European system of supervision, which does not mean a single supervisor. It means a European system of common rules that can be implemented nationally.

Got it.

So what you think we need is a way to avoid political confrontation. After all, if you start taking Brussels Directives and saying, 'Mr Blair – we are taking over the FSA and Madame Merkel, give us BaFIN' and so on, you end up in a political war.

Nope, no points there. Bankers 2, politicians 0.

9.4   END OF ROUND TWO

In fact, what really struck me at this point was how the politicians were sitting next to the bankers and the juxtaposition of their earnings.

How much does Mr Schaub earn per annum: €100,000 a year? €200 000?

And the gentleman sitting next to him, Antonio Borges, vice chairman of Goldman Sachs International? €10 million a year? €20 million?

No wonder bankers and politicians and regulators do not get on. I mean, the financial guys are making all the money out of the impoverished politicians and citizens, aren't they?

Maybe this is the point.

The politicians see bankers and insurers making loads of dosh (if you prefer moolah, spondulicks, you name it) out of the citizens, so they whip the regulators into action. The regulators try their best to interpret what the politicians want but are purely acting as go-betweens between politicians' dreams and market realities. In other words, the regulators will never win.

Alongside all of this, the industry may complain about the cost of regulation but continue to rake in the profits. The Top 1 000 world banks showed record pre-tax profits of $544.1bn and a record return on capital of 19.9 % in 2005, after-tax profits grew by 30.3 % compared to 65.4 % in 2004. Not great, but still a healthy delivery of cash.

The industry claims this is a temporary bull market high and various folks have been predicting a banking bust in 2006. This would be due to a variety of factors such as consumer demand for lending reaching breakpoint, the housing sector going belly-up, interest rates and inflation rising, stock markets blowing apart through hedge fund systemic risk and so on.

But it has not happened. . .yet.

However, the fragility of the markets is one of the reasons why all these regulators are hitting us with regulation – to try to avoid a banking meltdown. Not forgetting the other objectives, such as to liberalise their markets, promote free trade and increase globalisation and competitiveness.

The result is that to be in banking, banks need licences from governments and regulators and, to get those licences, they have to comply and spend.

- The average bank has to keep up with over 100 regulations from dozens of regulators.
- One in five Tier 1 European banks are spending over 15 % of overall costs on compliance.

- 45 % of Europe's biggest banks will spend over $ 60 million 2006–2007 on Basel II.
- 36 % of that spend will be on IT systems and interfaces.
- HSBC spent over $ 500 million on regulations in 2004, up 25 % from the previous year.

They have to spend to be in banking to get the great returns when risk is minimised and markets are liquid.

Another reason they have to comply and spend is that, during these buoyant periods of high returns, banks can get greedy. Shockingly, some might even abuse their clients as US State Attorney General Eliot Spitzer can testify.

The politicians want fairness, while citizens want safety, open community and respect. They just do not trust the financial institutions to provide this without being forced into it.

Bang goes any idea of self-regulation.

Therefore, as we go through this sea change of financial markets worldwide over the next five years, all I can think about is where will we find stability and growth? The more the regulators meddle with the markets, the less stable the markets become. After all, as you change things you create instability, and markets and people want stability. We do not like change.

9.5   ROUND THREE

Round Three was moving towards concluding comments until Henri de Castries, chief executive of the largest global insurance firm AXA Group, piped up. Mr de Castries made many highly lucid points such as:

> Supervision should mean safety, not stability, at the right cost and with the right levels of capital. The right level of capital means the right level. Too little creates risk and too much creates wastage. There should then be incentives to make investments of that capital in the right categories of assets. All of this should be supporting innovation, rather than creating stagnant market. . .We are starting to create a world where we are spending too much capital on a system that is not supporting the safety of the customer.

As the point sank in, I think I saw a little wobble amongst the politicians.

He then illustrated the consequences of the meddling with the markets with a potentially lethal point for Europe...and the GCC, China, India:

> Every national regulator, every quarter, adds bells and whistles to the European framework. This means we are less and less convergent at higher and higher cost. For example, European Solvency II regulations mean that AXA has to reserve € 23 billion to cover capital requirements for solvency. An equivalent USA insurer with a Triple-B S&P rating only has to reserve € 19 billion (AXA is A3a rated) according to our risk models. That means AXA is reserving € 4 billion more than it needs to because the EU does not recognize the strength of our diversifications. If that € 4 billion were invested, we would realise € 900 million a year in additional growth of investment funds. The result is that we lose € 900 million a year in lost opportunities on that € 4 billion.

In other words, the European Union is forcing our institutions to invest in weak assets and poor returns in order to comply with regulations. As this occurs, global firms with global ambitions could relocate.

The politicians fell to the floor but managed to stagger up again slightly shakily.

At this point Henri de Castries, in a kind of Rocky Balboa moment, launched in with a right hook to the chin:

> The benefits of the EU construction of the FSAP must be for the EU constructors. If the EU penalises EU firms, compared to other regions, then capital moves and companies move to where the markets are the most efficient. This means that prices rise in those markets that are inefficient.

The politicians were down and out for the count.

9.6   A CLEAR KNOCKOUT, BUT WHO CLEANS UP?

In the small skirmish I saw in Brussels, the financial industry clearly won on points, but they do not own the governmental controls, the legal authorities, the issuing of licences and the regulatory mandates.

The politicians and regulators are shaping the markets the best they can and know that somehow they have to make this work. The question is how?

The answer is that they do not know how. They are trying to compromise, to gain agreement amongst warring cultures, countries, companies and markets. It is not a pretty sight to watch because in any boxing bout, there will be blood on the floor.

Some will be from the banks, some from the banks' customers, some from the banks' home countries and some from the banks' host countries.

But, just as Rocky Balboa got knocked out by a Russian, banks around the world will be knocked out and consolidated, merged and acquired as MiFID is implemented. During this dramatic reshaping of Europe's investment markets, only a few will win and, just as in war, the only folks who will make money are the arms dealers.

Who supplies the arms to each side here I wonder?

10

MiFID and RegNMS: Changing the DNA of the Capital Markets

Michael Heinz and Bernhard Schüller

The aim of this chapter is to draw a bigger picture of the emerging dynamics of the future capital markets. Our aim is to describe the forces and implications of factors that are responsible for a major transformation in these markets. Technology innovations as well as regulatory changes will have the power to alter the DNA of the current capital markets structures. Specifically, the changes in the USA and EU regulatory regimes for securities firms and Exchanges will lead to a much more complex and competitive environment with the likely result of better customer service for both retail and institutional customers.

Looking at Europe particularly, there are heavy discussions under way about what the winds of change will bring to this continent, referring to the now much published new regulatory framework called 'Markets in Financial Instruments Directive' (MiFID).

Without doubt, there are many implications from MiFID, and a lot of questions for the different players concern what it really means for the nature of customer service, for marketing and sales, for internal processes (trade execution, order handling) for legal, audit and compliance departments and, last but not least, for information technology. IT organisations must take a close look at a variety of applications such as the relevant market data infrastructures and processes platforms in the area of order management, trade execution, trading strategies and overall IT systems, right down to the server and network connectivity layers because of the need for better data latency and trade execution quality.

All market participants have to look at whether their business models are still in synch with these changes, and whether the expected

---

The Future of Investing in Europe's Markets after MiFID   Edited by C. Skinner
© 2007 John Wiley & Sons, Ltd

competitive outcomes and the necessities stemming from the manifold implementation of the MiFID rules provide new *opportunities* for growth, in terms of customers, trade volumes, pre- and post-trade services and higher profitability.

Now, let us review what is taking place in the capital markets arena and who the affected parties are.

10.1 CONSOLIDATION AND COMPETITION BETWEEN BANKS AND EXCHANGES

For the last two decades capital markets have been on the radar of both regulators and IT vendors, respectively application service providers.[1] Trading volumes and the number of transactions have been growing extremely, worldwide. Emerging securities markets – like China, India, Brazil and Russia – have been added in the last ten years, and are now preferred by customers of the western hemisphere for investments with a big appetite for ever-growing returns. Large- and even small-sized firms move to the capital markets in search of international finance to leverage their risk carrying equity capital. Private customers are also eager for attractive investments around the world, making sure their retirement monies are invested wisely and more and more often replacing the simple savings and time deposits with the retail banks.

In particular, the search for higher returns of the superrich individual and large pension and mutual funds was, and still is, a factor that stirred the emergence of alternative investment schemes, with hedge funds the most notable and visible form of that part of the capital markets structure. The rapid evolution of the hedge fund sector in the last decade is a synonym for worldwide growth of capital markets overall. These funds, which are largely unregulated, today command nearly $ 1.3 trillion in client assets managed by around 9 000 hedge fund firms who command a very significant portion in trading activity worldwide. For example, insiders estimate that these funds represent 50–70 % of the trading volumes on the NYSE and LSE.

All of this creates a complicated mix of market players, systems and business models, where each individual player tries to maximise

---

[1] Editor's note: Application Service Providers (ASP's) are the organisations who deliver software solutions to the markets. Purely for illustration purposes, these include firms such as SunGard.

their share of market and profitability. Now there is another wave of increasing competition, new technological capabilities for trading and calculating analytics, and a more comprehensive regulatory framework to ensure better execution, transparency and lower trading costs.

The most challenging tasks for capital market participants stem from USA and EU regulators (SEC, EU) as they adopt two new regulations, namely the US-driven RegNMS and the European MiFID framework. Many industry experts believe that one of the likely outcomes will be that new players will jump into the securities markets, with high-tech Multilateral Trading Systems (MTS) or re-designed internal systems, in order to find new areas for value generation. The abolition of the concentration rule in some European countries like France and Italy, and the competitive moves by investment banks, will bring the existing Exchanges under pressure. This will result in the critical mass of transactions flowing rapidly to new electronic and alternative execution systems, as is already happening in the USA after the start of the ECN Archipelago.

There will be no protected areas in the markets anymore.

With the advent of more electronic communication networks, banks functioning as internalisers and/or establishing trading platforms with partner banks, a struggle is accelerating for the new positioning in the markets, and for the largest possible share of revenues and customers. To get a handle on who is involved in this struggle, one needs to look systematically at the different categories of market participants:

- Organised Markets (Exchanges);
- Electronic Market Place Providers, including

  - Electronic Communication Networks in the USA (ECN);
  - Multilateral Trading Systems (MTF) in Europe;
  - Alternative Trading Systems (ATS); and
  - Other crossing network/execution venues.

- Investment Banks (sell-side);
- Asset Managers (buy-side);
- IT and Market Data Solutions Providers.

All follow their own rationale for securing market share and future profit growth.

Similarly, to fully understand all the dynamics of this industry, one must now take a look at the driving forces that are responsible for the re-shaping of the DNA of this critical part of the financial system.

The most important influencing factors are:

- new complex and strict regulatory frameworks like MiFID, RegNMS, but also Basel II, IFRS and the ECB TARGET system, currently used for wholesale payment systems settlement;
- technology innovations that drive the speed of securities processing and trading towards real-time only applications, in combination with high speed networks and grid servers; and
- newly emerging electronic trade execution venues alongside the more traditional Exchanges.

Looking back at recent history, one begins to realise that all of this is happening within an evolutionary pattern, although the dynamics today are making life for the players tougher in terms of responding to the changes in play. The start of this pattern was the consolidation of organised and regulated markets.

The consolidation of the Exchanges began with the IPO's of the Exchanges and some of their service providers a decade ago. Since then, things have been in flux, with these developments transitioning into a more heated-up phase of consolidation over the last couple of years, and more mergers anticipated over the next few years.

In order to illustrate these changes, let us look at the markets.

First the derivatives markets in Europe are dominated by EUREX, operated by Germany's Deutsche Börse and the Swiss Exchange.

The Deutsche Börse AG in Frankfurt, with its daughter companies Clearstream International and Deutsche Börse Systems AG, successfully launched a public listing on the board of the Frankfurt Stock Exchange in 2001. This listing changed its focus towards shareholder value, profitability and cost efficiency with nearly all of the German stakeholders – many representing Germany's major banks – leaving the group of owners. These banks are now considering returning to investment in the Deutsche Börse because of the enormous profitability of that institution. Meanwhile, the new stakeholders are mainly hedge funds from the UK and the US.

Deutsche Börse has a very well diversified business model comprising a full-blown vertically-integrated services chain. It comprises operation of a traditional trade floor in Frankfurt, called the 'Frankfurter Wertpapierbörse', and the electronic execution venue model for cash equities called Xetra. Complementing the trade execution function, Deutsche Börse offers broad clearing and settlement services, plus delivery of pre- and post-trade analytical market data.

The highly successful derivatives Exchange EUREX is run by the Deutsche Börse in conjunction with the Zurich-based Swiss Exchange, which was a development partner. The Swiss Exchange, the fourth largest in Europe by volume, is very determined in its approach to continue to go it alone in the meantime, and is promising not to give up its mutual charter by staying independent and seeking not to merge or be acquired. Whether this can be successful remains to be seen if we look to the experience in the USA.

For example, a new competitive landscape was formed during October 2006 in the derivatives side of the capital markets, with the $ 25 billion merger of the two main American derivatives Exchanges, the Chicago Board of Trade (CBOT) and the next-door neighbour Chicago Mercantile Exchange (CME). That merger has created the largest derivatives exchange in the world carrying the new name CME Group Inc., which will be operating the most diversified derivatives market place in the world with tremendous liquidity. This market will represent an average daily trading volume close to nine million contracts per day, and approximately $ 4.2 trillion in notional value.

Can EUREX continue to compete with this market under the management of two separate entities?

Equally, we see the same things happening in the USA and European equities markets.

The US Stock Exchanges underwent considerable consolidation in the last three decades, driven primarily by the introduction of new technology. The winners against the regional Exchanges have been the New York Stock Exchange (NYSE) and the National Securities Dealers Association Quote System (NASDAQ). Nevertheless, New York's financial centre is no longer the undisputed top Exchange in the world, as was the case thirty years ago.

What happened?

The bond market moved away from New York to London during the 1970's and Europe has gained much more ground since 1996 in many areas. This was strongly supported by various competitive EU regulatory changes, such as the transparency rule, and is now driven further by means of the MiFID framework, replacing the 1993 Investment Services Directive.

Other developments impacting the Exchanges in New York are the advent of computer based trading systems (ECNs), forcing the NYSE and NASDAQ to leave behind the once dominating open-outcry, floor-based trading model, in favour of automated trading. Although the NYSE still operates the trade floor, it now represents only 5% of the total traded volume per day.

These markets are now impacted further by the regulatory powers of RegNMS, introduced by the SEC in April 2004 and effective in 2007. RegNMS further allows for alternative trading venues, by defining order execution with trade-through rules and opt-outs for example, and will fragment liquidity further by facilitating more intelligent trading strategies in search of 'Best Execution', with speed being a critical component.

This is one of the reasons why, given the already changing landscape of Exchanges, the NYSE decided to buy the very successful 'fast market' Archipelago at the end of 2005. Archipelago was one of the successful new ECN operators which gained critical mass – liquidity via increasing order flow – from both the incumbent NYSE and NASDAQ, the automated exchange venue.

This consolidation has continued, with the NYSE Group successfully launching a $ 14 billion acquisition of Europe's four country exchange Euronext, thus creating the largest exchange group in the world and the first cross-Atlantic merger of Exchanges. The NYSE Euronext Group will comprise nearly $ 27 trillion of value in listed companies on both sides of the Atlantic, and a combined daily trading volume of $ 100 billion.

In the past, Deutsche Börse AG failed to acquire Euronext because of political and cultural problems between the leadership of these institutions but, in our view, this is not the end of that transitional process.

For example, NASDAQ has tried to acquire the leading European bourse, the London Stock Exchange (LSE),[2] with the aim to create the second largest global exchange with 6 400 listed companies, representing some $ 11.3 trillion in market value. The two-and-a-half century old London Exchange has been fighting for its independence for a while, with successful rejections of bids from Europe (Deutsche Börse AG), Australia (Macquarie Bank) and Scandinavia (OMS). It is now only a question of time as to how long the LSE will maintain its status quo of independence and rules set by the FSA. Nevertheless, it is worth noting that the LSE is already in the hands of some foreigners

---

[2] Editor's note: at the time of publication, this acquisition had not succeeded.

as a third of its shares are owned by hedge funds,[3] and the aspiring NASDAQ itself has close to another third.

All the recent major changes in market structure have led USA regulators to call for a more unified structure and governance of the US securities sector, as far as the Exchanges are concerned. Consequently, the SEC merged the two different regulatory bodies which govern the NYSE and NASDAQ in 2007, in order to streamline efficiency, costs and provide a single-source of policies and rule-setting for the 5 100 USA investment institutions. NYSE and NASDAQ have merged their previously separated Regulatory Units and consolidating the NYSE and NASD members will change the way regulation is conducted as there will be, in future, a single set of rules, examiners, and staff.[4]

Finally, there are many other exchange activities. A re-start of EASDAQ under the new name Equiduct[5] has been launched in Europe as a Multilateral Trading Systems. Nomura's Chi-x is an organised market launched under Belgian Law in 2007.

You may also have noted that Asia is not discussed in much depth here.

The leading marketplace in that region, the Tokyo Stock Exchange (TSE), will perhaps embark on closer cooperation with the NYSE, agreeing on a possible contract with the NYSE for a mutual investment stake of up to 10%, based upon proposals submitted by the board of NYSE. That would be the first concrete step towards establishing deeper links for interconnectivity of the capital markets between Asia and the USA.

Besides the TSE there is activity of Nomura Holdings, Japan's leading investment firm, which stands out. Nomura Holdings acquired Instinet, the global agency broker for institutional clients, in November 2006 for $1 billion, thus driving consolidation of the trade execution area within Japan, and clearly giving Nomura a much more global reach.

Outside these activities, there is less consolidation observed in Asia, although booming stock markets in emerging markets such as India, China and Korea have regularly grabbed headlines and attracted retail and institutional investors.

---

[3] The most prominent being Samuel Heyman with nearly 9%.
[4] See Chapter 8 for more on this in Europe.
[5] See Chapter 14 for more on this.

10.2   UNDERSTANDING THE IMPORTANCE OF ORDER FLOW, LIQUIDITY AND FEES

The changes in New York, which the investment banks have long desired, are a response to the rise of a global marketplace. Integration among world markets will give chances to both investors and securities firms in multiple markets and leads to another key development in the USA, that will also occur in Europe under MiFID, namely that the leading investment banks and brokers are turning away trade orders from the two dominant Exchanges, the NYSE and NASDAQ, in order to maximise fee income and reduce trading fees paid to the Exchanges.

For example, Credit Suisse's Alternative Exchange System (AES) is connected to twenty execution venues and will have up to thirty connections in 2007. The three big players, UBS, Goldman Sachs and Credit Suisse, already steer 12 % of the USA stock trades away from the main Exchanges and execute via their own internal liquidity pools. That percentage rate is expected to rise to 18 % by 2010,[6] thereby saving significantly on trading costs levied by the Exchanges and improving 'Best Execution' for clients.

With technology available to mimic exchange functions internally, banks can begin to operate those functions for themselves. As one head of trading of a leading investment bank stated, 'More internal flow gives you a bigger chance to get more trades for your customer and for yourself'.

The latter part of this statement is important because several of the investment banks earn significant proportions of their profits by trading off their own account, which is defined under MiFID as systematic internalisation. The best examples are Goldman Sachs, Morgan Stanley, Merrill Lynch and Deutsche Bank.

The head of another bank expresses this core idea about why liquidity becomes key in the future competition between banks, Exchanges, ECN's and ATS's: 'Less transparency could increase the value of the liquidity that a broker has, since nobody else can see it'.

That is why these internal crossing networks are often called hidden or 'dark liquidity pools'. That is because they do not display quotes to the market generally, as orders are matched internally in order to

---

[6] According to specialist research firm, Aite Group of Boston.

address one of the buy-side's biggest problems, which is transacting institutional-sized orders with limited market impact.

Large orders are difficult to transact due to information leakage and due to decimalisation, which makes it costly for investment managers, pension funds and others to execute large trades. This is why such a large order is often divided into portions of hundreds of smaller orders to search for 'Best Execution'. In the last years the volume of a single executed order went down from $ 1 400 to $ 450. As a result, it needs more than 2 200 trades to execute a $ 1 million order. Hence the reason for dark pools and cross networks.

'Dark pools of liquidity' are a hot topic for traders and execution venues as these many new execution venues launch in a post-MiFID world. This means new electronic networks have been created with built-in functionality to cross all networks, including dark pools, in the search for all available sources of liquidity.

Today, almost all Wall Street Firms are operating in-house electronic trading systems to match incoming orders internally, before sending the order to other brokers, Exchanges or ECN's:

- UBS runs a system with the name of 'Direct Strategy Access';
- Morgan Stanley has 'Passport';
- Goldman Sachs has 'REDIPLus';
- Lehman has 'Electronic Trading Services';
- Credit Suisse has 'CrossFinder'; and
- Merrill Lynch has 'Posit'.

Credit Suisse's 'CrossFinder' manages one of the largest dark pools, and uses it to offer their institutional clients anonymous block trades. Parallel to this activity, broker-dealer Merrill Lynch formed a joint venture with ITG to utilise their system called 'Posit', which is one of the oldest dark pools on Wall Street. That deal, which marries Merrill's voluminous order flow with ITG's important and trusted crossing technology, puts Merrill onto a similar footing with Goldman Sachs, Credit Suisse and Morgan Stanley.

Within these systems, many of which are registered with the Securities and Exchange Commission as Alternative Trading Systems (ATS's), brokers can cross order flow from various silos including customer agency orders, principal orders, retail and institutional flow, correspondent clearing business and so on.

Surely, in the near future Crossing Networks will also appear in Europe. Especially smaller Exchanges in Europe like Madrid, Milan, but also those in Eastern Europe will face greater challenges because of such networks, and the big units already formed by Euronext and others.

As a result of these developments we will see consolidations of venues and at the same time a growing number of electronic venues.

So, how will all these top firms proceed in the near future?

The search for lower trading costs, a better cost structure and the efforts to gain competitive edge, thereby building more differentiation, is behind all of these efforts. It is all about future profitability.

Financial market firms have traditionally been very profitable, with return-on-investment ranging from 15–18 % over the last decade, compared with just 8–9 % for the average company. In addition, financial services firms are by far the most dominant sector in terms of market capitalisation. Respective figures underline this forcefully. As of August 2005, financial services firms in the UK and USA represented some 29 % of the total market capitalisation while the next largest sector, IT, represented only 12 %.

For these highly profitable firms, times are getting tougher.

Clients of those institutions now have fast online access to information about financial products and fees, are looking at lowest trading costs, and are managing investment research on their own.

A recent IBM study[7] focused upon the future of Exchanges and buy- and sell-financial markets institutions found that agency trading, prime brokerage and post-trade asset services will not be a safe harbour for earnings in the future. Adopted and revised business models are needed, to deal with a new dimension in the global markets in combination with risk assumption and mitigation. Greater focus on risk assumption and risk mitigation roles are potential revenue-generating core competencies of the future.

Researchers interviewed hundreds of market participants where the future earnings would be generated and Figure 10.1 depicts the expected profit margins and domains for revenue growth between 2004–2015 for the various players:

---

[7] IBMs 2006 Financial Markets study entitled "The trader is dead, long live the trader" is available under: www.ibm.com/ibm/ideasfromibm/us/finance/may02/feature_story.html.

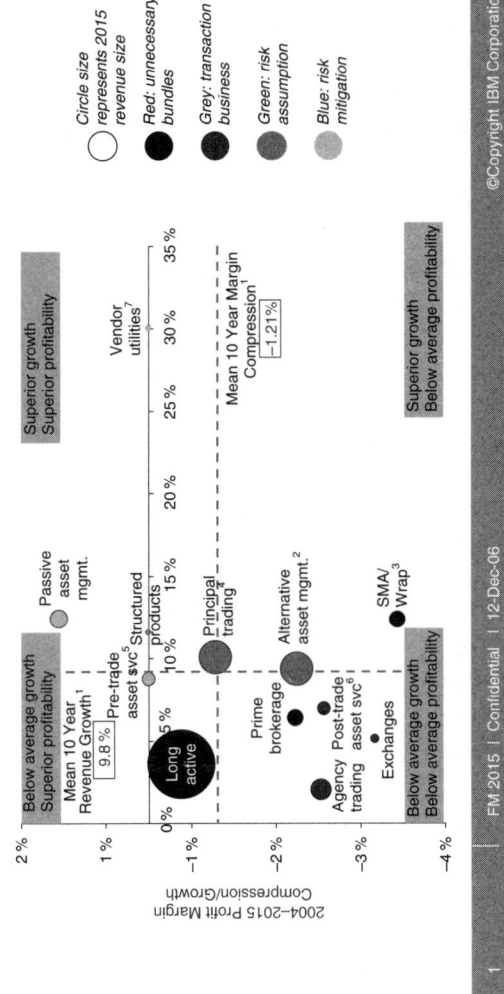

Figure 10.1 Expected profit margins and domains for revenue growth between 2004–2015. Reproduced by permission of IBM Corporation.

10.3   RECENT MARKET DYNAMICS

Similar to the aforementioned activities of US investment banks, a new platform was announced for European equity trades in mid November 2006 by many of the same group of banks that were actively fighting the USA Exchanges, namely the global investment bank players Morgan Stanley, Goldman Sachs, Merrill Lynch, CitiCorp, Deutsche Bank, Credit Suisse and UBS.[8] That news made headlines exactly on the day when, in Frankfurt, a European group of MiFID experts discussed the implications of the framework for the existing Exchanges.

If that planned venture became reality during the course of 2007, as is intended by the originators, then this could be a nightmare for all execution venues in Europe, because half the critical mass is concentrated in those banks' trading books as far as institutional trades are concerned.

Tough times are ahead for the major incumbent Exchanges in Europe, and competition is getting graver. The balance of power in equity markets is already shifting, and the struggle for greater market share and increased fee income will become even hotter over the next few years. One can only speculate about the loss of fees and earnings for the existing bourses, and the reduced transaction costs for the banks and their clients. But this was always the intention of MiFID: to reduce fees and transaction costs in order to make Europe's capital markets much more efficient, competitive and thus enable a better allocation of capital. This is critical to meet another important macro-economic goal, which is to lower the 'cost of capital' overall within the EU, and create one big, nearly harmonised European capital market structure.

Trying to judge how competing execution venues will be affected by the new rules in the USA through RegNMS, and in the EU through MiFID, one must therefore look at how they are intended to work.

10.4   COMPARING MiFID WITH REGNMS[9]

To recap in brief what we have covered so far, the EU initiative on MiFID is primarily about customer protection and greater transparency

---

[8] Project Turquoise.

[9] Detailed resources on RegNMS are recommended as follows: http://www.sec.gov/spotlight/regnms.htm (Securities and Exchange Commission); http://www.nasd.com/web/idcplg?IdcService=SS_GET_PAGE&nodeId=1278(NASD); http://www.nyse.com/marketinfo/hybmarket/1127349068564.html(NYSE); http://www.nasdaqtrader.com/trader/tradingservices/regnms.stm (NASDAQ).

across all trading activity. However, it must be borne in mind that the ultimate goal is to improve competition, and to unify the EU countries around regulation, creating a so-called single passport, and stimulate vibrant capital markets. The EU's objective is also to drive down the 'cost of capital', enabling growth throughout the EC countries. That should result, according to Commissioner Charlie McCreevy, in an improvement of the EU's competitive position in global markets, with Europe then taking a reinforced position as a growth engine and not falling back vis-à-vis the powerful emerging countries.

RegNMS, adopted by the SEC on 6 April 2005, is a very broad regulation framework affecting the national security Exchanges, such as AMEX, NYSE, PCX and so on; the national securities association (NASD) with approximately 600 broker-dealers including 585 broker-dealers that internalise order flow; and finally, the ECN's and ATS's that trade 'NMS stocks'. RegNMS introduces four new substantive initiatives aimed at modernising and strengthening the National Market System for equity securities and complementing section 11a of the Securities Exchange Act of 1934.

The four major categories of the RegNMS rules include:

(1) Sub-Penny Rule (Rule 612);
(2) Order Protection Rule (Rule 611);
(3) Access Rule (Rule 610);
(4) Market Data Rules (Rules 601 and 603).

One of the most critical of the four rules is to drive improvement in 'Best Execution' by restricting trade-through of orders via the establishment of certain policies and procedures under the 'order-protection' rule. That has to be made applicable in all market centres and execution venues.

The relationship between 'Best Execution' under RegNMS and MiFID therefore means that both regulations have similar objectives, implying that common themes are covered by these regulations.

What is relevant for European banks to look at, and how can the USA utilise common areas in these rules for banks that operate in both the US and European financial markets?

First, if a particular rule is already implemented in the US markets then these can definitely be leveraged in the European region as best practices. Typical examples would be the client KYC (Know your Customer) and client identification programmes.

Second, if a common theme is not implemented in the respective regions covered by these regulations, the solution implemented for one set of rules can be transferred to the other. Since RegNMS was introduced much earlier it can act as a stepping-stone for MiFID.

Third, it is now possible to break down these huge regulations into smaller, manageable implementation modules, enabling the compliance efforts for both regulations to occur in a coordinated way.

There are also a few specific areas where RegNMS and MiFID have a common impact, specifically:

- Orders and Quotations;
- 'Best Execution';
- Data Management;
- Algorithmic Trading.

10.4.1   Orders and quotations

Both RegNMS and MiFID have a strong impact on the front office IT systems of investment banks, which are generally the order and trade management systems. This impact is in the following areas:

- The trade-through rule of RegNMS and the ending of the concentration-rule under MiFID heavily promote best quotation order routing. Orders should be routed to market centres, either Exchanges or electronic communication networks (ECNs), which provide the best quotations and where the buy side cannot 'trade through' for the best quote. In MiFID however, orders must always be routed to the principal Exchange where the stock was listed, rather than to the best quote location. This is a serious issue, because some sort of intelligence has to be built in to the order routers and OMS to recognise the best location for routing orders. It becomes more complicated when one considers the number of systems across algorithmic, program trading and manual systems to be changed.
- The trade-through rule and end of concentration directive means that there should be connectivity to all the various market centres for orders to be routed.
- It is implied that market and quote data from all of the market centres has to be available for the respective systems to make any decisions. RegNMS also clarifies the storing of market depth data for each market centre, which unavoidably leads to huge storage

implications. IT vendors will address this area as one of the hottest, in their endeavours to provide regulatory systems support.

- For RegNMS, the concept of the National Best Bid Offer (NBBO) exists, and is being delivered via the market data vendors as conduits, that information is being displayed on the trader's workstation. For MiFID, the concept of a European Best Bid Offer (EBBO) across the European market centres is new, and may imply a lot of change at the trader workstation. This does not mean that the quotes displayed are restricted to trading workstations in Europe, and may also impact trading desks in the USA that handle cross border trading or quote information.
- MiFID will permit the internalisation of client orders as the norm, while also allowing distribution of the internalised prices to the market place. Similarly, RegNMS states that quotes should be classified as automatic or manual, so that orders can be held to the automatic quotes but not the manual ones.
- New classes of orders have been defined in RegNMS, such as the Inter-market Sweep Orders (ISO) with Immediate Or Cancel orders (IOC). These will be broken up and routed to different marketplaces to sweep the order book depth. Even though this is not a requirement under MiFID, the order management systems still have to be adopted to this rule and have to comply with the 'Best Execution' criteria.
- Even if the coverage of asset classes by MiFID has been defined as all instruments other than FX and commodities, the majority of the impact of the two regulations will be felt in the Exchange traded instruments more than the OTC (typical fixed income and credit derivatives) because of the sheer volume of quotes, orders and market places.

10.4.2 'Best Execution'

'Best Execution' is one of the toughest requirements for both regimes, both RegNMS and MiFID, with neither, however, detailing the process for achieving 'Best Execution'. It is left to the interpretation of each investment bank, and thereby makes it difficult for the IT organisations to define the exact degree of necessary change. In order to comply with the regulations, a common solution needs to be decided that can be leveraged across the USA and Europe.

'Best Execution' by itself can be viewed in two ways:

- pre-trade 'Best Execution', which is real time and is referred to as the transaction cost analyser; and
- post-trade 'Best Execution', normally used as a compliance tool.

Even though the actual computation of 'Best Execution' is elementary, the inherent complexity arises from the following factors:

- determination of benchmarks to compare 'Best Execution';
- a decision as to whether to include the depth-of-the-market-quotes to determine the benchmarks;
- calculation of 'Best Execution' on different order types such as basket orders, combination orders, strategy orders, or orders that have been internalised by the sell side firm; and
- computation of 'Best Execution' based on various asset types, as the benchmarks for comparison will be different for each type of financial instrument.

For any 'Best Execution' application, these factors must be taken into account:

- storage of all market data on a tick by tick basis;
- configurable rules for computing benchmarks;
- configurable tolerances by the various asset classes.

10.4.3   Data management

RegNMS and MiFID require a huge amount of data to be stored, to generate compliance reports for violations as well as to prove 'Best Execution' to the regulator. In many ways, these requirements are actually ahead of current storage capabilities in terms of complexity.

In the last five years, data volumes have been growing at an increasing rate, with the current trend being the merging of 'pools of liquidity' and rising markets. Data management will impact the firms in a number of ways:

- A large amount of transaction data has to be funnelled into a data warehouse that will require transformation, staging and loading, as data will be coming from varied systems across the firm.
- The capture of tick-by-tick market data in a centralised place, and disseminated to order management and order routing systems that provide information on the best venue routing and enable order splitting logic.

- Capturing market data without dropping a tick is a huge task by itself and, since the benchmarks are calculated on these ticks, missing information will result in wrong exceptions and false positives.
- A huge messaging infrastructure to enable this to happen.

For MiFID particularly, client data will become dynamic as opposed to its current static state, as the re-classification requirements are on a transaction by transaction basis.

All of this implies that firms need a defined reference data and market data strategy to cater for the data requirements of the different systems. Also, data quality maintenance will be one of the biggest challenges that firms are going to face.

How important is the future market data infrastructure overall, and what are the linkages to the aspects of latency and speed of execution of relevant trading strategies, especially algorithmic trading techniques? We believe that improved automated trading strategies, such as algorithmic trading, will drive market data message volumes enormously and, because of higher competition between the trading venues and the need for a larger share of the trading volume, trading strategies must adapt to this while, at the same time, delivering ever faster speeds of trade processing.

There is also a link between trading profitability and market data, and an emphasis on accuracy, speed and distribution of data between and across firms. Recent developments in the USA are harbingers for what is expected in the EU:

- between 2003 and 2006, market data volumes rose by 1 750 %[10];
- the volume of messages more than doubled between 2005 and 2006;
- projections indicate an exponential growth over the next few years.

What has caused this huge increase in data volumes?

The development started with decimalisation, which drove down spreads, and because of the advent of advanced trading systems, including algorithmic, black-box and automated trading. All of these systems can trade quicker and can scale across thousands of symbols and instruments.

Margins are also thin and getting thinner. Spreads are requiring immediate responses, so the only technically feasible way to trade is to trade utilising rule-based algorithmic systems. Real-time analysis of

---

[10] According to ComStock, a market data supplier.

market information is a key driver for ever-improving trading strategies, especially advanced electronic trading.[11] For this to be optimised, banks are in need of improved data infrastructures in their trading environments.

While market data traffic is soaring, trading counterparties must focus upon reducing data latency whilst increasing their bandwidth.[12] One of the answers is for trading institutions to locate their models on the site of the market centres and ECN's with many examples already in play, such as INET, Archipelago and NASDAQ offering what are called 'Colocation' services.

What are these services? These services enable trading partners to house their trading models and algorithms at the execution venue's data centre itself. Such an approach cuts down data latency and reduces data delivery times to milliseconds, tremendously improving the speed of trading.

The trend for fast execution will remain predominant, placing huge pressure upon banks, brokers, Exchanges, ECN's and MTF's to upgrade their market data infrastructures with modern hardware, grid servers and increased bandwidth.

10.4.4 Algorithmic trading

Algorithmic trading has hit the mainstream in the US equities market, and is increasingly becoming the execution tool of choice for both the sell-side and the buy-side. More than half of all equities trading in the USA will be performed using algorithmic dealing systems by the end of 2010 with, at the end of 2006, the share of algorithmic trading representing around a third of total USA equities trading volume, rising to 53 % by the end of 2010.[13] The leading Wall Street Investment firms currently account for over 65 % of all algorithmic trading volume, followed by agency brokers with 31 % of the market. Nevertheless, the adoption of first-generation algorithms appears to be nearing the end of the cycle in the US markets. Brokers have moved on instead to develop more sophisticated algorithms capable of supporting more complex portfolio trading, adapting to real-time changing market conditions and seeking darks pools of liquidity.

---

[11] According to specialist research, TaBB Group.
[12] Editor's note: the speed of networking and data transfers across the network.
[13] Aite Group of Boston.

A good example is one leading Wall Street Bank, JP Morgan Chase, which has built TAO, a new system with capabilities that signal the next level of trading.

What does TAO do?

JP Morgan Chase's TAO represents an optimal 'algorithm-of-algorithms' approach, using both portfolio trading business models and a modified version of its own algorithmically based market-making business. Using these intelligent trading tools, it beats risk reduction levels achieved via the more traditional Volume-Weighted Average Price (VWAP) strategies for a long-short basket. The bank claims that this approach detects the risk of adverse price movements much earlier in the process, as opposed to VWAP which reduces the market impact of costs alone. The main aim of this tool is to reduce trading costs and manage intraday risk and liquidity.

TAO is an algorithmic trading system for portfolios incorporating an interactive web page which can integrate directly into the traders' OMS. TAO is also capable of reviewing pre-trade analytics, configuring algorithmic parameters, optimising an efficient trading frontier of algorithm listings and monitoring execution performance against multiple benchmarks in real-time, all from one web screen.

For us, it is one of the ultimate trading systems on the markets right now.

10.5 CONCLUSIONS ON RegNMS AND MiFID

What will be the likely impacts of RegNMS and MiFID?

We believe transparency and speed are causing the elimination of intermediary profits, accelerating competition between banks and Exchanges and new electronic trading venues. The most difficult of these requirements is the ability to provide a market snapshot at a specific point of time to prove 'Best Execution', if regulatory scrutiny were ordered. This is a really tough challenge due to the large amount of data that must be made available and stored, without missing a tick. This represents a challenge of the first order because data quality is of the greatest importance in calculating 'Best Execution' benchmarks. For this reason, developing a 'Best Execution' setup is going to be difficult for the experts in the bank.

New market players may fill this gap by acting as execution 'authenticators' or 'verifiers', who will certify 'Best Execution' for securities firms that do not want to assume this function themselves. The market data vendors are the most suited to expand into this area, but big investment firms who are planning for the storage of the market data on a tick-by-tick basis may also push for this domain.

Finally, compliance reports or surveillances for RegNMS and MiFID based on these common themes will be almost the same, except for some minor regional differences. Therefore, surveillance design to capture non-adherence to the regulations will be common and generic.

10.6   THE SHAPE OF THINGS TO COME

The following trends emerge and play their role in the transformation of the capital markets landscape in the future.

First, under pressure from customers, primarily institutional/buy-side customers, the world's equity markets are moving energetically to consolidate, to reduce transaction fees and offer global services. Through merger and consolidation, Exchanges can pool their liquidity and offer better prices to buyers and sellers.

MiFID drives further the componentisation of functions in the capital markets, alongside an ongoing trend toward a deepening of division of labour amongst the different players and the spread of speciality advisory houses, trading institutions, product providers, securities processing entities and custodians.

More specifically this means:

- Europe will see more institutions taking business away from traditional Exchanges, such as Archipelago and new MTF's like Equiduct.
- More change comes from the much needed clearing and settlement side which is a highly fragmented area within Europe with the consequence of high costs, as outlined in the Giovannini Report commissioned by the EC. The ECB has announced its intention to set up a Pan-European settlement facility for securities, using the existing TARGET platform designed for the clearing of wholesale payments within the Eurozone.
- Exchanges trying to maintain leadership in their respective markets, as well as the other trading venues, are investing heavily in state-of-the-art technology in order to cope with immense market volume increases. This is caused by new hardware and software reducing response times down to milliseconds, and the moves by investment banks to invest in algorithmic trading systems.

- For trading rooms at both buy- and sell-side firms, there will be less traders per desk because of algorithmic trading and new IT systems. This trend is already underway in the USA and UK.

Open outcry, face-to-face trading is nearly extinct in this brave new world of automated, computer-based algorithmic trading. The latter is making big gains and will finally dominate as part of the new DNA of market structure. The cosy times of human-based trading will be viewed as fossils by 2015.

Given the new emerging landscape, banks and Exchanges need to adopt and take action in four areas:

(1) Understand their company's competitive edge by defining the company's key competencies, adopting the underlying business model, innovating around new services and new outsourcing possibilities, such as 'Best Execution' services, to streamline the company's true value proposition and exact winning market positioning for sustained growth and profitability development.

(2) Align the new business model with an underlying robust IT infrastructure and a modern Service-Oriented Architecture (SOA) in order to integrate legacy systems with cutting-edge new applications, such as high bandwidth, network connectivity, market data dissemination and low latency trading.

(3) Develop, nurture and grow a culture of systematic innovation and learning, combined with the application of best practices, in order to improve in the three major of competition: products, quality and excellence in service.

(4) Utilise a selective partnering model in order to best exploit the firm's strengths.

In conclusion, MiFID embodies the largest overhaul ever of the capital markets business, its practices and deployed IT systems, and removes quickly the monopolies of the national stock Exchanges in the EU.

MiFID presents an IT and compliance task that must be tackled, whist the business impacts of MiFID can hardly be underestimated. For example, higher levels of competition forces all banks, Exchanges and securities services firms to re-visit their value chain, the risk dimension of value creation and adopt better business models.

This exercise across Europe will bring the EU into a much better position vis-à-vis their US counterparts. As a result, the competitiveness of European securities firms will be much better in the next decade, the 2010's.

Fear amongst banks and securities firms, especially vertically-integrated Exchanges, has been in existence for many years, primarily because of technology-induced competition conquering various areas of the value chain: trading, pre- and post-trade analytics, clearing and settlement. The fear for many institutions of this leading to losses of business and profit streams has been held for long and for some it has, and for others it will.

The new DNA of the capital markets will create new levels of competitive pressure and will, because of increasing fragmentation of liquidity, further drive technological innovation. Here we foresee a strong interdependence between regulatory forces, competition and the rapid deployment of modern, innovative trading and analytics, along with straight through processing technologies, across all markets.

Who will be the winners? No-one knows. One thing is clear though, that the competitive nature of capital markets will continue to make life difficult for CEO's and CIO's.

The question for all will be: what is the new winning formula? The answer is a new understanding of risk. Some firms will be strong in risk assumption while others, perhaps the majority, will strive on risk mitigation for customers. Continued adoption to speed, transparency and true customer orientation represent key elements for long term survival in the capital markets business.

Part 3
MiFID's Implications: the End
of the Exchanges?

'MAKE OR BREAK FOR EUROPE'
BY CHRIS SKINNER, CHIEF EXECUTIVE, BALATRO

This chapter outlines the really big implications in the post-MiFID world, particularly the changing dynamics of Europe's Exchanges and the likely cost implications for Systematic Internalisers.

'EXCHANGES, MTF'S, SYSTEMATIC INTERNALISERS AND DATA PROVIDERS – WINNERS AND LOSERS IN A POST MiFID WORLD'
BY STEVE WEBB, PARTNER AND
KHAVER CHUGHTAI, SENIOR CONSULTANT, CAPCO

This chapter provides an excellent analysis of the impact of MiFID upon the four key constituencies of Exchanges, Multilateral Trading Facilities, Systematic Internalisers and Data Vendors who, effectively, will all now be competing head-to-head against each other in the post-MiFID World.

'EUROPE'S INVESTMENT MARKETS IN A POST-MiFID WORLD: THE FIGHT FOR VALUE-ADD'
BY CHRIS PICKLES, DIRECTOR, BT RADIANZ AND
CHAIR, MiFID JOINT WORKING GROUP

One of the biggest issues raised by MiFID is, 'What will be the future role of the Exchanges?' This issue is reviewed in several chapters, with each providing a valuable perspective as to what the Exchanges' role will be in the future. Here, Chris Pickles looks specifically at where value will be generated in the markets and how the Exchanges need to look for value.

'TAKING THE COST AND RISK OUT OF MiFID IMPLEMENTATIONS' BY BOB FULLER, CHIEF EXECUTIVE OFFICER OF EQUIDUCT

Bob Fuller was Director of IT Strategy at Dresdner Kleinwort, but was headhunted to take over a new exchange, Equiduct, which announced its arrival in November 2006. Equiduct's announcement was the first of the new Exchange services created explicitly as a result of MiFID. Bob reviews why this new Exchange service was needed.

'WHAT IS THE OUTLOOK FOR EXECUTION VENUES POST MiFID?' BY RICHARD THORNTON, PARTNER, SUNGARD CONSULTING

Richard covers a similar discussion to those preceding, regarding the role of Exchanges, MTF's and SI's, although his emphasis and conclusions are slightly different. This chapter also introduces the specific implications of new exchanges, such as Equiduct, and therefore follows nicely after Bob Fuller's chapter.

'HOW MiFID CHANGES BANKING BUSINESS ACROSS EUROPE' BY MICHAEL MCKEE, EXECUTIVE DIRECTOR, THE BRITISH BANKERS' ASSOCIATION

Further to reviewing MiFID's implications for exchanges, Michael McKee of the British Bankers' Association looks at the specific implications for the many different bank constituencies across Europe.

'MiFID'S IMPACT UPON THE RETAIL INVESTMENT MARKETS' BY ANGELA KNIGHT, CHIEF EXECUTIVE, THE BRITISH BANKERS' ASSOCIATION (BBA) AND FORMER CHIEF EXECUTIVE OF THE ASSOCIATION OF PRIVATE CLIENT INVESTMENT MANAGERS AND STOCKBROKERS (APCIMS)

Angela's executive title is one of the longest in this book. This is because she wrote her chapter as CEO of APCIMS and, by the time the book came out, had moved across to be CEO of the BBA. This chapter is an excellent review of the retail market implications of MiFID.

11

Make or Break for Europe

Chris Skinner

MiFID is a critical moment in European development, as it completely recreates Europe's capital markets from being many national investment and liquidity pools, into one pan-European investment market. As a result, investing in Europe's markets will be transformed over the coming decades, with trading strategies moving away from national Exchanges and equities, and towards regional strategies. This evolution will be particularly dramatic for the Exchanges, but also challenges the large investment banks as it demands transparency and 'Best Execution' as part of this process. The end game is one where off-exchange trading and traditional stock Exchanges become obsolete.

11.1 WHAT IS MiFID?

MiFID came into being in early 2004 although it was actually dreamt up back in the early 1990's when the European Commission released the Investment Services Directive (ISD) in 1993.

In that first Directive, the Commission tried to force concentration rules into the European equities markets. These concentration rules tried to ensure that all trading activities took place through the national Exchanges: the Deutsche Börse, Euronext and the London Stock Exchange. After a decade of implementation, those concentration rules were clearly not working, as many broker-dealers were trading off-exchange using their own book of business. This is a generally recognised activity called 'internalisation', and commonly takes the form of Over-The-Counter (OTC) trading.

In practice, OTC internalisation means that you hold large blocks of trading instruments internally, and buy and sell them in a 'virtual exchange' internally. The issue with this form of trading is that, because

The Future of Investing in Europe's Markets after MiFID   Edited by C. Skinner
© 2007 John Wiley & Sons, Ltd

it is not transacted through the national Exchanges, it is not visible to the general access of the public or the regulator. Therefore, OTC firms can provide better trading prices to preferred clients than to the general investor. Equally, the investment throughput and liquidity in firms across the Eurozone can be impacted by such trading, as firms can make markets from such trading.

It should also be noted that although MiFID's wordings apply to all trading, it is particularly firms who trade on an 'organised, frequent and systematic basis' that are affected, as these firms are classified as 'systematic internalisers'. That is why firms known as 'market-makers' are the real target of MiFID.

These firms are the focus for transparency and 'Best Execution', which are the two key principles behind MiFID. Transparency requires firms to declare and publish their trading prices publicly, including the pricing that used to be purely for the internal book of business. 'Best Execution' requires that these firms also guarantee that when they trade on behalf of a client, they will guarantee contractually the best price, lowest cost or fastest speed of processing, dependent upon the choice of the client in that contract. As in the client chooses between best price, cost or speed.

It is the largest OTC traders who truly make markets because the largest market-makers are the preferred trading entities and venues for Europe's largest stocks. ABN Amro, Citigroup, Credit Suisse, Deutsche Bank, Goldman Sachs, HSBC, Merrill Lynch, Morgan Stanley and UBS are examples, which is why these firms created their own Exchange as a result of the impact of MiFID. This is discussed in more detail later, but the fact that over 80 % of Europe's equities are traded through only 20 % of the firms is one of the key reasons why MiFID was created.

11.2   THE BACKGROUND TO MiFID

MiFID has its roots in the introduction of the Euro, and that process began in 1992 when Europe's politicians signed the Maastricht Treaty that created the European Economic and Monetary Union (EMU).

Since 1992, there have been many debates, discussions, arguments and even displacements of Europe's political leaders, but the drive towards Union continues at a pace. The reason for EMU's existence is the vision to create a European economy that can compete on an equal footing with the USA and other global markets. However, the vision is continually challenged by the hiccups of political and commercial agendas which seek to change it from being an Economic and Monetary Union to either being a federated Europe at one extreme or an abandoned Europe at the other.

This is why, within this debate, the financial markets of Europe have such a key role in either supporting or blocking the Union. Kicked around like a political football, Europe's financial markets are at the core of the Economic and Monetary Union, because it is the financial markets that provide the capillaries and arteries to allow the trade to flow without clots or blocks across Europe's borders. That is why Europe's political leaders have focused so heavily on driving change into the financial arena.

Specifically, the development of the Euro currency has implied a lot more than just dropping the French franc, the German mark and the Spanish peseta. There were the cultural and infrastructural changes dictated by European governments in re-issuing currencies and also a greater need to change practices to enable transparent movement of currencies between European countries.

In the investment and trading arena, the key issue was the fragmented and disparate nature of trading across the European markets. Each country had different policies, Exchanges, capabilities and clearing. Infrastructures and rules differed from each Member State, resulting in confusion over which markets worked and how.

Bearing in mind that the fundamental heart of the Lisbon agenda was to make Europe as competitive as the USA as an investment region, this has been a major barrier to the region's success. For example, in the USA, you contract a broker to act on your behalf and can then immediately invest in all fifty states, with a single securities clearing process. In Europe, you contract a broker to act on your behalf, and are typically restricted to investing in one country. If you want to invest across all of Europe – currently twenty-seven countries and soon to be thirty – you have to contract a broker and have clearing operations in each country as such. It is for these reasons that MiFID and the need to rationalise the European financial industry became a focused desire amongst European leadership.

The result was a gathering of Europe's political leadership in Lisbon, Portugal, in March 2000. The meeting discussed many areas and resulted in the critical announcement to create a single financial market across the Europe as a foundation for making Europe a leading global economy by 2010.

After consultation with the industry, it was soon realised that creating such an integrated marketplace would not be simple. For example, it would require a complete restructuring of virtually all financial market activities within the region, from mergers and acquisitions to securities and settlements, from electronic transfers between deposit accounts to insurance sales.

In order to make this happen, the European Commission has created a comprehensive set of legislative changes represented in the Financial Services Action Plan, or FSAP.

The European Commission produced the FSAP Consultation on 11 May 1999, as the Euro was born. The FSAP was subsequently adopted by the European Council in Lisbon and, within the FSAP, are recommendations that form the framework for the creation of a single market in financial services in Europe. In particular, they are the framework for a single wholesale market, an open and secure market for retail financial services and state-of-the-art prudential rules and supervision.

It is these recommendations that are now being implemented as European statutes of law known as Directives, of which the Markets in Financial Instruments Directive (MiFID) is critical for the European investment markets, although there are several others such as the Payment Services Directive, the Transparency Directive and the Savings Directive. In fact, overall, there are forty-two measures in the FSAP and each potentially implies significant restructuring of systems, products, services and infrastructures.

However, the one Directive that has caused the most major debate since its first wordings were released in April 2004 is MiFID, is the Markets in Financial Instruments Directive, which came into force in 2007.

11.3   THE LAMFALUSSY PROCESS

Another little quirk of MiFID is that Alexandre Lamfalussy had just delivered his principles for better regulation of the securities markets. The European Commission had asked Baron Lamfalussy – the respected former president of the European Monetary Institute – to investigate how their regulatory process affected Europe's financial institutions. This was a requirement of the Lisbon meeting of 2000 when the Financial Services Action Plan (FSAP) was first created.

Baron Lamfalussy and his Committee of Wise Men, known as the Lamfalussy Committee, came back with a four-level process that said:

Level 1   European Commission State the Principles of the Directive through a new body known as the EU Securities Committee (ESC) whilst another new body, the Committee of European Securities Regulators (CESR), develop the detailed wordings of the Directive.

Level 2   Consultation Period with industry representatives, governments and regulators of the Member States of the EU, before the Directive is endorsed by the European Parliament.

Level 3   The Directive is ratified by the European Parliament and passed into Member States' governments and regulators to implement national legislation.

Level 4   The Directive is Law.

These four levels were presented by Baron Lamfalussy to the European Commission in February 2001. Once agreed, the new process of regulation awaited its first test and although a few Directives had challenged the process, the first to really test the Lamfalussy process was MiFID.

The Lamfalussy process is a critical point in MiFID's development as the process allowed for the Level 2 consultation period which, in MiFID's case, generated a great deal of debate and disagreement, and changed the target dates for its implementation.

For example, when the European Commission began the Level 1 process, the aim was purely to redraft the ISD of 1993. At that point, MiFID was purely the principles being developed, which were that concentration rules did not work because firms were dealing extensively off the national Exchanges. The Directive therefore aimed to increase transparency and 'Best Execution' by focusing on internalisation issues. These principles introduced the new term: 'systematic internaliser', which is any broker-dealer who trades off their own account in an 'organised, frequent and systematic' manner.

Everything seemed fine until CESR (the Committee of European Securities Regulators) drafted the detailed wordings for MiFID which took these principles into a version to be implemented by national regulators. These wordings were released in April 2004 and moved the process from principles to consultation, as in from Lamfalussy Level 1 to Level 2.

During the process thus far, most of the discussions had been between regulators, compliance departments of securities firms and some industry leaders. However, when the consultation period started in April 2004, a slow burn began as others read the words and saw wider implications. In particular, many technology experts in the markets were concerned about the impact the way in which MiFID was being released would change their technology structures. Exchanges were concerned about how MiFID might change trading structures and impact their core business. Internalisers became worried about how MiFID might change their reporting and compliance requirements.

This is why the Level 2 consultation period that began in April 2004 created so much discussion as, upon release of the draft Directive, the European Commission had set the date for MiFID implementation for April 2006. This is when Level 4, national implementation and enforcement, was meant to be in place. That Level 4 implementation was pushed back twice during the consultation period though, so that the final implementation date was November 2007, eighteen months later than originally planned.

These slippages were not because the European Commission were causing issues or blockage. The Commission was in fact surprisingly accommodating in their consultative approach. That is the spirit of Level 2, which proved to be even more consultative than expected due to the massive amounts of pressure to change. Pressure from sell-side firms in particular, as well as some Exchanges, buy-side firms, industry regulators, treasury departments, even vendors, consultants and others.

This pressure built during 2004 like a slow-burning pressure cooker and exploded during 2005. The explosion was that MiFID was wrong. What was wrong? A lot.

To start with, MiFID's detailed wordings from 2004 were viewed to be ambiguous, and did not represent the actuality of how the markets worked.

For example, Article 29 focused upon pre-trade transparency requirements for Multilateral Trading Facilities (MTF's). MTF's are typically electronic networking venues such as an ECN (Electronic Cross Network) or ATS (Alternative Trading System). Article 29 in the original MiFID wordings read as follows:

All MTF's must '. . .make public current bid and offer prices and the depth of trading interests at these prices. . .on reasonable commercial terms and on a continuous basis during normal trading hours'.

Now this may seem picky, but some folks wondered what 'normal trading hours' meant. Nine till five? When the markets opened and closed? When all of Europe's Exchanges were open? Is there any issue with the fact that London opens and closes an hour later than Frankfurt due to the one hour time difference? Equally, what level of 'depth of trading interests' do systematic internalisers have to make public, as they have never had to do this before?

These are just a few examples of the many questions MiFID's draft text raised as broker-dealers, Exchanges and vendors picked through the detail. In particular, many of the issues raised were related to technology change.

For example, MiFID had words around being able to reconstitute a trade in its entirety for a period of five years. That raised fundamental questions around what does 'reconstitution' mean because if it included all data and voice transactions, as in telephone calls, then the implications for data storage and retrieval are horrendous.

None of these questions were raised initially because the interface between MiFID's wordsmiths and the industry were the compliance managers, who were not technologists. It was only when the technologists read MiFID that they realised it could be a nightmare. In particular, a few people in London realised the full extent of the havoc MiFID might create in the technology rooms and have been championing the campaign to change it.

One particular catalyst in this campaign was the launch of the MiFID Joint Working Group (JWG) in May 2005. The MiFID JWG mobilised the key industry associations of FIX Protocol Ltd, ISITC Europe, the Reference Data User Group (RDUG) and SIIA/FISD to work together to analyse MiFID's true costs. The JWG was followed by the formation of another group, known as MiFID Connect, in November 2005.

MiFID Connect combined the forces of the major UK Financial Market Trade Associations, including the Association of British Insurers (ABI), the Association of Private Client Investment Managers and Stockbrokers (APCIMS), the Association of Foreign Banks (AFB), the Bond Market Association, the British Bankers' Association (BBA), the Building Societies Association (BSA), the Futures and Options Association (FOA), the International Capital Market Association (ICMA), the Investment Management Association (IMA), the International Swaps and Derivatives Association (ISDA) and the London

Investment Banking Association (LIBA). The purpose of this group was to establish a programme for reducing the legal risk and simplifying the implementation of MiFID.

The MiFID JWG and Connect groups lobbied the European Commission heavily throughout 2005 and 2006, as well as other bodies involved in the investment markets including the regulators and treasury departments of governments of the Member States of the EU. That is one of the reasons the final form of MiFID is viewed as being much less onerous to the markets than the original April 2004 draft. Key sections were cut back and redrafted and, in its final form, the biggest impact appears to be upon Europe's Exchanges.

11.4   THE CHALLENGE IS FOR THE EXCHANGES

As mentioned in the opening paragraphs, MiFID replaces the Investment Services Directive, which tried to force concentration rules for trading activities to take place through the national Exchanges. Because this did not work, MiFID aims to make trading on or off Exchanges transparent. However, in that process, the Deutsche Börse, Euronext and the London Stock Exchange all become pure trading venues. This means that you could just as easily use other trading venues under MiFID, including systematic internalisers and Mulitlateral Trading Facilities.

That is why late 2006 saw some interesting developments with the launch of Project Boat, Project Turquoise and Equiduct.

Project Boat was formed in October 2006 by a group of leading investment banks. These banks, including ABN Amro, Citigroup, Credit Suisse, Deutsche Bank, Goldman Sachs, HSBC, Merrill Lynch, Morgan Stanley and UBS, formed a consortium to aggregate European trade data and market data in competition with the traditional Exchanges. The aim was to take advantage of the MiFID regulations that allow trade reporting to any compliant entity, rather than forcing participants to report to the relevant Exchanges – the concentration rules. Those rules meant that market participants were meant to report OTC trades to Exchanges, who charged fees to receive this information, then generate further revenue from collating and selling this information. The Project Boat approach will allow members to retain the fees for themselves and create opportunities for revenue generation. Another interesting feature of Project Boat is that any qualified market participant can use the platform.

This was followed rapidly in November 2006 by the announcement of Project Turquoise. Project Turquoise combines the focused efforts of seven leading investment banks to run their own exchange, in competition with other European Exchanges which they claim are too expensive. In particular, the seven banks involved – Citigroup, Credit Suisse, Deutsche Bank, Goldman Sachs, Merrill Lynch, Morgan Stanley and UBS – generate half of the volume of trading on the London Stock Exchange (LSE). LSE's share price dropped 10% on the day of the announcement.

Similarly, in November 2006, Equiduct was launched. Equiduct is based upon a revamped version of EASDAQ, the European exchange that disappeared in the internet bust. The service became available in April 2007 offering a pan-European pre- and post-trade reporting service with 'Best Execution' for equities trading, again taking advantage of the opportunities presented by MiFID.

The result of these services is that a Frankfurt based trader might have a direct connection to the Deutsche Bourse and then use Project Boat or Equiduct to access the other Exchanges and equity prices. This ensures that they avoid the high costs of having to build infrastructures to connect to all of the internalisers, MTF's and national Exchanges if they were trying to build a pan-European trading service, and is particularly relevant to smaller trading firms, which is one of the key intents of MiFID: to make Europe's trading venues more liquid and transparent.

The issue for the traditional Exchanges however is how to compete. As Charlie McCreevy, the Commissioner in charge of the Internal Market and Services responsible for MiFID, stated in an address to the British Bankers Association in October 2006, 'We believe the scope for competition and innovation that the MiFID will generate will be significant and lasting. We are already seeing consolidation moves by Exchanges, and new transaction platforms for market players. I look forward to seeing even more creative developments in the wake of the MiFID revolution.'

This referred to the bottom-line of consolidation of the national Exchanges which is part of the outcome of MiFID and other moves. This was illustrated by the rapid growth of Euronext. Euronext was formed in September 2000 when the national Exchanges of Amsterdam, Brussels and Paris merged. From there, various other Exchanges consolidated into Euronext, including LIFFE (London International Financial Futures and Options Exchange) and the

Portuguese exchange BVLP (Bolsa de Valores de Lisboa e Porto) in 2002.

It is this style of consolidation that MiFID seeks to deliver, and certainly the huge debate over the future of the London Stock Exchange (LSE) illustrated this well and is one of the factors as to why the LSE became a target in a three-way battle between the New York Stock Exchange and NASDAQ of the USA, along with Macquarie Bank of Australia. The result was that LSE's share price tripled in value from a lowly £4.53 in April 2005 to a peak of £12.76 one year later, in May 2006.

In addition, the value of national Exchanges is also challenged in the post-MiFID world as MiFID also introduces 'liquid shares'. Liquid shares are defined using a number of factors, including the idea that they have a free float of more than €500 million and more than €2 million and five hundred transactions traded. In other words, they are the most popular shares in each of Europe's markets.

The big question here is that there is currently a range of market indices, such as the FTSE100, DAX 40, CAC 40, MIB 30, IBEX 35, not forgetting the Euronext100 and 150 and DJ Stoxx. These indices are run by, and dependent upon, Member States' national Exchanges. Well, all of that will disappear in the post-MiFID world of trading, as MiFID defines a Euro500. These are the five hundred liquid shares defined under MiFID which market-making internalisers must now publish as transparent share pricing and trading. Bang goes the FTSE, Euronext and other indices and, potentially, the Exchanges that go with them.

The result is a major war over Europe's Exchanges, as more exchange services and MTF's appear, and more merger and consolidation occurs.

11.5   THE COSTS OF MiFID

The costs of implementing MiFID vary from €1 billion to €20 billion. This is why some people refer to MiFID as Big Bang II,[1] because of the magnitude and impact of the changes required.

---

[1] The first Big Bang was a major change to the UK Stock Markets implemented back in October 1986; the impact was massive as the traditional gentleman's style of trading between 'chaps' and 'blokes', brokers and jobbers, was replaced with a transparency model similar to American practices of the time.

For individual firms, you hear numbers ranging from €5 million to €150 million. The fact is that few know the real cost of MiFID. However, some are investing heavily to gain advantages from MiFID. By way of example, one large internalising European market-maker budgeted €120 million in 2007 for MiFID implementation: €80 million for the investment bank and €40 million for the private bank and other investment-related areas of their corporation.

Generally, the average broker-dealer firm who deals regularly over the counter and is categorised as a systematic internaliser, is estimated to have spent an average €20 million in reorganising their systems, structures and processes, to comply.

Half of that spend was on a broad range of technologies including data storage and retrieval, networking overhaul to exploit IP-technologies, algorithmic trading and order management and routing applications to improve straight through processing, and so on. This is a considerable investment with the bulk of it going into data warehousing and interoperability. Interoperability being driven through conformance with standards, with the FIX Protocol being a winner in setting the standards for the pre-trade and trade area. Meantime, most OTC firms have undergone extensive business process change to enable 'Best Execution' compliance. The result is a radical shake-up and transformation for most firms.

This is not just for the systematic internalisers though, as the networking, linkage and operations for most buy-side to sell-side firms changed too as other factors came into play, such as the unbundling of services by brokers such that the charging for connectivity, execution, research and commissions also became transparent.

Historically, brokers have bundled their services into a single charge on a monthly billing statement for trade services. Under the new post-MiFID world, many of those charges are being made explicit, as buy-side firms and institutional investors want to know the costs for execution, versus the costs for connection and the costs for research. Some of these buy-side firms will then only pay for the parts they use. For example, many firms view research as being of less value today, in the Google-enabled instant access world. As a result, research is being spun-out of broker firms into specialised research houses or, alternatively, being moved offshore into lower-cost research bases in India, the Philippines and China.

The result is that the trade lifecycle for European investing has been comprehensively transformed and, the more you think about it, the more extreme the implications of change are for the European securities markets, as national Exchanges are opened to direct competition and sell-side firms pricing is stripped bare.

The result is that all securities firms involved in trading equities, options, derivatives, bonds and foreign exchange have had to overhaul their operations to avoid being railroaded by the Directive.

11.6 LOOKING AHEAD

MiFID is just one of the many Directives being implemented as part of Europe's Financial Services Action Plan (FSAP). There are many other Directives of note, including the Payment Services Directive, the Mortgage Credit White Paper, revised Banking and Insurance Directives relating to Mergers and Acquisitions, Giovannini's Clearing and Settlement standards, the Retail Financial Services Expert Group, the eMoney Directive. . .

Until all of these Directives are finalised and implemented, Europe will remain a fragmented market with huge differences between the approaches of Member States to their financial operations. It is this disparity which lies at the heart of the European Commission's agenda. For Europe to work, there needs to be one financial market, not many. This is why the Payment Services Directive, for example, aims to create a single clearing house operation for low value payments across the region; and this is why MiFID aims to create a single exchange and trading environment for Europe.

All of this is wrapped up within the FSAP which, in itself, is still only half-way through its cycle of development and implementation. With Directives such as MiFID, it has its basic pillars and foundations built on paper. The brickwork and roofing is still to be built by Europe's banks and regulators.

Europe's biggest pan-European operators – ABN Amro, ING, Deutsche Bank, BNP Paribas, Societe Generale, and so on – as well as the other banks in Europe with pan-European capabilities – Citi-Group, Bank of America, JP Morgan Chase – should see MiFID and the Financial Services Action Plan as a great opportunity.

An opportunity to create an integrated pan-European banking operations that can compete across Europe for the business of the world's largest organisations.

For the pan-European bank, it means they can finally consolidate and create a competitive European financial zone. One that competes on equal status with any geography in the world. One where the biggest banks can only get bigger and where they can truly leverage the economies of scale that a harmonised and integrated European market offers.

Meantime, for the central banks and national Exchanges, clearing houses and infrastructures across Europe that support these activities, there will be blood on the floor when the inevitable fall-out from these changes hit.

For the corporate investor it means they can potentially run their complete European business through a single account, rather than having an account in every nation. That should mean considerable cost savings. Equally, under MiFID, corporate investors can now manage a pan-European portfolio of investment and asset allocation from a single view, rather than having to deal with twenty-five, twenty-seven and ultimately thirty national schemes, regulators and Exchanges.

In the time left to implement the FSAP, and the years that follow as banks, clearing houses, brokers, asset managers, insurers, intermediaries and the rest fight for position, there will be a great battle. A battle for Economic and Monetary Union supremacy and survival. Only the fittest will survive.

12

Exchanges, MTF's, Systematic Internalisers and Data Providers – Winners and Losers in a Post-MiFID World

Steve Webb*

...it is clear that MiFID will be the catalyst for significant market changes. It will dramatically increase levels of competition among and between execution venues and investment firms. It will definitely increase cross-border competition...

Commissioner McCreevy
European Commissioner for the Internal Market and Services[1]

Once MiFID is fully implemented, the new regulatory framework is intended to facilitate significant change in the entire financial ecosystem of Europe. Not least affected are the key players in the trading and information dissemination infrastructure of the union: the Exchanges, alternative trading venues and information providers. Into this mix we must add the investment banks that will take the role of Systematic Internalisers (SI's).

In this chapter we consider the implications of MiFID to these players and predict how the market may alter, once the new European landscape begins to evolve. Of course it is important to reflect that the

* Steve would like to acknowledge the contribution of Khaver Chughtai, Senior Consultant at Capco's London Office who co-wrote this chapter, and Dr Shahin Shojai, Director of Strategic Research within the Capco Institute.
[1] Annual Lecture at SUERF (Société Universitaire Européenne de Recherches Financières) Brussels, 30 November 2005.

The Future of Investing in Europe's Markets after MiFID   Edited by C. Skinner
© 2007 John Wiley & Sons, Ltd

European politicians and legislators can only create a legal environment that they hope will bring about their vision for a unified European financial marketplace. They must then stand back and watch as market forces and Darwinian economics, the survival of the fittest, determine what does come to pass.

This chapter analyses the strengths and weaknesses of each of the participant groups, discusses the major impacts of the regulation on each player and highlights the opportunities for them. We will also postulate some potential outcomes, though in such a complex environment this is definitely not an exact science. We have looked for available historic parallels that can help us draw conclusions about what will change and, whilst we would be surprised if we are totally correct in our predictions, it has not stopped us from trying.

12.1 KEY MiFID CHANGES TO CONSIDER

The following is a recap of the key MiFID changes that will impact on the area that we are examining. These changes are interlinked, in the desire to create greater competition between trading venues while at the same time maintaining transparency and an effective but fair market.

- MiFID sweeps away rules that forced the majority of trades in some markets to be conducted on the national exchange – the so-called 'concentration rule'.
- In return alternative trading venues (Alternative Trading Systems and Electronic Communication Networks) become more heavily regulated. MiFID defines such venues as MTF's (Multilateral Trading Facilities).
- Investment banks that internalise client orders and cross these against their own books also provide trading venues. These firms are defined in MiFID as Systematic Internalisers and, through 'pre-trade transparency' articles, they are obliged to quote their prices on the liquid shares that they internalise.
- In order to maintain high levels of transparency MiFID also defines 'post-trade transparency' requirements, so that firms publish details of trades that are conducted off exchange in near to real time, making these available on a reasonable commercial basis.
- 'Best Execution' requires that firms establish a policy that will achieve the best result for their clients taking into account price, cost and risk. They must follow this policy and keep it up to date. In

achieving the wider aims of MiFID, this rule is intended to ensure that competition between trading venues results in a better situation for the investor, in particular the retail investor.

12.2 EXCHANGES

A stock Exchange performs two fundamental capital market roles, providing both a primary and a secondary market. It is the latter activity that produces the bulk of income for the Exchanges.

The Exchanges provide a platform which facilitates transactions in an array of financial products. Exchanges will ordinarily derive income from amongst the following sources:

- Listing Fee;
- Data Processing Fee;
- Market Information Fee;
- Trading Fee;
- Regulatory Fee;
- Facility and equipment Fee.

Existing European Exchanges have a number of natural advantages to consider with respect to their responses to MiFID:

- Proven scaleable technology platforms;
- Existing connectivity to their broker-dealer and investment bank members;
- Track record, reputation and experience of running markets;
- Reliable and well regulated public image;
- Pools of existing liquidity.

12.3 WHICH MiFID RULES HAVE THE MOST IMPACT UPON EXCHANGES?

12.3.1 Elimination of concentration rules

In many Member States, national Exchanges will be exposed to competition for the first time. This is not isolated to smaller states but will affect core Member States including France, Italy and Spain. Exchanges in these countries, up until this point, have enjoyed the comfort of a guaranteed source of income and limited scope for competition.

The simple fact that their protection is eliminated will not necessarily cause the flight of trading from these previously protected venues.

There will be more competition with other Exchanges, MTF's and Systematic Internalisers. All of these now have the opportunity to attack market share.

The most significant repercussions could be felt by those Exchanges that have a very small number of highly liquid stocks. For example, the Borsa de Barcelona and Budapest Stock Exchange earn more than 50 % of their transaction fees from a small handful of stocks. These stocks are also the most heavily traded by the large international banks who will seek to internalise. Even before considering the impact of other Exchanges and MTF's therefore, it would be reasonable to assume that some of Europe's smaller Exchanges will suffer significant reduction in revenue.

Even though the evidence is that liquidity moves from existing venues only slowly, the combination of threats and, in particular, the impact of the Systematic Internalisers will have a material impact. The historic evidence that supports this is explored in more depth later.

12.3.2   Post-trade transparency

MiFID rules stipulating the requirements for trade reporting state *what* must be done but remain silent on *how* it is to be achieved.

When considering what this means for Exchanges we should reflect that many of them have a pseudo regulatory role today, whereby all members must report off exchange trades to them. This results in major banks paying for the privilege of reporting trade data and paying again when data is bought back, either through exchange feeds or through aggregation by data vendors.

The extent of this threat is potentially considerable when one examines the proportion of revenue that Exchanges make from data and information. The LSE, for example, earned 42 % of its total revenue from information services in 2004/2005, exceeding the 38 % of total revenue earned from brokerage.[2]

It is now certain that this part of the landscape will change. For example, on 19 September 2006, a consortium of nine banks[3] announced their intent to pool trade transparency information across Europe and to create a trade reporting platform under a project named Project Boat.

---

[2] Capco Institute's research finds that not all of this revenue relates to trade reporting fees, which are estimated to have been less than 10 % of revenue overall.

[3] ABN AMRO, Citigroup, Credit Suisse, Deutsche Bank, Goldman Sachs, HSBC, Merrill Lynch, Morgan Stanley and UBS.

It is possible that Exchanges will be able to offer their trade reporting platforms to the consortium or to other banks. However this will certainly be on a new commercial footing as the banks look to reduce or eliminate trade reporting fees and to make money by commercialising their data asset. It seems safe to assume that, for the majority of European Exchanges, this revenue stream is also under threat.

12.3.3 'Best Execution'

MiFID rules require that firms have a 'Best Execution' policy, follow it and review it regularly. An effective policy therefore will have to take into account the performance depth, price and cost of all available liquidity pools.

Firms will have to adjust their policies to account for multiple trading venues which give rise to two key considerations:

(1) Firms 'Best Execution' obligations will drive them away from venues that are expensive or have poor prices.
(2) Exchanges could potentially offer services that will help firms achieve 'Best Execution' through connectivity with other venues, as with the 'trade-through' approach defined by the USA's RegNMS. This could be offered by Exchanges working together in alliance as a service that would simplify life for their clients; in particular the small to medium size broker members that may otherwise be challenged to meet 'Best Execution' obligations.

The 'Best Execution' rules therefore represent both an opportunity and a threat for Exchanges, accelerating the flight from poor quality venues, and offering an opportunity to gain revenue by providing innovative service to small to mid-tier members.

12.4   MULTILATERAL TRADING FACILITIES

Multilateral Trading Facilities (MTF's) are platforms that essentially bring together a number of participants that buy and sell financial instruments, although it is neither a buyer nor seller itself. The MTF's electronic trading system purely facilitates trading in transactions, including shares, bonds and derivatives.

MiFID stipulates that the MTF should operate a system that applies a set of defined, non-discretionary rules in bringing together buyers and sellers.

In recognising the existence of the MTF's, and by bringing these entities within the scope of greater regulation, MiFID not only balances the elimination of the concentration rules but also recognises the development and proliferation of new technology that allows trading solutions to be developed, both alongside and in competition with existing Exchanges.

There are a number of different types of MTF's in existence:

- Bulletin boards that allow bids to be posted and negotiations concluded within the system.
- Crossing systems which import orders to buy and sell and match on an anonymous basis.
- Quote driven systems that bring together buyers and sellers with Market Makers that quote continuously and bring liquidity to the market.
- Order-driven systems which match buy and sell orders in an order book, either through periodic auction or continuous trading.

MTF's make their money from their ability to attract and conduct transactions and, as such, are in competition with national Exchanges. In order to assess the impact of MiFID on the MTF's we need to first examine the potential benefits that they offer:

- **Cost**: MTF's compete directly on explicit transaction costs.
- **Speed**: the potential for higher speed of throughput through more advanced technology.
- **Greater trading opportunities**: for example by offering out of hours trading.
- **Reduced market impact**: through the ability to work orders in multiple venues.
- **Customised and/or innovative services**: that adds new functionality to a market or provides a mechanism to deal with specific types of transaction, for example, block orders.

12.5   WHICH MiFID RULES HAVE THE MOST IMPACT UPON MTF'S?

12.5.1   Elimination of concentration rules

The elimination of concentration rules in those Member States affected by MiFID opens those markets to competition in the trading of shares in those markets. This gives MTF's the chance to compete for market share in a new range of securities. For this opportunity area, they are in competition with both the incumbent national Exchanges, and the other large Exchanges that will wish to expand their listings into previously protected markets.

In reality this does not appear to present a huge change for the MTF's. There are already a significant number of MTF's in Europe, and their ability to attract significant volume away from traditional equity venues has been limited. The number of MTF's identified by CESR rose from twenty-nine to forty-eight between 2000 and 2004. At the same time the total percentage share of the market commanded by these firms remained in single digits.[4]

The modest success of MTF's in the equity marketplace would appear to be due primarily to the relatively high efficiency and automation of the European markets. The only instances of new trading venues gaining significant market share appear to be driven by the ability to offer significant change to the existing operating models. The relatively low growth of existing European MTF's, shows that competing on price alone is not good enough.

The quality of the market provided by the new-comer is the key driver to challenge existing markets successfully, as illustrated by these two examples:

- Electronic Communications Networks (ECNs) made significant inroads into NASDAQ's markets, gaining 29% share by early 2001 after starting operations in the late 1990's. Analysis of the key reasons for this success identifies that the quote driven market maker model of NASDAQ was a key weakness at the time, and gave the newcomers significant advantage with their order book approach, introducing an alternative model that lowered the spreads of dealers.[5]
- The International Securities Exchange (ISE) launched the first fully electronic US options exchange in May 2000. By September 2006 they were the largest US Equity Options Exchange. This can be attributed to the fact that they offered the first automated trading platform for US options, with lower fees and instantaneous execution. This was a significant differentiation over traditional open outcry trading.

---

[4] Alternative Trading Systems: a catalyst of change in securities trading, Marion Mühlberger Deutsche Bank Research 2005.
[5] 'Alternative Trading Systems and Liquidity', Hans Degryse and Mark Van Achter, Paper prepared for SUERF-conference.

Given the relatively high levels of automation and efficiency in the existing European equity Exchanges therefore, there is limited significant additional opportunity for the MTF's simply by being able to list more stocks. We predict that for MTF's, the impact from the concentration rule change in MiFID is slight.

12.5.2 More regulation of MTF's

The majority of existing MTF's were previously subject to regulatory oversight. In theory, MiFID should simplify their ability to utilise their existing regulatory approval and passport to other markets. Whilst there may be some additional regulatory work undertaken prior to the implementation of MiFID, the main impact would appear to be beneficial in allowing wider use of a passport, assuming minimal 'gold plating' by national regulators.

12.5.3 Pre-trade transparency

MiFID specifies a range of pre-trade transparency requirements for MTF's to meet. These are achieved either through proprietary means or through links to data vendors such as Reuters, Bloomberg and Thomson. Given the nature of their business it would appear that existing MTF's already largely comply with the transparency Articles of the Directive, and that the impact is minimal.

From an opportunity perspective, the obligation for SI's to make their prices public on a reasonable commercial basis may present them with an opportunity to exploit price publishing and order management technology to offer services to the SI's. Similar services may also be offered by market data vendors (either in a complementary or competitive form).

12.5.4 Post-trade transparency

The opportunity to change post-trade reporting arrangements presents MTF's with an opportunity to provide services around trade reporting. Again this requirement could exploit technology and infrastructure assets that are already in place.

Given the announcement of the Project Boat consortium, the extent of this opportunity remains to be seen. Nevertheless, any MTF that is able to either work with the consortia or capture a significant number of lower-tier players should find a market for the service. Competition is set to be fierce and the margins very low however, so there will be a limited number of winners. These will certainly need to find other income streams by providing more than just trade reporting services, which will not command premium prices.

An example of the fierceness of competition that exists is the Chi-X platform. This firm, a subsidiary of Instinet, is offering trade reporting at a monthly fee of £210 per month per venue at the time of writing, a significantly lower price point than those offered by LSE and virt-x.

12.5.5 'Best Execution'

The pressure on brokers to deliver a policy that results in 'Best Execution' may lead to opportunities for the MTF's to benefit. They already have infrastructure and technology to exploit. This means that they could work alongside traditional Exchanges, acting as routers to 'Best Execution' or as competition by being cheaper, faster venues. This means that investment firms would find them difficult to ignore as these firms needs to be compliant with the requirement to have an up-to-date policy.

Instinet was one of the first MTF's to use MiFID as a selling tool, through their Chi-X subsidiary. Chi-X is positioned as a MiFID compliant MTF that can help deliver 'Best Execution' through cheaper execution and settlement. Whether there is sufficient liquidity and depth generated by the MTF will determine the extent to which investment firms need to utilise it in order to meet 'Best Execution' requirements. If a threshold is reached, MiFID could work in the MTF's favour, forcing firms to incorporate Chi-X into their policy. As discussed earlier however, liquidity does not readily shift unless there are fundamental differences in the way a market operates.

Outside the equity markets, MTF's have had more success in Europe.

The MTS Group, for example, has become the most important market for trading in Euro-denominated government bonds. The growth of automated trading for other bonds has however, been limited by the non-standard and illiquid nature of corporate bonds and derivatives. These are predominantly traded over-the-counter, and the size of orders and established trader practice has limited demand for automated platforms.

Whether MiFID changes this situation remains unclear at present. The industry has lobbied in advance to propose minimal changes to current practice around 'Best Execution' in illiquid dealer markets and we predict that, immediately following the implementation of MiFID, there will be little in the way of change.

However, the EU law makers will pursue tighter interpretation of the regulations where they perceive that this is in the best interest of investors, and especially retail investors. As retail investors across Europe diversify away from equities and increase their exposure to other instruments, it is likely therefore that the need for tighter and more transparent 'Best Execution' policies will come. We predict that starting with the bond market, pressure for greater trading automation will then increase, and some of the established MTF's, such as EuroMTS, will benefit.

12.6   SYSTEMATIC INTERNALISERS

Systematic Internalisers (SI's) are investment firms that trade shares from their own books of business on an 'organised, frequent, and systematic basis', away from an exchange or MTF. The Directive will require all Systematic Internalisers to provide quotes on those liquid shares[6] that they internalise on a reasonable commercial basis. Those quotes must be comparable to quotes available in other markets and SI's must keep a record of quoted prices. SI's must also have a policy available for executing orders, that allows clients and potential clients to gain access to execution on a non-discriminatory basis.

The Systematic Internalisers are a newly defined entity in MiFID.

Some of the early publicity surrounding MiFID picked up on this part of the directive and generated headline catching quotes about the number of Exchanges that could exist in Europe. Around four hundred was the much touted figure. In reality, off-exchange trading against own book is not a new phenomenon and has been going on around Europe for some time. In particular, the practice is well understood in the London markets.

Unease in other parts of Europe was highlighted in 2001 and 2002 when Euronext first declared that they were totally against the practice and then changed tack to highlight specific concerns. In a paper in

---

[6] Liquid shares are defined as shares with a free float of €500 million and an average daily number of transactions of 500 or a daily turnover of €2 million (Commission Regulation (EC) No. 1287/2006).

2002 they proposed greater pre- and post-trade transparency in order to ensure investor protection alongside internalisation.
The paper stated:

> For a central order book market, if firms are permitted to internalise order flow unconditionally, pre-trade transparency will be reduced and their clients' orders will no longer contribute to price discovery. Less pre- and post-trade transparency reduces investor protection.[7]

MiFID would appear to meet these specific concerns.
The banks that internalise today are primarily the investment banks that make money on transacting business, and on the margin that they make transacting business against their own book. In addition, by internalising orders, they have the opportunity not only to reduce exchange transaction fees but also to net their trades and reduce settlement costs.
The major investment banks have a number of benefits:

- The ability to offer constant access trading across their own books, taking on the other side of the trade while taking a few points on the trade.
- The ability to offer investors the chance to avoid exchange fees with whilst retaining control of more precise timing than is possible with crossing networks.
- The scale, capital, risk appetite and trading skills to internalise.
- Relationships with a wide network of investors providing internal flow.
- Connectivity to Exchanges and data providers so that they will have access to price information (allowing them to set price based on market conditions).

12.7   WHICH MiFID RULES HAVE THE MOST IMPACT UPON SI'S?

12.7.1   Elimination of concentration rules

The removal of the concentration rules in some markets opens up new shares to internalisation. As these rules did not exist in the most

---

[7] Euronext, 'Internalisation', 2002, http://www.bondmarkets.com/europe/euronext_proposal.pdf.

heavily traded markets of Germany and the UK, the major global and European investment banks already internalise trades. The impact for these firms is through the availability of a limited number of new stocks from the markets where protection is lifted.

The question of new entrants to the business of internalisation is less clear because the barriers to entry are quite high, as firms require:

- technology investment to meet transparency requirements;
- the risk appetite and ability to manage trading risk;
- capital;
- trading expertise.

We believe that this will limit the number of new entrants to this arena. At most we expect a small group of major banks from mainland Europe to join those primarily London-based investment banks that already internalise, to form the core group of Systematic Internalisers. We would expect that some of these new entrants will come from markets that were previously subject to concentration rules, and we would further expect that several banks will exit the business in the medium term, as they struggle to compete in a world of ever tighter margins. We also believe that some banks that currently internalise will see the new requirements as onerous and may try to avoid being classed as an SI, either by adopting business practice changes or potentially by registering their platforms as MTF's.

In summary, there are significant entry barriers that will limit the number of firms that wish to internalise. Given the likely competitive responses of Exchanges and MTF's, the business case will be difficult to justify and we do not expect to see the creation of the large numbers of SI's reported in early MiFID stories.

12.7.2   Pre-trade transparency

Firms that become Systematic Internalisers need to comply with the requirement to make quotes public on a reasonable commercial basis, and to offer clients and prospective clients access to execution on a non-discriminatory basis. The mechanisms by which firms make the price public are to be determined, although it is likely that firms will utilise either existing data standards such as FIX, or existing platforms such as MTF's, or consortia approaches such as the post-trade plans of Project Boat.

The Project Boat consortia are also working together on a quotation platform, Project Turquoise, which could in time become an MTF or exchange. Whilst it is a possibility that the platform could provide a mechanism for quote dissemination, the progression on to a full Exchange is less certain. In terms of complexity, the consortium will already have a significant platform to deliver to meet their initial aims. At the outset, we predict that the firms will focus on trade reporting and will not, initially at least, develop MTF type functionality.

12.7.3   Post-trade transparency

The post-trade transparency rules impact upon the SI's as they will have the obligation to report off-exchange trades in near to real-time. This formalises at a European level the kind of trade-reporting obligations that already exist in the rules of some national Exchanges, such as London.

MiFID therefore does not introduce an entirely new obligation, although it does throw open the mechanism by which that obligation can be fulfilled.

As highlighted in an earlier section, nine of Europe's largest investment banks have unveiled plans to build a platform for publishing post-trade data for OTC equity trades. Project Boat represents the investment banks' desire to be less dependent on external entities consolidating and providing market data information. It also highlights the irritation the banks feel at being charged, not only to report trades but also to buy the data back from data providers.

The likely impact of Project Boat on competition will be added to the desire of MTF's to compete with traditional Exchanges for trade reporting services. This is likely to result in greater price competition. The SI's will therefore benefit in terms of long-term savings. Whether or not the major SI's that report to the Project Boat platform are able to gain significant revenue for their data remains more doubtful. The firms that aggregate and deliver data will argue that they need to protect their commercial position against the added work of consolidating data from multiple sources. It will be this consolidated data rather than a subset of it that is a truly valuable asset.

12.7.4 'Best Execution'

'Best Execution' rules will need to be accommodated by SI's in the same way as other investment firms. The largest investment banks that have connectivity to multiple markets and also choose to internalise, may see opportunity to offer 'Best Execution' services that assure smaller players of meeting their 'Best Execution' obligations. This will allow the biggest investment banks to exploit their investment in connectivity, routing and algorithmic trading technology, to capture flow from small to mid-tier players.

12.8 DATA VENDORS

Whilst data vendors are not directly impacted by regulation, the effects of MiFID will undoubtedly touch on their business models because data vendors own information distribution and trading businesses require that data in order to operate.

The current market is dominated by three vendors: Reuters, Thomson and Bloomberg. In terms of screen count, Reuters have around 37% of market share, followed by Thomson and Bloomberg each with around 25%.

All around the trading floors of Europe, data vendor screens, distribution pipes and embedded analytics drive a huge amount of front office spend. The traders compile their mosaics of price bulletin windows on various markets and global news information screens in order to, at a glance, perform an 'at the second' review of their markets, executing deals whilst managing market risks. Not only do the data vendors service traders, but increasingly feed the information that drives the algorithmic trading applications that computerise much of the equity market decision making.

The existing data vendors have a number of advantages:

- Trader familiarity with the specific tools (those that have undertaken market data rationalisation programmes will appreciate how much customer loyalty to familiar data products exists on the trading desk).
- Proven ability to deliver data with high reliability and low latency.
- Scaleable, robust collection and dissemination infrastructure.
- Embedded API's and interfaces that will not lightly be redeveloped by investment firms.

- Analytical tools embedded within the product.
- Other information such as news and analysis.
- Concentrated market share amongst a small group of vendors with limited room for new competition.

12.9   WHICH MiFID RULES HAVE THE MOST IMPACT UPON DATA VENDORS?

12.9.1   Elimination of concentration rules

It is the combination of rules that will lead to more fragmentation of trade reporting and instrument pricing, rather than specifically the concentration rules themselves, that will give rise to the major impacts for data vendors.

With more venues reporting trades and competing prices, work is required to consolidate this information and present it in a manner that does not reduce transparency. The role of data aggregator has been proposed, which could be taken by existing Exchanges, MTF's or data vendors. Reuters, for one, has stated that it is considering whether to act as an aggregator.

Whilst this role may represent an opportunity for a data vendor it is likely that the investment required will be high and the potential for revenue limited. In addition an aggregator must be prepared to offer their data to all market data vendors, so there will be no particular additional benefit for the aggregators in their core competence of information dissemination. We would expect that a very small number of participants, including existing Exchanges and possibly one of the data vendors, will compete in the aggregator space.[8]

The amount of data to be reported will increase in terms of volume and complexity. However as previously stated, we do not believe that this will be the predicted blizzards of data caused by a proliferation of SI's. We would therefore expect growth in data to be very much business-as-usual for the data vendors.

---

[8] This prediction is subject to there not being any additional regulation that creates 'accredited' aggregators. The FSA have discussed an accreditation process that we believe if implemented across the EU would introduce national self-interest and encourage a sub-optimal environment with a number of national aggregators.

12.9.2 Pre-trade transparency

The projected competition between trading venues will generate growth in the amount of pricing data to report. We expect this to have limited impact on data vendors.

12.9.3 Post-trade transparency

The potential changes to the trade reporting landscape represent something of a threat to the market data vendors. The potential power shift that will come about from the biggest investment banks taking control of their own trade reporting in Project Boat are most likely to be felt most acutely by national Exchanges. However data vendors such as Reuters have until now enjoyed somewhat cosy relationships with Exchanges, such as the LSE. These will be disrupted, and the data vendors may now find themselves negotiating with suppliers that are the same banks that are their largest customers. As such, we predict that data vendors will be placed under commercial pressure from the banks, resulting in either a reduction in revenue or increased costs.

12.9.4 'Best Execution'

The requirement to have a 'Best Execution' policy and to review this on a regular basis represents a challenge to investment firms. For data vendors there is an opportunity to develop services to help firms, both with the establishment and the validation of their policies. Data vendors that distribute price information will be well positioned to provide services around the storage of historic pricing data. This will position them to provide data through which investment firms can test their 'Best Execution' policies and results.

An extension to this service would be to provide detailed Transaction Costs Analytics (TCA), so that not only instrument price but also the cost of transacting business can be accounted for when policy is reviewed. A viable extension to the service would be for data vendors to offer a 'back testing' service. Such a service would use historic price data and TCA analysis to test samples of trades, and provide firms with a report indicating the degree to which their 'Best Execution' policy achieves the desired results.

We expect to see such services develop, and would expect data vendors to benefit either directly as a provider of the service or indirectly as a provider of data.

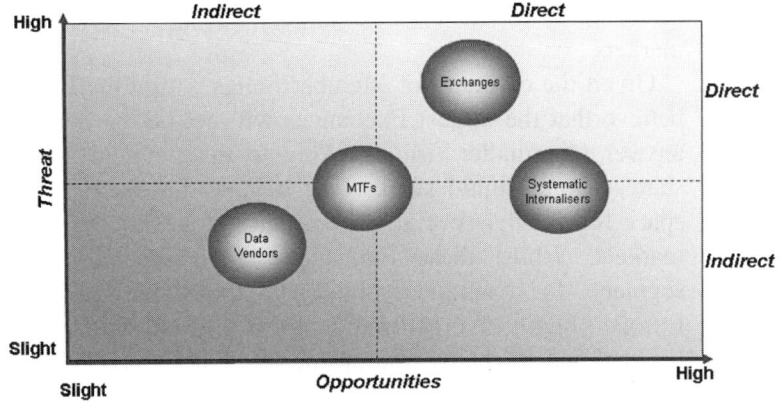

Figure 12.1   Threats and opportunities radar

12.10   SUMMARY

Figure 12.1 above represents the entities that we have examined in this chapter against the degree of threat and opportunity that MiFID represents.

When considering the degree of threat/opportunity we have considered whether MiFID impacts the entity directly, as in the regulatory change has direct impact, or indirectly, as in the changes in the wider landscape bring about the impact. The conclusions are:

Exchanges   The threats and opportunities for Exchanges are direct, with both the elimination of concentration rules and the impact of trade reporting having significant impact. We expect that competition will increase, with Exchanges, MTF's and SI's all competing for transactions and for trade reporting revenues.

As discussed earlier, there is ample evidence that liquidity does not shift readily from established venues, unless there are fundamental structural reasons for it to do so. However, over time, we believe that intense competition will drive consolidation and we will see the most liquid markets in Europe concentrate into two, or at most three, highly efficient hybrid model Exchanges[9] – the 'hyper markets'.

Given the diversity of Member States within the EU, we believe that the largest Exchanges will not be the complete answer for smaller firms looking to raise capital and for shares in non-liquid stocks. We believe that there will be space for smaller specialist Exchanges alongside the hyper-markets. Whilst these Exchanges could specialise upon segment, for example technology stocks, we think that Europe's highly divergent national structure will support satellite regional Exchanges alongside the hyper-markets. These will offer smaller firms access to 'local' capital.

MTF's   The threats and opportunities for MTF's are direct although the impact is considered lower as they do not lose any protected commercial status. They are merely brought into a more highly structured regulatory environment.

As discussed at length, MTF's in Europe have had relatively limited impact, in terms of capturing market share. We believe that they will continue to occupy a niche in the equities markets, operating alongside the main Exchanges, providing services that support particular types of trading. For other markets, such as the fixed income market, we predict that a market shift to more electronic trading will occur over time. This will slowly lead to an increase in the volume of transactions handled by firms, such as the MTS Group. In such circumstances, the MTF's can grow their business. However, we believe that once alternative trading venues reach a certain size, there is a strong chance that they will merge with one of the hyper market Exchanges.[10]

SI's   There are direct impacts for the Systematic Internalisers, as they have additional obligations to accommodate. These obligations will lead to the need for investment in IT

---

[9] The hybrid model is attributed as being the most successful in the extensive study 'Institutional Design and Liquidity at Stock Exchanges around the World' by P. K. Jain.

[10] A historic parallel could be drawn from the Island ECN, which originally won significant market share from NASDAQ but ultimately struggled to continue their growth once NASDAQ responded with Super Montage. They ultimately merged first with INet and were then sold to NASDAQ.

infrastructure but we believe, for the major investment banks that will play the role of SI, the investments are manageable.

There is also direct opportunity for the same banks, as they have the opportunity to compete with previously protected national Exchanges through the elimination of concentration rules and the opening up of trade reporting options.

There have been dire predictions in some quarters that over-regulation of investment firms will lead key market participants to move to other 'light' regulatory financial centres, such as Dubai or Singapore.

Given the importance attached to financial services in Western Europe, and the impact that the industry's invisible earnings make to the economies of the EU, we firmly believe that regulators will continue to work with the markets in order to avoid regulating to such a degree that such a scenario arises.

In summary, we believe that the changes MiFID brings for SI's is, in fact, an adjustment to the way that the marketplace works rather than a revolutionary change. It will result in changes to the investment banks that internalise historically, rather than a rush of new firms chasing the SI opportunity.

We believe that those firms that do register as SI's will be the larger investment banks that are the best equipped to benefit from MiFID. For these firms, we believe that although there is an initial cost impact, there is a real opportunity overall to either increase revenue or reduce long-term costs.

Data Vendors The threats and opportunities for data vendors are indirect, as they result from the wider changes to market practices that MiFID creates.

We would expect to see that all major data vendors will seek opportunity to add services alongside their current offerings. Those that can be most innovative in helping investment firms address the challenges posed by MiFID will strengthen their position with customers.

The changes in trade reporting arrangements may have a slight negative impact for the data vendors but, given both their dominant market share and the 'stickiness' of their presence on trader desk tops, we do not see this as a major threat.

13

Europe's Investment Markets in a Post-MiFID World: the Fight for Value-Add

Chris Pickles

One of the continual trends in financial markets and financial technology has been that of disintermediation: being able to do things yourself rather than being forced to use an intermediary. MiFID follows this trend, and legitimises it at the market level, the operational level and the technology level.

In many ways, this is one of the most surprising aspects of MiFID. As Charlie McCreevy, European Commissioner for the Internal market, says himself, 'MiFID goes with the grain of the market; not against it'.

MiFID allows market participants to do business through a value chain that they consider to be most appropriate to their needs, rather than being forced to use existing value chains that may not, in reality, be as efficient as they seem. The reason for some of this has been the usage of technology.

13.1 TECHNOLOGY IN THE MARKETS

Technology has been used as both an enabler and as a barrier within financial markets. Back in the 1970's, when a mainframe computer would fill a house, and cost as much as an office block, sharing the cost of expensive technology was vital. One of the roles that Exchanges filled was to be the agency that allowed brokers to share the use of this expensive technology, and this approach saw the Exchanges thrive through the 1980's.

The Future of Investing in Europe's Markets after MiFID   Edited by C. Skinner
© 2007 John Wiley & Sons, Ltd

The 1990s saw the Exchanges capitalise on this central role, not only in a figurative manner but in a literal manner as well, when many of the major European Exchanges became publicly-quoted, for-profit commercial enterprises.

Meanwhile, technological change moved along inexorably, and not necessarily in the direction that was in the greatest long-term interest of Exchanges.

This was further illustrated by the EU Investment Services Directive (ISD), which allowed and encouraged cross-border trading and multi-market trading. The systems installed in major investment banks could now equal or surpass the systems of major Exchanges. Investment firms had to become lighter and more nimble, to take advantage of fast-moving changes in the market, which also changed their approach to the use of technology-based services.

Has technology run away from Exchanges?

In hindsight, one could say that the moment that technology was introduced into Exchanges, the end of the world as we knew it was already in sight.

Back in the 1960's, General Electric went into the financial market data business, building a network and installing terminals internationally. When the time came to carry out its first technology refresh, and replace its first generation terminals with the latest hardware, General Electric realised straight away that it was not worth it. It would cost more to replace the technology than all of the future revenue that the technology would ever generate. So General Electric pulled out of the financial market data business.

When an Exchange replaces its current electronic trading system with the latest hardware and software, it probably doesn't generate a single additional client order. As a result, if it costs a major Exchange €50 million to replace its trading platform, it can cost the Exchange's members one hundred times that amount to change their existing systems to fully utilise the new exchange platform.

But no extra business is necessarily generated as a result.

In times of great change, sales-oriented firms understand that it is only too easy for customers to make big decisions and to change the whole way that they do business. Those decisions include moving away from suppliers with which they have long-standing business relationships, and potentially bringing in new suppliers.

When investment firms are faced with major structural and technological changes in their markets, there is always a new opportunity for investment firms to change the way that they do business. European markets are faced with such changes now, as the structural changes that MiFID not only permits firms to ask these questions, but actively encourages them to do so.

13.2   CHALLENGES FOR THE EXCHANGES

An Exchange's interests and its members' interests are clearly not the same thing as the two types of organisation are in two different types of business. This was highlighted when MiFID was being created, and the 'concentration rules' of Europe were addressed. Should trading be forced onto Exchanges, which would then have a monopoly on trading and market transparency? The answer from the European Parliament was clearly 'no'.

This was a key learning from the early 1990s, just as the internet went commercial and internet-based trading kicked off. The watchword then was 'disintermediation'.

At the time, the thinking was that investors would be able to bypass the intermediaries – brokers – and trade directly with each other. Exchanges asked themselves if they should consider setting up their own execution-only broker operations, to compete against their own members. Exchanges and brokers wondered if new trading platforms would emerge, to allow buy-side firms to trade directly with each other.

Today, it looks like the 'intermediary' whose future business may be in question might not be the broker but the Exchange instead. Do the large investment banks in Europe need twenty different stock Exchanges in order to trade securities with each other? If the majority of client order flow is controlled by a very small number of major investment banks, what do Exchanges do that those banks cannot do themselves?

Matching transactions, publishing data and interconnecting market participants is no longer 'rocket science', but is something that banks do as an everyday part of their business. Exchanges have a role to play in the market, but that role is not necessarily the same one that they played twenty to thirty years ago.

In a changing international market for services, the traditional value-add of Exchanges is not what their traditional customers want to pay for. For example, Charlie McCreevy describes the financial services industry as a 'network industry'. Networks, as in computer networks, have helped to define the shape of Exchanges today. From just inter-connecting broker desks round the Exchange floor, and delivering market data to information vendors, Exchanges have expanded their reach to be international trading networks.

As Exchange membership fees have had to fall to attract new members, and Exchange transaction fees have fallen to attract more order flow, a greater proportion of an Exchange's revenue is being generated from market data and network services. This puts Exchanges into three areas of competition with other market players. They compete against investment firms, against information vendors, and against network providers.

The major banks, including their investment banking arms, have made it clear that they want to do business with each other directly, wherever they can do so more cost-effectively than using interme-diaries. This is as true in activities covered by the EU Payment Services Directive and SEPA (the Single Euro Payments Area) as it is around MiFID. Investment firms can run their own quote-driven Systematic Internaliser platforms or order-driven Multilat-eral Trading Facilities (MTFs), and will not be forced to use Exchanges. If they want a shared, multi-national or pan-European market infrastructure as well, they have a choice of waiting until one or more Exchanges is able to offer this, or they can work together to construct their own. It's a 'build or buy' decision: do they buy into what the Exchanges might build, or do they build what they want themselves?

It is also worth remembering that competition is not just one-way though it is two-way. When the European Commission says that MiFID is intended to generate competition between Exchanges and investment firms, it is not just investment firms competing against Exchanges but also Exchanges competing against investment firms.

One should not expect that investment firms would necessarily want to support Exchanges or to help them compete against investment firms.

Exchanges have also been the focal point of domestic market trans-parency for the asset classes that they address. This has been partly biological, because the majority of trades were naturally carried out on-exchange; and partly artificial, because trades were forced by regu-lation to be executed on-exchange. As MiFID withdraws all of the latter 'concentration rules', Exchanges may not be able to hold on to this central transparency role.

A further challenge is around their information usage with the argument that has raged for years as to who owns the information. Exchanges, investment firms and information vendors have all been trying to show that they each had a fundamental and superior right to the information that flows through their systems. We are now seeing the investment firms, which are closer to the source of market data, moving to take control of this information flow.

This was illustrated by the announcement of 'Project Boat',[1] a multi-firm collaboration to concentrate and deliver MiFID-related market data. The investment firms involved in Project Boat have made it clear that they welcome participation from all investment firms across Europe. The result is that Project Boat might change the shape of the market data industry in a similar way to the way in which EBS changed the shape of the foreign exchange trading sector.[2] This is especially true as an Exchange that wanted to collect and concentrate market data from investment firms could now be seen to be competing against the major investment firms' own collaborative effort, in the form of Project Boat, as well as against the normal business activities of the information vendors.

Exchanges would have the additional problem that they typically aggregate only domestic market data. With market participants wanting more consolidated, pan-European or global views of the markets, the solutions that Exchanges find easiest to offer appear parochial. Exchanges are also only a centre for data about the asset classes that are traded on the Exchange, not the whole range of asset classes covered by data vendors. For Exchanges to extend their market data coverage, they have to compete head-to-head with the major market data vendors. These data vendors are a major source of revenue for

---

[1] Editor's note: Project Boat was formed in October 2006 by a group of leading investments banks including ABN AMRO, Citigroup, Credit Suisse, Deutsche Bank, Goldman Sachs, HSBC, Merrill Lynch, Morgan Stanley and UBS, to aggregate European trade data and market data in competition with the traditional Exchanges. At the time of writing the chapter, Project Turquoise had not been announced, but Chris was certainly alluding to the next logical stage where these banks create their own exchange which is exactly what the November 2006 announcement of Turquoise revealed.

[2] Editor's note: EBS was launched in September 1993 by a group of the world's largest foreign exchange market making banks. Shareholders include ABN AMRO, Bank of America, Barclays Bank, Citigroup, Commerzbank, Credit Suisse, HSBC, JP Morgan Chase, Lehman Brothers, S-E-Banken, The Minex Corporation, The Royal Bank of Scotland and UBS. EBS claims to be the world's pre-eminent provider of foreign exchange and precious metals technology trading solutions with 2 000 dealers on over 800 dealing floors in more than forty countries using EBS to trade an average of $ 145 billion in interbank spot foreign exchange and an average of 700,000 oz. in gold and 7 million oz in silver.

the Exchanges, and would take it unkindly if the Exchanges they help to fund become direct competitors.

There is clearly a great potential for friction, not only around who owns the data but also around who adds the value in the data distribution chain.

13.3   THE NETWORKED ECONOMY

In the area of networks, most European Exchanges operate a competitive 'silo'.

Typically an Exchange only makes its own trading platform accessible via its own private data network. This means that the Exchange requires an investment firm to buy one service from the Exchange if the investment firm wants to use another service from the Exchange. In other words, the services are not separated but bundled together so you cannot just buy the piece(s) you require.

This approach to bundling its services allows an exchange to maximise on its unique position in the market, to cross-subsidise its activities that are less financially viable, and to hide areas of commercial inefficiency behind a 'take it or leave it' approach. For example, the private network that an exchange operates is, by definition, extremely small with the largest European Exchanges having only a few hundred members, whilst the smaller Exchanges have only a few dozen members.

This means that Exchanges can never achieve the levels of economy of scale of commercial network operators, with the result that firms wishing to access an Exchange's trading platform or market data delivery system may have to pay ten times the market price that they would pay for a similar type of network service on the open market. For firms in other countries that wish to access an Exchange's systems, the cost of cross-border use of the Exchange's private network can be an even higher multiple.

In a post-MiFID world, where the aim is to have no barriers to cross-border trading throughout the EU, the private networks operated by Exchanges are a clear barrier. It would therefore be understandable if investment firms decided to avoid such barriers and go around them by withdrawing their order flow from these Exchanges. MiFID not only allows this or encourages this; it demands for this to be the case, if the results provide 'Best Execution' for a firm's clients.

It seems that many Exchanges have made little effort to provide truly cost-effective access to their services. An example is the Exchanges' use, or rather their general lack of use, of industry standards. The recent Giovannini Consultation[3] showed that only around half of the central securities depositories in the EU made use of international messaging standards. A similar study of the over forty Exchanges across the EU would find that almost none use international messaging standards at all.

This lack of standardisation makes it more expensive for investment firms to access an exchange's market data and trading systems, and to access multiple Exchanges' systems results in a multiplication of costs for investment firms.

As an example, it costs around € 55,000 for an investment firm to develop a software interface to the market data system of a single exchange. If it were to do the same to access the forty-plus EU Exchanges, it would be faced with a development cost of over € 2 million. Multiply that by the number of firms that are members of Exchanges across the EU, over 2 000 firms, and the cost to the industry comes to over € 4 billion if all of these firms wanted to have access to all of the Exchanges in the EU.

This is also not a one-time cost, as Exchanges change their systems throughout their lifetime. Each time these change, the investment firms have to change and adapt their own interfaces accordingly. On top of these costs would come exchange membership fees, transaction fees, market data fees, etc.

Hence, there are billions of Euro costs being wasted on proprietary interfaces and changes to systems to maintain connectivity with Europe's Exchanges. This situation has similarities to the one described earlier, in terms of the problems faced by General Electric back in the 1960's.

Add into this equation the fact that even if every Exchange across the EU agreed to change the way that it offers access to its systems, so that every Exchange could use a single industry standard, the resulting changes would still be a considerable cost to investment firms. One might wait until perhaps all of the Exchanges consolidated and merged into one, which might result in a greater degree of standardisation of

---

[3] Editor's note: the Giovannini Group is a group of financial-market participants, under the chairmanship of Alberto Giovannini, which advises the European Commission on financial market issues.

exchange access, though it is not clear that such an all-embracing consolidation will ever happen. Another alternative is that the major investment firms that control most of the order flow in the market, rather than waiting for all of the Exchanges to 'get their act together', decide to use alternative trading platforms that use the standards that the investment firms already use themselves. Rather than waiting for a consolidation of multiple Exchanges to get a single pan-European trading platform that delivers particular services that investment firms might need, it could be cheaper and quicker for investment firms to build a single new platform from scratch to meet the market's requirements.

13.4   GET RID OF THE WASTE

The financial services industry has to cut out waste and to compete around the value-add in the market. Waste includes not only wasted money, but also wasted time.

IT systems are now so fast and so optimised that how long it takes an electron to get from point A to point B is a critical factor for business success. The only way that some processes can be speeded up significantly is by reducing the distance that the electrons have to move.

This is changing the architecture of IT systems that underpin trading markets.

In the early days of electronic exchange trading, the trading systems were centralised within the Exchanges. Later, some Exchanges changed their systems to use client/server-type approaches, requiring the installation of the Exchange's technology as an interface on the member's site. Now some of the most demanding Exchange members want to put this client-site technology back inside the Exchange, to reduce the intrinsic latency involved in a distributed trading system. Members like these want to place their own trading technology as close as possible to the Exchange's trading system for the same reason. Overall, service users want to have less and less of a service provider's technology on the user's own site, as this also means that the user had to become a technology manager. And technology is something that is not its core business function.

As the European Commission sees the financial services industry as a 'network industry', in which hopefully everyone can do business with everyone, the justification for having so many private networks appears to be more and more questionable. There are too many similarities to the very earliest days of the introduction of telephone networks, when individual commercial enterprises ran the local network in their cities, and those networks did not inter-link with each other. It also echoes back to the 1960's, when users had to dial an operator and ask to talk to another user if they were located in another town. It is definitely a historic left-over from before the days when customers had network choice, and it bears little relationship to today's modern world of communications where anyone can communicate with anyone, irrespective of where in the world they are located.

Networks can be used for communication: they can also be used to create barriers that lock customers in and lock competition out. Now that more and more Exchanges have become listed, for-profit commercial companies, it should not be surprising if they try to extend the range of their business operations, address new areas in which they feel that they can add value, and if they compete head-to-head against other Exchanges and against their own members that would rather provide such value-add themselves. However, their closed-network, non-standardised approach to business results in a barrier to cross-border trading. This barrier is similar to the one described by the Giovannini Group as 'Barrier 1' in its recommendations about increasing the efficiency of securities clearing and settlement.[4]

Are such barriers in the interest of investors, of the market as a whole, or of the competitive economy of the European Union?

There is a saying that 'Nothing can stop an idea that has found its time'. The idea that 'communication should be easy and inexpensive' is now part of our everyday life and yet, only thirteen years ago, this was not the case. In 1993 the Internet went commercial, and altered everyday life across Europe from our private lives to our business lives and especially across the whole of the financial services industry. The idea found its time, and communication now therefore has to be easy and inexpensive. Artificial barriers that would otherwise hinder this new idea are being removed

13.5   STANDARDISATION IS KEY

One very small example of this is the telephone connector.

Since the early days of telephony, the vast range of different telephone connectors acted as a practical barrier to communications.

---

[4] Giovannini Barrier 1 is focused upon the issues of national differences in information technology and interfaces used by clearing and settlement providers.

Despite years of inaction, the problem of the different telephone connectors has now largely disappeared. Why? Partly as result of deregulation, but more because it was killed off by the 'universal' connector used in every laptop computer, which has since been overtaken by the arrival of low-cost broadband internet connectivity and internet telephony.

Business people used to have to carry around a bag of different telephone adapters for their laptops when travelling internationally. Today, those adapters no longer have a value, and probably never get used. Barriers to communication have been removed.

The EU's Investment Services Directive of 1993 also aimed to remove the barriers to cross-border trading, but it only went part of the way. MiFID has the same goal and, by replacing the Investment Services Directive, intends to go all the way.

At the end of MiFID implementation, we will not still have a Europe that is identified by dozens of different trading platforms, running on dozens of different closed and non-standardised private networks. We should see other new ideas, which have a profound effect on the market instead.

The value-add that Exchanges offer within this new world cannot be protected by using artificial barriers to change and competition. The market will merely flow around those barriers, and may not even use up the energy required in order to try to erode those barriers.

The challenge for Exchanges in the new post-MiFID trading world will be how to stay in the mainstream, by adding value in an even more competitive market where their users want to add that value themselves.

14

Taking the Cost and Risk Out of MiFID Implementations

Bob Fuller

Trading in Europe's investment markets in a post-MiFID world will be very different to Europe's traditional markets, potentially changing how we all think of equities trading in Europe.

At the time of writing, there's a significant increase in M&A activity across European Exchanges, either through abandoned bids, co-operative initiatives or acquisition moves, as the traditional American and European Exchanges position themselves for an uncertain future. Currently, within Europe, we have twenty-nine markets across the extended European Economic Area (EEA), and an even larger number of different Exchanges in existence. As a result, larger Exchanges are feeling the need to consolidate. Examples include Euronext and the NYSE, Deutsche Börse and Borsa Italiana, and NASDAQ's move for the London Stock Exchange. However successful these consolidations prove, and some have already failed, the reality is that there are still too many Exchanges across Europe.

For some while, there's been a general perception that Exchanges have been too expensive. Despite increases in trade volumes, prices have remained high, and many investment firms are tired of the costly process of having to report all their trades, including off-exchange trades, to their local national exchange. Not surprisingly this led to frustration, and a general consensus that there simply must be a better way of doing things.

That's why MiFID is so important.

Despite many firms choosing to focus on the extensive re-engineering and cost burden that MiFID initially imposes, it is essential

The Future of Investing in Europe's Markets after MiFID   Edited by C. Skinner
© 2007 John Wiley & Sons, Ltd

to remember that MiFID is intended to promote cost-effective pan-European trading, effective capital flows, and to ease the move away from trading in isolated national Exchanges.

Highlighting the opportunities that MiFID presents, EC Commissioner for Internal Markets and Services, Charlie McCreevy has stressed that: 'MiFID will lead to a step-change in competition between investment firms, stock Exchanges and other trading venues, for the right to host transactions in shares.'[1]

So why is MiFID such a catalyst, and what changes can we expect to see?

To establish this, it's worthwhile first clarifying what MiFID aims to do:

- MiFID is attempting to create a single European market place to rival the United States in global terms.
- MiFID will allow any firm in any EEA country to have full access to Exchanges, customers, clearing and settlement in any other EEA country without the need to open a branch or subsidiary in that country.
- It will repeal the concentration rule for equities in those parts of Europe where it still exists, such as France, and create a new class of activity called 'Systematic Internalisation'.
- MiFID will allow current Exchanges to compete with each other to become the predominant European player.
- MiFID will codify and enforce 'Best Execution' for most traded products.

So MiFID will significantly affect how we all trade across Europe.

14.1   POSITIONING EUROPE AS A TOP-CLASS, DYNAMIC FINANCIAL MARKET

MiFID is certainly capturing the market's attention and it's a topic that senior politicians, such as Charlie McCreevy, are convinced will play a key part in positioning Europe as a top-class, dynamic financial market. Today the EEA has nearly forty separate equity Exchanges, while the USA effectively has two plus the futures and derivatives

---

[1] Charlie McCreevy, European Commissioner for Internal Market and Services, Speech to the Institute for European Affairs, Dublin, 30 June 2006.

markets in Chicago. So economic and market logic would indicate that rationalisation in the EU is both necessary and inevitable.

The EU's vision is to create an integrated financial services market across Europe, with unified structures to provide the lowest cost of financing to small businesses, corporate borrowers or national Treasuries, and a market where multiple reporting markets are progressively phased out.

While outlining a very upbeat picture of trade services in a post-MiFID world, Charlie McCreevy has been quick to point out the challenges:

> MiFID is close, but not close enough. Governments, regulators and companies have to implement it, and the costs of implementation will be front-loaded while the benefits will take time to emerge. But we believe that the scope for competition and innovation that MiFID will generate will be significant and lasting. We are already seeing consolidation moves by Exchanges and new transaction platforms for market players. We look forward to seeing even more creative developments in the wake of the MiFID revolution.[2]

Commissioner McCreevy, however, also highlights the opportunities:

> For those prepared to adapt and to make the necessary preparation for MiFID, the opportunities in this new landscape of open and competitive marketplaces will be enormous. However, those market ostriches that leave their heads in the sand will be seriously weakened.[3]

Charlie McCreevy has also been clear about the importance of MiFID and its role in the EU vision to create an integrated financial services market across Europe. MiFID is intended to open up the European financial instruments trading market from the investor's viewpoint, and as a result is expected to increase the overall ease of trading, whilst reducing the costs. Projected outcomes post-MiFID include an increased ease in the movement of capital and potentially higher net returns for investors.

---

[2] Charlie McCreevy, European Commissioner for Internal Market and Services, Speech to the British Bankers' Association, London, 11 October 2006.

[3] Charlie McCreevy, European Commissioner for Internal Market and Services, Speech to the London Stock Exchange Christmas Lunch, London, 16 December 2005.

According to Commissioner McCreevy:

In the MiFID world, financial services firms will be able to deal in a wide variety of financial instruments and undertake investment services right across the EU. This will be possible on the basis of a single passport and under the control of a single regulator – that of their 'home' Member State. Post-MiFID there will be no more monopolies of Exchanges for trading of securities, and this will lead to a significant increase in competition – both across borders and domestically – between the Exchanges and other trading venues.[4]

14.2   WHAT WILL THE POST-MiFID WORLD LOOK LIKE?

Because MiFID fundamentally changes the shape of the European investment market, there are some key questions that we need to consider:

- Will the current Exchanges change their behaviour to achieve post-MiFID success and how?
- What happens to the smaller Exchanges in Europe? How quickly?
- How will the publication of the makeup of the 'liquid' equities that define 'Europe' affect customer behaviour, both inside and outside Europe?
- How many Investment Firms will want to 'enter the fray' and become Systematic Internalisers or create MTF's?
- Will these SI's and MTF's still provide their liquidity to the Exchanges?
- Do all these changes alter the definition of 'cross-border'?
- How will Clearing and Settlement be affected?

None of these questions are easy to answer.

The bidding war for various Exchanges during the mid-2000's demonstrated that some Exchanges are more equal than others.[5] Similarly, the impact of MiFID on European Exchanges is not uniform,

---

[4] Charlie McCreevy, European Commissioner for Internal Market and Services Speech to the British Bankers' Association, London, 11 October 2006.

[5] Editor's note: specifically the bidding war for the London Stock Exchange (LSE) which, during 2005–2006 became the focus in a three-way battle between the New York Stock Exchange (NYSE) and NASDAQ of the USA, along with Macquarie Bank of Australia. The result was that LSE's share price tripled in value from a lowly £4.53 in April 2005 to a peak of £12.76 one year later.

and some smaller Exchanges will disappear early in the post-MiFID years.

We are also likely to see the listing of stocks, not just trading, becoming more complex as issuers start to have a real choice of where to list. This will be especially true if the local exchange of the country, where issuers are based, is not the main liquidity pool for similar stocks. We also expect that the liquidity of lesser known stocks in the European 'liquid list', not currently actively traded in volume terms, end up being moved quickly if there is consumer demand for them due to the creation of new European indices. There is a strong chance too that the effect of MiFID will initially be quite volatile execution policies, as liquidity moves rapidly and finds its way to these new centres.

14.3   PRESSURE TO BECOME AN SI?

No one knows just how many Systematic Internalisers there will be post-MiFID, although it is quite possible that the numbers may be higher initially than in the longer term. We suspect that certain large banks, or investment firms with a large number of retail customers, might feel bound to become an SI as a 'badge of honour'.

Similarly, it will be an interesting measure of just how far individual countries across the EEA have accepted the reality of a single European financial services market, by seeing just how many insist on having their own local SI, so as to be a part of the ongoing discussions regarding 'Best Execution'. At least initially we would expect there to be quite a few, thereby increasing the number of execution venues for each stock significantly.

14.4   WILL THERE REALLY BE ONE EUROPEAN MARKET?

From a regulatory point of view, the answer should be yes. Not only MiFID but other initiatives such as the Single Euro Payments Area (SEPA) will play a key role in simplifying pan-European trade. SEPA aims to overcome the imbalance between bank fees and costs for cross-border payments processing. By providing a common interoperable infrastructure, SEPA will bring about further European integration and market efficiency. This consolidation of infrastructures will spur competition and increase the need for rationalisation of financial services companies.

SEPA is just one example of the strong drive towards European financial services integration. Another, which has significant implications for the post-MiFID world, is the Committee of European Securities Regulators' announcement of its European liquid list of some 537 European equities. At the time of writing, this has not been released, but is expected to comprise 140 UK equities, eighty German and sixty French, with the rest made up from the entire EEA including countries such as the Czech Republic and Cyprus. The final list containing equities from most, if not all, of the different EEA countries.

At the moment there is no single venue offering execution services on this list, so it would be difficult for EEA investors to invest in the European 537. If for example an investor wanted to trade this 'index' they would currently be trading in thirty countries in seventeen currencies with multiple clearing and settlement.

It will of course take time to answer these kinds of questions.

Buy-side firms will be working to create new pan-European products that make it easier for customers to invest in the European index. This index will also provide a focal point for new pan-European trading services, which will be keen to trade in both Euros and local currencies and to provide investors with an immediate snapshot of their current portfolio worth.

The European 537 is just the start, as there should also be Euro 100, 200, 300, 400 and 500 indices, as well as end-investors who want to buy into them. The question here is how do customers get their quotes? Does the customer get to choose from a UK price or a European-referred price? How do firms secure 'Best Execution' if the stock is offered by multiple liquidity pools?

These questions and new customer demand, not just from Europe but also from global non-European players, will open up equity trading to a whole new set of market players. These are not just MTF's and SI's, but new pan-European Exchanges based upon technology not history. Think about the universal connectivity and availability of eBay...then apply it to the European trading markets!

14.5   NEED FOR A NEXT GENERATION EXCHANGE APPROACH

It is probably fair to say that while the larger global investment banks will have all the resources, skills and technology infrastructures, they need to address these challenges. There are also a significant number of smaller firms, at both a regional and a niche market level, who really do not have the resources available to plug into the twenty-nine different Exchanges they may need to. These organisations need to pursue three key strategies to close this gap on their larger colleagues. First, they need to collaborate by talking to each other or taking part in a MiFID Joint Working Group or some other forum. Second, they need to have a commitment to standards that are open and not proprietary. Third, they need to find ways to take advantage of common central services for key functions, such as transaction reporting, 'Best Execution' and trade reporting.

Let us look at 'Best Execution' and liquidity in more detail.

Any such open, next generation approaches to this issue will need to take account of the three different types of liquidity, namely execution, clearing and settlement liquidity. It is clear that settlement liquidity is the most difficult to move, as the cost and time required to physically move stock from one depository to another is very high. Clearing liquidity is slightly easier to move, and a smaller number of providers leads to less cost to investors. But it is execution liquidity that is the main thrust of MiFID, with firms now having to execute their customer orders wherever they can obtain the best results. This will, for the first time, cause fundamental shifts in execution liquidity.

Almost every trading system will need to be upgraded to support MiFID's customer protection, data retention and reporting requirements, as well as supporting projected new trading process flows. Typically this could involve, for example, the instant routing of trades to the most appropriate external venue and ensuring 'Best Execution'.

MiFID encourages organisations to look externally, making it far more difficult for firms just to keep on going to the same Exchanges that they have always used. MiFID also defines the shares that are 'liquid', effectively creating a new pan-European index, and necessitating the requirement for a pan-European execution venue to reduce the costs to investors.

Currently if you want to buy French, Polish or Czech stocks, you need three different connections with three different venues subject to three different rulebooks. Clearly, after MiFID, there is a need for a new kind of pan-European exchange that makes all these connections for the firms, and helps them to take advantage of the opportunities that MiFID brings.

That is why we launched Equiduct, a new Belgian regulated pan-European exchange to help organisations meet the challenge of the EU's vision of an integrated financial services market across Europe.

14.6   BUILDING A NEW REGULATED EXCHANGE FOR EUROPE

Why do we need another regulated Exchange in Europe? Especially when there are already so many and when some of them will not survive in a post-MiFID world?

The first and major reason is that there is a big difference between traditional capital-based national Exchanges and new entrants, which can be pan-European from the start using the latest technology models.

Today's technology models are ideally suited to the requirements of a post-MiFID market, as they can be built using the most advanced processing to achieve turnaround times from order to execution of milliseconds. In addition, they can truly exploit open standards, such as FIX, making it as easy as possible for organisations to connect and trade.

With this type of high performance engine, new Exchanges can provide low risk, low cost platforms for high quality MiFID services, including the consolidation of pan-European equities ticker tapes, full pre- and post-trade transparency, facilities for internalisation across an exchange in a single regulatory environment, and proof of 'Best Execution' in equities.

New Exchanges can therefore help organisations to cut the cost of their MiFID implementations and give the desired end user result to the investors of reduced costs and better prices. They can fully take advantage of the new MiFID-enabled business opportunities.

That is why we focused upon enabling our customers to reduce the cost of connecting through to pan-European trading, in order to leave them free to spend their money on other areas that required further internal investment, such as dealing with their customer classification requirements.

These connections should be as pain-free as possible by delivering proven connectivity to front-end dealing systems, data vendors and network providers. By using the FIX protocol standards, customers can connect simply and, wherever possible, can use their current clearing and settlement providers. Similarly trading firms should be able to us either use their current data vendors or choose to receive a direct feed. Collectively, this is all about giving European investors increased confidence about trading in the post-MiFID world and reassurance that they do not need to change their existing trading and settlement processes more than absolutely necessary.

14.7   APPROACHING MiFID IN DIFFERENT WAYS

Through Equiduct and similar exchange services in the post-MiFID world, organisations should be able to access a single pan-European exchange service, rather than having to trade in all of the existing national Exchanges. This is effectively delivering on MiFID's key goal of making Europe more liquid and transparent.

This also demonstrates that MiFID will be the catalyst for significant market changes. I expect these changes to increase levels of competition dramatically among and between execution venues and investment firms. At the same time, MiFID will definitely increase cross-border competition, and lower costs for issuers and investors wishing to access Europe's capital markets.

Given the requirements and complexity of MiFID, investment in IT systems is likely to take up a bigger part of firms' budgets. The largest players will no doubt want to develop their own solutions, whilst smaller firms will look to either co-operate or take advantage of proven MiFID solutions. For those firms prepared to adapt and to make the necessary preparations, the opportunities in this new landscape of open and hyper-competitive marketplaces will be enormous.

Investment firms that try to ignore MiFID will find themselves fatally weakened, as first-mover advantage is demonstrating itself to be all-important.

Post-MiFID, I suspect some of the characteristics of the European market will also change. MiFID is all about improving Europe's financial services competitiveness, and that is going to attract more trading volume across Europe, and more investment from outside of the EEA. We are also going to see firms getting smarter rather than bigger. The successful firms are those that manage to make compelling services out of what they are good at, and then outsource what they are not good at.

14.8   WELCOME TO A BRAVE NEW WORLD OF OPPORTUNITY!

For many MiFID seemed like a complex and expensive issue, and it was often far easier to focus on the challenges rather than the undoubted opportunities that MiFID created for organisations across the financial services spectrum. These opportunities come through greater speed, greater connectivity and greater reliability.

Equiduct and other new exchange services are following the example of organisations such as eBay by offering a centralised technology platform that is easy to communicate with, and that gives customers what they want through uniform, repeatable and measurable behaviour.

In conclusion, at times of great change, such as MiFID, it is always worthwhile to remember the lessons of the past. Almost half a century, ago Machiavelli wrote in *The Prince*:

> Leading the introduction of a new order is hard. There is nothing more difficult to take in hand, more perilous to conduct, or more uncertain in its success.

That is why we are determined to take the cost, and the risk, out of MiFID compliance and implementation.

15

What is the Outlook for Execution Venues Post MiFID?

Richard Thornton

There is no doubt that MiFID will have a fundamental impact on the structure of the European Financial Markets. The Directive's scope is so ambitious that the outcome in five to ten years might be quite different from the creators' intention. What will be the impact and what will the financial markets look like ten years from now?

Many believe MiFID to be the most significant piece of European Financial Services legislation since the Big Bang.[1] Only time will tell whether it brings the growth that the latter provided as a catalyst and November 2007 is only the start of change for where and how trades are executed across Europe.

This chapter is focused upon exploring potential models which may develop for execution venues, whether they are Exchanges, as in Regulated Markets, Multilateral Trading Facilities (MTF's) or Systematic Internalisers (SI's). There is a significant variation in the number of trading venues which are predicted to be established in the next few years. Some predict that the number could be in excess of two hundred. Whilst this might not be the case, it definitely appears to be true that the number will be at least double the amount we have today. Some will become SI's in a broad range of stocks, some will become niche SI's focusing on small numbers of stocks or specific sectors, and some will join or form MTF's. The larger players are likely to be both SI's, and have an involvement in at least one MTF.

---

[1] Editor's note: the first Big Bang was a major change to the UK Stock Markets implemented back in October 1986; the impact was massive as the traditional gentleman's style of trading between 'chaps' and 'blokes', brokers and jobbers, was replaced with a transparency model similar to American practices of the time.

The Future of Investing in Europe's Markets after MiFID Edited by C. Skinner
© 2007 John Wiley & Sons, Ltd

In the case of Exchanges, a combination of MiFID and market forces is changing the playing field, for example, the announcement of a new European electronic exchange, Equiduct,[2] in November 2006 was just a start. It is highly likely that the vision of having only a small number of very large Exchanges may never happen, but a completely new model might emerge driven by market participants.

Firms that internalise trades supported by technology allowing fully automated crossing and internal matching are *de facto* Systematic Internalisers. Any argument which states that trades are carried out on an *ad hoc* basis would be difficult to defend. Clearly the definition of 'Systematic Internaliser' is likely to be a contentious issue which will be challenged.

The fundamental question firms need to address is whether sufficient liquidity can be attracted, from day one, to make venues viable as an execution venue under 'Best Execution' rules. This is equally applicable to SI's and MTF's, however it will be critical for MTF's if they are going to survive.

The old cliché remains true: 'change is the only constant'. It is essential that firms appreciate the competitive advantages and threats MiFID will bring, as doing nothing is not an option if firms wish to survive in the new environment.

15.1   REGULATED MARKETS: EXCHANGES PRESSURED BY COMPETITION AND CONSOLIDATION

MiFID will act as the catalyst for a major change in the number and function of trading venues. Change is not new in the Exchange space, with consolidation a key focus of the industry in a battle to gain control of more liquidity, and gain more economies of scale to drive down transaction costs.

There does, however, seem to be a mismatch between what the EU Commission would like to see and what is in reality taking place.

It would appear that the Commission would like to see a number of 'Super' Exchanges, with large amounts of pan-European liquidity being transacted across them. These would form the cornerstone of a

---

[2] See Chapter 14.

European capital market capability that could challenge the USA, as well as the emerging economies of China and India.

The consolidation we have seen to date, however, indicates a different model emerging which involves a number of Exchanges owned by a single entity, and operated autonomously within their respective marketplaces. Although this gives some economies of scales and allows the use of consistent platforms, it does not achieve the aims of creating large pools of liquidity. Investors and the industry would be better served by a model where all equities within Europe could be traded across any trading platform, and settled through any settlement agency.

The single biggest issue which will hold back the development of a true pan-European market is local protectionism, and self-interest of the Exchanges and exchange members. By way of example, the UK's FSA has stated that the LSE should remain an independent market if it were taken over by NASDAQ, to ensure that UK firms do not get subjected to Sarbanes Oxley. The paradox here is one of enabling investors to trade through global Exchanges without submitting them to local regulations.

In France, for example, the AMF's discussion paper on 'Best Execution'[3] has stated that they 'would consider that the price of execution of an equity order would benefit from a "safe harbour" as regards "Best Execution" if the order is executed at the price quoted on the organised market that commands the greatest liquidity in the stock in question'. In other words the 'Best Price' would be taken as the one in the most liquid market. This clearly favours established Exchanges at the expense of new, less costly trading venues.

A big question is whether politicians and regulators will allow local Exchanges to be replaced by bigger pan-European Exchanges with deeper liquidity.

Bigger Exchanges will allow companies a broader opportunity for raising finance, and would allow significant cost savings within the European Union. It is possible that market-driven forces will drive secondary markets away from existing Exchanges, and eventually force the politician's hands by making the smaller Exchanges unprofitable. The recent re-launch of the EASDAQ platform as Equiduct, aiming to

[3] 'AMF consultation on enforcing the "Best-Execution" principles in MiFID and its implementing directive', published by the Autorité des Marchés Financiers (AMF) in June 2006 http://www.amf-france.org/documents/general/7274_1.pdf.

offer a one stop shop for European equities whilst also offering 'Best Execution', is an example of the direction the markets might take.

An alternative model may be one where primary issues and admission to trading is provided on a local basis by local regulated markets as it is today. Secondary trading would move to large liquidity pools provided by new Super-Exchanges and highly focused MTF's, whilst niche trading would be provided through banks acting as Systematic Internalisers. In essence the current services provided by Exchanges would be unbundled and replaced, or complemented, by entities which best serve the market. This would allow countries to keep their local Exchanges and corporate finance functions, whilst at the same time providing a more competitive market for secondary trading.

15.2   THE ROLE OF THE EXCHANGE

One should consider the varying roles different Exchanges carry out today, and how they might change as a result of MiFID.

Exchanges provide some of the core functions needed to facilitate efficient operation of the securities markets. These include development and hosting of the trading platform, regulation and supervision of the market, listing processes, control and reporting. Under MiFID some of these functions may change, and the structure of how Exchanges serve their markets will inevitably change.

One of the core areas which will change will be reporting and market regulation, some of which will be picked up by the regulators in each country.

Under MiFID's pre- and post-trade transparency regime, firms will have to report transactions directly to the regulators or via a new data consolidator. This was a role that was traditionally carried out by the Exchange, and justified part of their execution fees. In addition, the Exchanges carried out market surveillance, which may also change under MiFID.

Admission to trading rules are being changed under MiFID, and although Exchanges will continue to be responsible for these functions, it is possible that these may be separated in the future.

Operation of the Trading Platform will not be directly impacted but each Regulated Market (RM) must ensure that access to its market is provided for all interested parties. This may change the membership criteria over time.

Other areas of the market will be impacted if the distribution of the liquidity of major stocks becomes more fragmented across multiple trading venues.

The way Indices are constructed may have to change to take into account this new model. Otherwise they will stop reflecting the true prices in the market. Therefore, futures based on them will cease to be effective hedges for portfolios or positions.

Index providers may well be forced to buy data from the new data concentrators to ensure that the indices continue to reflect the market. Far from increasing transparency, MiFID could make markets more opaque.

The functions the Exchanges carry out are not the only area under threat. Exchanges seem to believe that they are the custodians of the liquidity in their market. Any suggestion that they may lose any significant share of this liquidity is always dismissed. Were the creation of MTF's to be a success, the Exchanges could see large amounts of liquidity moving from their trading system. This will have a marked impact on their profitability, and could leave them with the smaller, lower volume, lower profit stocks as their secondary market.

This is clearly only one scenario but, for some of the smaller regional Exchanges, it could be sufficient to make their business difficult to justify.

15.3   MULTILATERAL TRADING FACILITIES: THE CHALLENGE OF ATTRACTING LIQUIDITY

Liquidity is critical in the world of trading venues, and a number of new trading venues have been set-up in the past with varying degrees of success. Jiway, launched by Morgan Stanley, and OMX lasted a little over two years before it closed its doors to business. NASDAQ Europe faced a similar fate after it took over EASDAQ, only to close in January 2004.

The main reason that these ventures failed was because of the mistaken belief that either Exchanges or broker-dealers, own or control market liquidity. Liquidity ultimately comes from the buy-side firms, who initiate the bulk of all transaction volumes on the Exchanges. Without these volumes, trading venues will have difficulty attracting the liquidity they require in order to survive.

If one truly believes that market liquidity derives from the buy side firms, then this could lead to a view that the only way to build a new trading venue with sufficient liquidity to survive would be to persuade the buy side to participate. Alternatively, the buy-side could collaborate with each other and set-up their own MTF.

Picture a situation where four to six of the major buy-side firms collaborate to start an MTF with the view of putting the bulk of their FTSE100 business through it. They could approach their broker-dealer community and persuade them to deal through the MTF, offering a more efficient market than that currently provided by the LSE. Certainly the buy-side firms could benefit from lower execution costs and the ability to 'cross' trades over the MTF. The impact to the LSE would be significant, with a large slice of liquidity moving to the new platform.

This scenario may be fanciful, but there are clear benefits from the model. There are however, a number of potential issues with the buy-side owning a market and controlling the liquidity pool.

Buy side firms must seek to provide 'Best Execution' for the funds that they manage. This might mean that they will find it very difficult to direct their business to new trading venues, other than the large liquidity pools which already exist within the Exchanges. If they were to set-up MTF's or become SI's they must prove that, by transacting across the new platforms, they were on average either equalling or improving upon the 'Best Execution' performance they would achieve over existing venues. In practice this could be difficult to achieve, and could generate a significant amount of conflict for a fund manager.

In addition, ownership of a trading venue by multiple buy side firms could allow these firms to abuse the already considerable power they yield within the markets. It could be argued that this level of control would run counter to protecting consumers, by allowing large funds to manipulate the market in their favour.

Other potential MTF's models could emerge based around Industry Sectors or market capitalisation. Multi-asset class MTF's may also emerge allowing trading and execution of all products associated with an underlying asset. For example; equities, bonds and all associated derivatives. They will all need to address the issue of how will they attract sufficient liquidity to remain in business.

15.4 SYSTEMATIC INTERNALISERS: WILL THE COSTS DETRACT FROM THE BENEFITS?

Internalisation has been around for a while in some European markets, with the main benefit being that the broker-dealers could execute efficiently across the floor. This internalisation, however, has also been opaque to the external investor community, with few real controls over whether the trades executed provided value for the investor or just favoured the broker-dealer.

The regulation around SI's is intended to change this by making the quotes and trades visible on the same basis as other trading venues. In doing so, however, this takes away some of the advantages to internalisation, which provided the ability to execute at a single price and not have to quote a true bid-offer price. The need to now quote externally to your customer base will mean that some of the attraction of internalisation is lost, but not the cost savings which come from avoiding exchange fees for internally transacted trades.

Most large firms will continue to internalise trades since they have sufficient liquidity in those stocks to make it worthwhile. Niche players, who only have sufficient liquidity in a few stocks, will increasingly find that being an SI may well cost more than it is worth. To some firms, the ability to offer the services of an SI to their client base will be regarded as a competitive advantage, giving a faster and cheaper execution venue. To others it will just be an unnecessary burden.

Initially, there may well be a large number of SI's across Europe. Over time, this number is expected to reduce significantly, as firms seek to reduce costs or find that the costs of executing over an MTF or Exchange converge on the internal cost of running an SI function. It is quite possible that in the longer term the concept of an SI will not survive, but it will be an important stepping stone to a lower cost environment for trade execution.

In a recent joint MiFID survey carried out by SunGard and Trade-Tech,[4] banks indicated that being an SI will provide them with a key competitive advantage as the cornerstone of their European expansion plans. In addition, another key finding was that the biggest losers post-MiFID would be Exchanges and locally focused banks. This could threaten small regional Exchanges and banks that, in the past, have been protected by legislation that made the cost of entry prohibitive into what were relatively small markets. Under MiFID's 'passporting' rules, firms will be able to leverage their existing infrastructure into other centres, and only need to set-up sales and advisory services. This allows firms to compete at a significantly lower cost in these markets which will clearly be to the detriment of small locally focused broker-dealers.

---

[4] Editor's note: readers can download this survey from http://www.sungard.com/mifid/.

15.5   SETTLEMENT IMPACT

In order to support these new execution methods, settlement will need to change.

The settlement of securities will need to become pan-European with true fungibility – substitution – between Central Securities Depositories (CSD's) and central counterparties. The model will need to become more standard than it is today, to allow investors the choice as to where their transaction settles.

This is also important in order to allow investors the flexibility to open a position on one trading venue and close it on another. The infrastructure to do this is not available to investors today, but will be essential if true trading venue competition is to take place. This does not, however, imply that Europe requires just one settlement entity, but does mean that existing CSD's exchange information in a consistent manner. In other words, the market needs to define and agree a standard for the sharing of information between CSD's.

An alternative approach would be for the CSD and Central Counterparty information to be attached to each trade, so the trade information could be routed to the correct parties post-execution for settlement.

Many of these issues may well be addressed if a Clearing and Settlement Directive is launched by the EU. The danger with any Directive in this space, is that the EU may well legislate to support one business model when the market decides to go in an entirely different direction.

Stock Exchanges and major clearing and settlement providers have recently committed to a code of conduct which is aimed at promoting more competition for clearing and settlement within Europe. This should pave the way for a significant reduction in cross-border costs in the future.

A Directive may not be needed if the industry starts to offer the services that a single European market requires, at a price which will allow Europe to compete in a global market.

15.6   SUMMARY

Politicians have Europe's long-term competitive interests at heart through the MiFID Directive. By tabling such an ambitious Directive, with so many facets, they might not get the results they aimed for, however, as financial markets develop in the direction which best suits the key stakeholders: the broker dealers, asset and investment managers, investors, trading venues and governments. Therefore, the outcome of MiFID may well be something completely different from what was envisaged by the EU regulators when drafting the legislation, in terms of the future structure of the execution venues.

In many ways there are too many powerful interests vested in the current model for major change to occur. November 2007 is the start of a change process which will emerge over time. One of the greatest inhibitors to change is the attitude of European governments, and particularly their focus in protecting their home markets from losing their Exchanges and, therefore, potentially much of their capital markets business.

Moving the listing of stocks to an exchange which has access to significantly more liquidity than local Exchanges could benefit local companies, as they will be able to access a much broader investor base than before. This in turn would allow those companies to prosper, and thus aid the balance of payments in their home country.

Sticking with the current model will only mean that in the long term European companies will lag further behind their international competition.

Another vested interest is maintenance of the broker-dealer and fund manager relationship. Ultimately, however, Exchanges exist to serve investors and firms seeking to raise capital. These parties will seek out opportunities where they can do business in the most advantageous conditions. The demand to secure liquidity on demand, together with best price and cost, will drive forward change. This is unpredictable, and may not always be as envisaged by the European governments.

Despite the wish to create more choice and greater competition for investors, by allowing the creation of more trading venues, there exists a conflict here.

Most new trading venues will start with low levels of liquidity and, over time, seek to attract new liquidity from existing venues. This fact will make it difficult for broker-dealers and asset managers to use the venues if they need to provide 'Best Execution' for their clients, since there may be insufficient liquidity to allow this to happen. Some models may survive by focusing on niche markets, whilst others will need to build rapid liquidity by significantly reducing the cost of execution.

There is no doubt the markets will change, but how quickly and in what direction is open to debate. Firms need to ensure that they have the ability to rapidly adapt to new market models as they occur, and need to be wary of promises made by new venues.

If the past is a predictor of the future some trading venues are in for a rocky future, competition will be fierce and the market may well evolve faster, and in a different direction, than some predict.

16

How MiFID Changes Banking Business Across Europe

Michael McKee

The implementation of MiFID raises significant issues for banks across Europe. There are few banks which are not buying or selling securities in some way or other, and consequently all banks, whatever their precise business model, will be affected by MiFID in some way or another.

The important difference between banks and other securities firms though, is the fact that banks already have a passport to do business across the EU under the Banking Coordination Directive (BCD). Consequently there are a range of provisions in MiFID, mainly organisational requirements, which do not apply to banks because they are already subject to them or equivalent provisions under the BCD.

The precise impact of MiFID depends, in particular, on whether or not a bank is principally carrying out wholesale investment banking, private banking or retail banking. Before discussing this, it may be worth making some general comments about the likely landscape for banks once MiFID is implemented.

16.1 COMPETITIVE IMPACT OF MiFID ON BANKS DOING BUSINESS IN EUROPE

It not possible to pick specific banks which will be winners or losers as a result of MiFID, although is it possible to make some general predictions as follows:

- MiFID will impose significant implementation costs on the European financial services industry initially. Large banks and

The Future of Investing in Europe's Markets after MiFID Edited by C. Skinner
© 2007 John Wiley & Sons, Ltd

Exchanges will be better placed to bear these costs than smaller financial institutions, particularly non-banks.

- Banks generally, particularly larger banks, tend to be better prepared for MiFID. Many of them have followed the negotiations closely and have well developed project teams. This means that the banks, and particularly the large banks, will be much better placed to take advantage of MiFID than many other market players.
- Overall, despite the costs of implementation, some banks are likely to reap a significant competitive advantage from MiFID as a result. At least one recent research report from an analyst in JPMorgan Chase suggests that US banks operating in Europe may be better placed to benefit than European banks. This is yet to be proved – but it is certainly the case that some US and investment banks have invested heavily in their MiFID projects.
- Other banks will still be able to benefit from MiFID, but will have to think hard about how they can best differentiate their service offerings to clients from the services of others.

16.2   WHOLESALE INVESTMENT BANKS AND UNIVERSAL BANKS

These banks focused on the importance of MiFID very early, as it was perceived to centrally affect their business. It is not possible to cover every aspect of their business in a short chapter, but key ways in which MiFID affects their business are as follows:

- Trading securities, particularly equities. Key provisions include pre- and post-trade transparency provisions, 'Best Execution' obligations and the provisions creating the concept of a systematic internaliser of equities.
- Improving the passport. A range of MiFID provisions are intended to strengthen the role of the home state supervisor and lessen the influence of host state rules. New passport rights are created, e.g. for commodities and multilateral trading facilities (MTF's).
- More common conduct of business requirements across the EU as a whole.
- A greater differentiation between the rules applying to business with retail customers and the rules applying to business with professionals and the most regular players in the markets (known under MiFID as 'eligible counterparties'). In essence lighter obligations apply when

dealing with professionals, and even more light when dealing with eligible counterparties.

16.2.1 Banks as systematic internalisers

The most controversial and potentially expensive requirements to implement for wholesale investment banks are the requirements relating to market structure for equities business, particularly if a bank is regarded as a 'systematic internaliser'.

However, a bank can choose whether or not to be a systematic internaliser, and can choose to structure its business so that it does not carry out such a role.

Banks are only likely to be systematic internalisers if they have a multilateral platform which is dealing with its customers in equities by quoting in a 'standard market size' for those equities to which the obligation applies. This 'standard market size' is likely to be a size consistent with retail equities trading, rather than the much larger sizes traded by wholesale investors. Consequently it is likely that institutions will structure their business to ensure that they are not systematic internalisers if they only wish to do equities business with wholesale investors.

It is less costly for many firms to adapt their structures in this way rather than to take on the obligations of a systematic internaliser. As a consequence, there will be far fewer banks taking on these obligations than might have been anticipated originally.

16.2.2 Banks' passporting rights

The value of passporting rights is likely to be of some advantage to banks who do a considerable amount of commodities business, or who operate an MTF. These advantages are more likely to develop over the medium to longer term, than in the first few years after MiFID implementation, because it is likely to take some time for regulatory practice to settle down with regard to these new passports.

16.2.3 Banks' and conduct of business rules

A more common approach to conduct of business rules could carry significant benefits. The UK's FSA will cut its own Conduct of Business Sourcebook by around 50 % for example and, although there will be initial implementation costs, it is likely that over time this will bring advantages. Wholesale banks will benefit more than retail banks if there is genuine convergence in conduct of business rules across Europe because most cross-border business is wholesale. However, there will still be scope for some divergence between rules in different states and, moreover, there are still risks of divergent interpretations. In view of this, the changes to the conduct of business rules are mostly helpful, but are likely to take some time to bed down as there remain risks of continuing differences. The benefits are likely to be medium to long term.

16.3   RETAIL BANKS

The most significant impact on retail banks will be in the area of conduct of business rules. MiFID does not apply to all of a bank's retail banking business; only to business in relation to financial instruments. Consequently, its principal application is to retail securities business. In the UK, where the BBA has its focus, this therefore applies mainly to the sale of equities, often on an execution only basis, and to the sale of tax-wrapped products containing securities such as pensions, ISAs and the like.

Strictly speaking MiFID does not apply to UCITS, which continue to be covered by the UCITS Directives, although there can be some unexpected indirect affects on firms, particularly those which sell UCITS and other fund management products from the same platform.

In the context of retail broking business an important issue will be the impact of MiFID on the existing retail service provider model, whereby brokers access shares on behalf of retail clients. There had been concerns that MiFID requirements relating to market structure might destroy this model of doing business. However, the belief is that this model of business will survive, albeit with some modifications.

There had also been concerns that MiFID might limit the ability of a firm to carry out execution-only business in a range of financial instruments but, again, it is expected that this business will generally continue. As a result, it will be possible to carry out most business which is currently considered to be 'execution only', because the correct analysis of this business under MiFID is that it is business subject to the requirement to carry out initial 'appropriateness' checks.

Most 'execution only' brokers now consider that their initial account opening procedures, whether online or not, already contain the right sort of checks to ensure the retail client is only carrying out the sort of business which it would be appropriate for him or her to do. If they do not believe the client should be engaged in that sort of business however, they will have to modify their account opening procedures accordingly.

An important constraint for retail business will be the limitations on carrying out derivatives business. In general most continental European Member States are very reluctant to permit retail clients to have access to derivative products. MiFID does not draw a sophisticated distinction between derivatives products which are generally regarded as relatively safe and low risk, such as warrants, and those which might be high risk. Consequently it is likely that it will be more difficult for retail clients to buy and sell derivatives in future, except on an advised basis.

16.4   PRIVATE BANKING

This may be the area of banking that will struggle most with MiFID. The reason is that most of the clients with whom private bankers deal are likely to fall into the MiFID retail category, and will have the full range of retail protections applied to them. However, traditionally private bankers have dealt with high net worth individuals, and most of these individuals have neither needed nor wanted these full retail protections. Similarly current rules in the UK, Ireland and some other European jurisdictions, permit most private banks to treat their high net worth clients as more informed, and consequently the full retail regulatory requirements do not apply to them.

As a result, many private banks have business models which are not geared up to follow the processes and documentation requirements required by the regulators for mass retail banking. This is why, in the UK, the FSA is using MiFID implementation as a means of removing from its rulebook many detailed retail documentation obligations they currently require, but MiFID does not. However where MiFID requires certain documents or warnings to be given to retail customers, private banks who may not currently be required to give such documents or warnings may find that they will now have to put in place processes to do this for their clients, even if they consider that the client is sufficiently sophisticated not to need them. This will mean that private banks are likely to have to think very carefully about their current business models, and the best way in which to adjust in order to comply with MiFID, while not drowning their client base in new warnings and documents.

16.5   OVERALL

Overall the precise impact on a bank will depend very much on its mix of products and services, and the nature of its client base. However, it is likely to have the biggest impact on wholesale banks and on private banking. The banks who are likely to be best placed to benefit from MiFID are likely to be found within the group of the largest wholesale investment and universal banks for two reasons. First, they will be best placed to reap the benefits of greater cross-border competition and trading, even though there may be substantial costs at the start. Second, because they are amongst the entities who have most closely followed the development of MiFID and are best prepared to implement the Directive the quickest.

17
MiFID's Impact Upon the Retail Investment Markets

Angela Knight

The Market in Financial Instruments Directive has an impact on every firm that operates within the financial services industry, whether it is inside MiFID or whether superficially the Directive does not directly impact on that firm. The reason for such a widespread impact is because MiFID actually changes the structure of the industry and the market infrastructure across Europe.

For some European countries, financial advice becomes regulated for the first time and so advisers are required to take examinations in a way that they have not had to do before. Spain is an example of this.

Other countries, such as France and Italy, have had to remove what is known as their Stock Exchange 'concentration rule' and open up trading to more competition. This, in turn, produces an environment which gives choice for all those who directly or indirectly trade equities.

A third example is the new 'Best Execution' requirements which cover equities, bonds and OTC markets and are relevant for both retail and professional business. Again this has not happened before and, even in the UK where 'Best Execution' is the norm, the current arrangements will change.

Lastly, MiFID 'demonises derivatives', or at least derivatives are deemed to be appropriate for the few and not the many. Yet what is and what is not a derivative differs widely. For example, fixed interest mortgages are extensively chosen by many borrowers in the UK, and yet they use derivatives. To consider all derivatives as high risk as implied by MiFID is too crude and generalised.

The Future of Investing in Europe's Markets after MiFID   Edited by C. Skinner
© 2007 John Wiley & Sons, Ltd

These are just a handful of examples of why the impact of MiFID is large and is not just a wholesale issue, but a retail one too.

Looking at the technicalities is one thing, but more important is what the real impact of MiFID upon investors and this chapter considers such impact upon three broad groups of customers. First, retail customers who use execution only or no advice products and services; second, the mass market individual; and third, the high net worth clients. For each, the impact will vary.

Firstly, for those who simply want to buy and sell an equity or a financial product without advice, the likelihood is that they will get more choice and, for some things, at a lower cost. Execution only costs vary extensively across Europe, and business tends to be cheaper in some EU countries than in others, partly due to lower regulatory costs. This is particularly noticeable in the Netherlands.

But investors should beware, as it is also the case that consumer protections are not the same elsewhere if something goes wrong. For example, for a UK investor, as long as the individual is buying and selling through a firm that is quartered in the UK and regulated by the FSA, then if a problem arises it is the UK arrangements of the Ombudsman and after that the Compensation Scheme that will protect that individual. If, though, they have use non-UK headquartered brokers or broker sites to do that buying or selling, then that firm will be regulated in another European country and if there is a problem, who steps in? The UK Ombudsman Service is not replicated elsewhere in Europe, nor is the Compensation Scheme, and whilst there are some 'loose' arrangements in place, a loose arrangement is frankly neither good enough nor safe enough for the inexperienced investor.[1]

Another related issue arises because the UK is proposing to be 'super equivalent' in some aspects of MiFID. These super equivalent areas are mainly in respect of retail business and, for practical purposes, it will mean that there are more protections and safeguards built in to the UK rules than that of other European countries.

---

[1] Editor's note: Angela is noting a UK specific impact which we also see occurring in other countries. The aim of MiFID is that these disparities will disappear such that Europe operates as single market with no significant difference in trading between each country of operation. However, the point she makes is a good one, e.g. you focus upon one area – transparency, 'Best Execution' and trading – but it has a knock-on effect into other areas that are not caught by the regulation. This is worth considering as you look at the restructuring of retail and wholesale products and services.

The UK justifies this super equivalence on the basis of consumer protection, and that may well be correct. After MiFID though, it will not be possible for the FSA to add any of those additional requirements to business which is 'passported' into the UK. What this means from a practical perspective is that before MiFID, a UK firm is able to offer to UK retail investors a collective investment scheme which tracks the FTSE All Share for example. After MiFID, a Polish quoted firm can offer exactly the same thing to UK retail investors. However, the UK firm will have to meet the cost of extra super equivalent UK regulatory requirements, but the Polish firm will not. Whose offer will the consumer buy? They may well go for the cheaper one, the Polish one. So being super equivalent is not necessarily going to bring any consumer protection benefits. Instead, it is more likely to lose the UK business to overseas firms whilst, conversely, resulting in fewer protections for individuals if the Polish firm, in my example, gets into difficulty. Does the individual have any access to the UK Ombudsman service or the Financial Services Compensation Scheme in my example? I doubt it.[2]

Next I turn to the mass market. The mass market is defined as those individuals who have some money to save and are prepared to pay for advice and a straightforward portfolio management service. For these individuals, MiFID does not change much. There may be more choice for them but then, right now, there is pretty good choice anyway. They may well have access to more and different financial products or investments, but that is going to be more as a result of an innovative marketplace than it is of open borders. And although firms will be able to be members of a number of Exchanges and clearing and settlement systems, it is unlikely to be cost effective.

Anyway, there are many other reasons why individuals will stay local. Language and culture are two, and tax, the greatest driver of individuals' behaviour after sex, is the third. For the mass market, the post-MiFID world for the majority of investors will look not a lot different from now – once they have got through the hurdles of new paperwork, more paperwork and new client agreements that is.

This brings me to the high net worth client.

There is no fixed definition of high net worth, but behaviourally they are those who can choose from a variety of types of firms, private

---

[2] Please note, I am not bad mouthing the Polish industry, rather I use this example because the UK has such a large Polish ex-pat population.

banks and others. They are individuals who know what they want, and they are individuals who have the money to purchase it. The high net worth client is usually an advisory client. They are international in outlook, international in location, and increasingly they have their money from either their own entrepreneurship or because their family has sold out a large stake in a family business. Interestingly the percentage of high net worth individuals who inherited money is still significant, but reducing.

The growth in high net worth clients is from people who are younger, are greater risk takers, more knowledgeable and want more things. To this group intuitively one would have thought that MiFID, with its open market effect, has got to be a huge success story. Has it?

Within MiFID there is section called client categorisation, which states that clients have either got to be classified as retail or professional. On the face of it that seems little different to now but looking at the detail one finds it is actually going to be pretty hard to call an individual 'a professional'. The objective tests that a firm has to make invariably means that that the high net worth client may start as professional, but will then not meet one or other of the tests. So, over a period of time, they will have to be reclassified as retail. But if a high net worth individual is classified as retail under MiFID, then the full suitability requirements kick in.

Suitability means that before a firm can invest or deal on behalf of the individual, they have to assess that individual's financial status, other financial commitments and their appetite for risk. They then have to ensure that the investments that are purchased on their behalf meet those requirements. It is not likely that this approach will work well with a high net worth client who knows what they want. They will not be happy if they are told that what they would like to do with their money cannot be done because they are classified as a 'retail' client, and so the investment is not 'suitable'.

A firm with this type of client has three choices. The first is that they refuse their high net worth client's request, with the result that he or she may well walk away to invest through Switzerland or another non-EU venue that has a strong regulatory environment and a high calibre financial services industry. The second is that the firm moves out of the EU itself. The third is that the firm stays headquartered in the EU, and keeps the client's business by moving the assets to an off shore jurisdiction.

The long-term outcome is likely to be a convoluted and contrived arrangement in order to ensure that the consequence of MiFID is not a shifting of the high net worth section of business out of Europe. So to summarise the issues:

- MiFID opens up the market for wealth management but, whilst making it easier for a firm to undertake the business of the ex-pat population resident elsewhere around Europe, it will also create extensive competition from firms in other EU countries into existing markets. This is a particular issue for the UK, especially if we retain the super equivalent rules which means that the British 'gold plating' problem is still with us.
- Many of those who form the mass market of individuals with wealth – the largest category – are unlikely to find the future any different from the past in the short term, with the exception that there will be a significant paper chase at start date of MiFID, and maybe some more costs to pay for the systems changes.
- The high net worth client firms are going to have to contrive a future arrangement, otherwise the implementation and enforcement of MiFID will be a deterrent.

This all sounds quite negative, especially since the high ideal is for broader, deeper, more liquid markets and fewer barriers across Europe. The reason why this is negative is that MiFID is an example of what happens when decisions are made before market analysis is undertaken, and where changes are agreed before any cost benefit analysis undertaken. MiFID is also a compromise, and has parts which are market opening for some countries but which will constrain markets in others. It is the product of good intentions but with many compromises.

This chapter is not about wholesale markets, but it is worth noting that the changes in wholesale markets may well result in more power being passed to the investment banks. Investment banks already have power because of their size, the amount of trading they undertake and because they hold stakes in the major Exchanges of Europe. After MiFID they will have the additional ability to retain to themselves that most valuable thing of all – the pricing information on their own trades.

If, as is widely reported, a number of these investment banks create their own information reporting system, then not only does that become the main part of the price formation process, but it also provides data for them to sell. This data will no longer be in the ownership of the

Exchanges. Also, their very size means that some will become entities similar in a number of respects to the Exchanges of themselves. The result will be that trading will shift around in continental Europe too, and the Exchanges that survive will be the ones that the investment banks decide are going to survive and there is precious little that anyone can do about that.

So the benefits of MiFID accrue to the big multi-national wholesales and the costs of MiFID accrue to the retail sector. It may not be Big Bang II,[3] but it is certainly much more than the costly whimper that some predict.

---

[3] Editor's note: the first Big Bang was a major change to the UK Stock Markets implemented back in October 1986; the impact was massive as the traditional gentleman's style of trading between 'chaps' and 'blokes', brokers and jobbers, was replaced with a transparency model similar to American practices of the time.

Part 4
MiFID's Technologies:
Standards and Latency

'WHAT IS THE ROLE OF PRE- AND POST-TRADE STANDARDS?'
BY ANDREW DOUGLAS, HEAD OF SECURITIES MARKET REFORM, SWIFT

This is the first of two chapters that review specific technology aspects implied by MiFID. Andrew's chapter reviews the key challenges of technology standards, or the lack of them, and why this needs to be resolved if MiFID is to work.

'MiFID: DATA LATENCY AND ALL THAT'
BY NIGEL WOODWARD, DIRECTOR, FINANCIAL MARKETS, INTEL

One of the most interesting technological dimensions of MiFID is the increasing need for speed – as in low latency. This is emphasised in Chapters 13, 14 and 18, so here Nigel explains the area in depth.

18
What is the Role of Pre- and Post-Trade Standards?

Andrew Douglas

National markets are held together by shared values and confidence in certain minimum standards but, in the new global market, people do not yet have that confidence. Kofi Annan, Secretary-General of the United Nations, 1997–2006.

The nicest thing about standards is that there are so many of them to choose from Andrew Tanenbaum, Professor of Computer Science, Vrije University, Amsterdam.

In this chapter, I will set out to answer the question 'what is the role of pre- and post-trade standards in a post-MiFID world?'. However, before we start discussing this, I believe a number of disclaimers and definitions are in order.

First, as a disclaimer, I am not a Standards geek. I am a business person. In this regard, do not expect pages of technical standards and detail. If you want that level of detail, I can recommend a number of excellent technical sources including www.iso.org, www.fixprotocol.org, www.fpml.org, www.mddl.org and so forth. Rather, in order to determine the role of standards, I will be concentrating on the business impact they have.

My second disclaimer is that I write this at the close of 2006, with the implementation of MiFID still ten months away. Unfortunately, I do not have a crystal ball. Consequently, some of what we will cover requires a degree of speculation. Time will judge the accuracy of such speculation.

The Future of Investing in Europe's Markets after MiFID   Edited by C. Skinner
© 2007 John Wiley & Sons, Ltd

In terms of definitions, and for the purposes of this discussion, I will be using the same definition of a 'standard' as was used in the Giovannini Barrier 1 protocol published in March 2006.[1]

18.1 WHAT IS A STANDARD?

A Standard is defined as having four component parts:

- **A single agreed business process model:** before messages can be created to support a specific business process, the business process must be analysed and the information flows between different participants fully mapped. Such 'business information maps' illustrate the relationship of all business components, such as security and cash related to instruments, to the activity flows representing business processes, such as trading, and the order in which processes must be carried out, as in trading prior to settlement.
- **A single agreed data dictionary:** a common reference point of terminology to ensure the same business data elements, such as trade date, security ID, etc., are referenced by all counterparties in all business interactions. This common terminology facilitates simple translation between syntaxes if required.
- **A recommended syntax, or syntaxes:** the syntax used to develop messages from the relevant business data elements should be independent of both the business process model and the data dictionary, so that if a new syntax is chosen in the future, or the use of a specific syntax is more appropriate than others for a specific set of market activity, the dictionary and the business models need not change. This ensures that there is no impact on a firm's applications that process the business content of messages. This flexibility also allows the models to be used to interoperate with messages developed using other syntaxes, for example, ISO, FIX and so on.
- **A set of agreed market practices**: market practice allows the application of additional logic layers. For example, messages can include rules in their structure that facilitate intelligent completion, for example in a PEP/ISA[2] transfer message. Once a security is identified as a PEP, the message is structured in such a way as to

---

[1] For more information, go to www.swift.com.
[2] PEP, Personal Equity Plan, was the predecessor to an ISA, the Individual Savings Account; both are retail investment savings products in the UK.

make it impossible to give information that would only be relevant for an ISA. Typically, such market practices are agreed by representative organisations, such as the Securities Market Practice Group (www.smpg.info). Most market practice today does not actually embed communication in this way, but it is published as best practice rules.

18.2 WHAT IS THE ROLE OF PRE- AND POST-TRADE STANDARDS IN THE POST-MiFID WORLD?

One way to illustrate this is to look at language as the phrase 'two countries separated by a common language' is often used to describe the USA and the UK. For example, the way we use the verb 'to table', as in 'to table a discussion'. In the UK, this means to put a subject forward for discussion whilst, in the USA, it means to remove a subject from a discussion. Without a standard definition of terms, such as those set out at the beginning of this chapter, the misunderstanding of terminology will continue to lead to confusion between counterparties.

At any stage in the securities investment lifecycle, from pre-trade through to post-trade, a simple set of equations summarises the potential end result of such confusion;

$$Process - Standards = Confusion$$

$$Confusion = Risk + Cost$$

So the role of standards appears very simple: to reduce confusion and therefore reduce risk and cost which are both good things, are they not?

If we agree that this is the case, then why have the financial markets not embraced standards wholeheartedly? The fact that markets have not embraced such standards is evidenced by the continued need for initiatives such as MiFID, Giovannini, Group of 30, CPSS-IOSCO, and many others. Each of these have, in their own way, promoted the need for and the value of standards and standardisation. But to assume that standards simply reduce risk and cost is to miss out on a raft of other benefits that standards can provide.

In order to examine the role of standards in more detail, we need to examine the answers to a number of related questions:

- Why are financial markets so fragmented?
- What is the impact of fragmentation?
- Can market standardisation be achieved?
- What are the barriers to success and how are they overcome?

18.3   WHY ARE FINANCIAL MARKETS SO FRAGMENTED?

Why are the financial markets like this, fragmented by:

- product line between cash, fixed income, derivatives, equities, etc.;
- geography: Europe, Asia, Americas, individual nation states, etc.;
- position in the investment life cycle: front office, back office, etc.; and
- type of participant: end investor, broker, custodian, infrastructure, etc.

The reason for fragmentation is self evident. Without a single authoritative or legislative body defining a global template against which markets and participants could develop their financial market solutions, we have inevitably seen the creation of a multi-dimensional patchwork of local solutions, using local standards and local technology to service local business requirements and local market practices. Indeed, in the absence of such 'guidance', we see the existence of overlapping and competing initiatives, as well as those which unintentionally or intentionally exclude other relevant business areas and/or participants.

The consequence is that there is no single standard that provides total coverage of processes from pre-trade right through to post-trade.

Since the original G30 report 'Clearance and Settlement Systems in the World's Securities Markets' was published way back in 1989,[3] many global markets and their participants have sought to engage in various forms of standardisation and harmonisation. These initiatives have increased the level of interoperability between markets, participants and solutions, but not eliminated the issue. They have also led to improvements in efficiency, as well as reductions in risk and cost. Further initiatives, typically geographically targeted, have sought to continue this work. MiFID is one of these.

---

[3] Editor's note: if interested, go to www.group30.org for more.

I can predict with a high degree of certainty that, whilst MiFID will lead to further improvement through reduction of some fragmentation, we will still operate in a world in which further standardisation can significantly reduce the 'Risk + Cost' side of the equation, not only within Europe but also between Europe and other markets.

Now, you might be asking yourself, 'Why is it that we are not simply implementing a single standard for the entire transaction lifecycle and what is the impact of not doing this?'

18.4   WHAT IS THE IMPACT OF FRAGMENTATION?

Front office versus back office, cash versus securities, derivatives versus cash instruments, USA versus Europe...sound familiar? As discussed earlier, for understandable reasons, individual markets have developed at different paces and typically adopt the technology and standards most appropriate to their business model 'at the time'. Such developments do not always subscribe to existing standards, due to participants not being aware of the existence of relevant standards; because existing standards may be inappropriate in content and functionality; and because of that age old enemy of common sense, politics or the 'not invented here' syndrome.

For this reason, the financial industry and particularly the securities sector, insists on reinventing standards with initiatives that:

- overlap with other initiatives, resulting in redundant spending, wasted time and loss of momentum as industry luminaries debate the marginal benefits of such initiatives, for example, FIX and ISO;
- seek to replace existing initiatives for no apparent benefit, and leave existing initiatives unfinished and therefore unsuccessful, such as the multiple languages and syntaxes that spring up seemingly every day; and
- leave a trail of 'previous versions in production', which risk compromising the standardisation objective itself, for example, FIX.[4]

The securities industry has in the past, found it far too easy to invent new standards, create new infrastructural bodies and define new transaction models. In so doing, this overlooks one of the primary

---

[4] Editor's note: there are multiple releases of the FIX standard, as it evolves. Many firms use older versions than the 'current' standard. See www.fixprotocol.org for more.

development considerations for standards: to leverage existing implementations and reduce development costs. For the long term, it would be better to improve what exists rather than devise yet another replacement solution.

Our industry seems to frequently confuse activity with progress and, as global markets seek to standardise, this provides a further reason why markets and participants might invoke the 'not invented here' defence.

In the recent past, proprietary standards and solutions were seen as effective mechanisms for locking customers into a particular market or service provider. Now, they are also seen as a legitimate way of locking competitors out. National and regional market-specific systems, standards and conventions, have thus emerged and become protected by the market system they were designed to support.

The post-MiFID world is one in which compliance with multiple standards will be cost-prohibitive. Investment banks and brokers in particular will be required to know which liquidity pools are likely to give optimum price with whole-lifecycle trade formation, and to be able to conduct business with them at very low latency. This implies, for every firm, either a vast library of different languages, network connections and syntax rules, operating with unprecedented efficiency, or a dramatic consolidation of standards and 'regional market variations' leaving little room for the 'not invented here' syndrome.

18.5   CAN MARKET STANDARDISATION EVER BE ACHIEVED?

At a high level, business processes can be defined as either competitive or collaborative. Typically, competitive activities are where market participants make their money whilst collaborative processes are those 'worthy but dull' commoditised processes that need only to be executed at least risk and least cost.

18.6   COMPETITIVE PROCESSES

In the post-MiFID world, standardisation will help address a number of anti-competitive issues including:

• proprietary trading formats operated by individual execution venues;
• inability to access fungible post trading arrangements;

- exchanges directly or indirectly making access to clearing and settlement arrangements difficult or impossible for a competitor;
- the lack of 'consolidated' pre- and post-trade information;
- delayed implementation of industry standards at Exchanges and central counterparties (CCP) making it more difficult for new service providers to compete for CCP services;
- a lack of standards as a barrier to the development of competition in the settlement area;
- differing formats and content of regulatory reports;
- a lack of pan-European thinking and vision.

Adoption of a common standard will facilitate remote access to market infrastructures as well as interoperability between market infrastructures, which in turn will promote both *competition in the market* as well as *competition for the market*, directly supporting the interoperability and access goal laid out in the European Commission's 2006 call for an industry Code of Conduct.

18.6.1 Competition in the market

Greater interoperability should be facilitated between all players:

- participant to participant for buy-side and intermediaries;
- participant to market infrastructure for the sell-side;
- market infrastructures to market infrastructures.[5]

Standardisation enhances the level of interoperability in a market and reduces the cost of switching between service providers, enhancing competitive pressure and therefore encouraging innovation in order to create and maintain added value.

18.6.2 Competition for the market

Standardisation creates a so called 'plug and play' environment which allows the displacement of historically monopolistic service providers, with the associated reduction in cost and risk. This ensures incumbents

---

[5] From definitions published by the European Commission, participants are defined to include both 'Demand Side' and 'Intermediary' actors whilst Market Infrastructures are considered to be 'Supply Side'.

maintain cost effective and fully functional products compared to other potential service providers in the market.

18.7   COLLABORATIVE PROCESSES

A collaborative process is one which provides no real competitive value. It is a process which all participants need to execute at least risk and least cost. Good examples of collaborative processes include the sourcing of static data and the satisfaction of regulatory reporting obligations. It is unlikely that such collaborative processes have any profit capability attached to them, only risk associated with 'getting it wrong'.

The adoption of open standards facilitates cost effective consolidation of data through the standardisation of data content. Typically this is achieved through the adoption of open ISO (International Standardisation Organisation) standards. For example ISO8601 is a standard for date and time representation, ISO10962 provides a standard classification of financial instruments (CFI) and ISO6166 is used for instrument identification (ISIN). Financial messages constructed under ISO20022 use these data content standards, as well as standard fields for such data elements as price and quantity.

However painful standardisation may be, it is necessary in the long term, simply because the clients of the global financial system require it. It will take a long time to work its way into the fabric of the industry. However, as the payments business continues to demonstrate via the implementation of industry wide solutions based on single standards, typically the ISO20022 standard as adopted by both SEPA and TARGET2, it is possible, practicable and even profitable for the securities industry to support standardisation, rather than oppose it.

The main problem with infrastructural projects designed to create or enforce standardisation is that, like government policy, they are long term projects. In a world in which thinking is dominated by short-term considerations, it is hard to keep sufficiently focused on these long-term measures. This is why it is so hard to allow them sufficient time to make their contribution.

In this regard, it is encouraging to note that the European Central Bank have announced their intention to adopt the ISO-based Giovannini protocol for the TARGET2 for Securities developments proposed in 2006. This will thereby cement the role of the ISO standard as the post-trade standard for both securities and cash management throughout the European Union.

Standards developments also need to be considered as evolutionary, not revolutionary. As an industry, we have mistakenly allowed ourselves to think that as new technologies and architectural conventions replace old, the same must apply to standards. As discussed earlier, we too easily confuse activity with progress.

I also referred earlier to the fact that open industry standards are available to provide relevant standard data elements and define an appropriate message structure for use in improving market data transparency. MiFID, supported by other initiatives such as the elimination of the Giovannini barriers in the clearing and settlement space, provides opportunities for the industry to significantly increase the usage of these standards, from pre-trade through to post-trade in both cross-border and domestic markets. If no action is taken, today's domestically focused proprietary solutions for data content and structure will continue to add cost and inefficiency to the trading, clearing and settlement process.

18.8 WHAT ARE THE BARRIERS TO SUCCESS AND HOW ARE THEY OVERCOME?

In the financial industry the use of open standards has been gaining increasing acceptance, such as the definition of a common communication protocol for cross-border securities clearing and settlement in the EU and the removal of Giovannini Barrier 1.[6] This work was published in March 2006. At its heart, the protocol recommends the adoption of the single standard, ISO20022, across the European cross-border clearing and settlement industry. More importantly, it establishes the case for adopting this standard outside of cross-border clearing and settlement, and recommends its adoption by the domestic clearing and settlement community, as well as by the front office, the community at which the provisions of MiFID have been clearly aimed. Work has begun with key clearing and settlement infrastructures and institutions to implement this recommendation within a five year timeframe.

---

[6] Editor's note: the Giovannini Group, as advisors to the European Commission, published a report in 2003 identifying fifteen barriers to creating efficient EU securities markets; Barrier 1 cites national differences in information technology and interfaces used by clearing and settlement providers.

Euroclear's move to adopt open ISO standards as an integral part of their single platform development is a good example of progress being made already in this direction.

A similar approach, based around open standards for key trans-action and data flows covered by MiFID, appears to be essential if competition is to be promoted, and the attendant costs and risks to be managed and reduced accordingly. The European Commission and CESR are instrumental in this context, by providing direction to the market following appropriate industry consultation.

The real key to the success of standardisation is the acceptance that standardisation is inevitable if our industry is to provide the most cost effective, risk free and profitable service to its clients. This acceptance, together with a genuine effort to leverage existing investments and allow the evolution of standards rather than create continued standards revolution, will enable standards to play their true role to their fullest advantage. In simple terms, we must minimise the voice of the 'not invented here' constituency which requires all participants, including standards organisations, to be less parochial and to be more industry focused.

The conclusion I hope you can all draw from this, as implied by Kofi Annan's opening quotation, is that the purpose of standards pre- and post-MiFID is continually to build and reinforce a global platform of transparency, resilience and trust in all market operations throughout the financial services sector.

19

MiFID: Data Latency and All That

Nigel Woodward

There is a general expectation of change in the market today. Is this about the various regulations that have recently been implemented, or a dawning renaissance in financial services technology, a catalyst for new approaches after half a decade of post dot.com indigestion and lost confidence?

Without doubt there is a sense of timing in the air as a result of the firms where systems renewal is on the agenda and amongst the vendor community, where new technologies and approaches to building solutions are being developed in order to satisfy a regulatory enabled appetite for investment in new infrastructure.

We can sum up the challenge as being all about data. From front through middle to back office, and across the market's infrastructures, data and its usage is exploding.

The challenge lies in many respects not simply data volumes, handling, maintenance and storage, which are relatively well known disciplines, but in the emergence of new interactions between producers and consumers of data, and the information derived from it. Behaviours will change and current systems, although yet to be proved inadequate, will without doubt have to perform different tasks. In the short term, such systems are likely to require major adaptation and, in the medium term, wholesale overhaul. This means that there is no single answer to the questions raised, but a journey of change starting in 2007 for many, as they implemented MiFID, Basel II, and other regulatory changes. The result is that all aspects of the market should be positive moving forward in order to embrace new paradigms and not try to force fit old models.

The Future of Investing in Europe's Markets after MiFID   Edited by C. Skinner
© 2007 John Wiley & Sons, Ltd

Nevertheless, at the start of 2007, there is a disappointing paucity of hard evidence around the future shape of data management across the transaction life cycle. It appears instead that most folks are just talking about change. The change required for the high levels of storage necessary for record keeping, the change required for the possible on-demand regulatory scrutiny that may arise, and the change required for the audit trails to support professional practices across the transaction lifecycle.

I argue that MiFID is just one driver for change and we are, in fact, ready for an overhaul of the Financial Services technology, systems and services market.

19.1   FRONT OFFICE

Buy side and sell side front office will see change.

After all, there is nothing new in the function of systematically internalising trades. It is a natural commercial behaviour. The data implications of reporting this practice in a regulated environment with current systems, processes and technology are significant however.

Front office data processes are more about receiving market data and distributing that data around the room to the trading positions with massive levels of efficiency. This is followed somewhat later with contributions by the data vendors from the pricing engines. The sophistication of the current MDS (market data system) for market data consumption is not matched with the explosion of publication that becomes necessary for Systematic Internalisers (SI's) in the post-MiFID New Age World.

Similarly, price contribution is not new. . .but this function will now have to be extended across instrument and asset classes, with deeper and more far reaching implications around storage and tracking of prices. The industry's favourite systems and applications in front office data infrastructure will need re-architecting to reorient themselves to new demands.

In particular, data latency[1] is of high concern in the automated trade environment, especially in the areas of statistical arbitrage and

---

[1] Editor's note: in the trading world, data latency refers to the time delay of the transfer of data between the moment a trade is initiated to the moment the trade is executed. As volumes of data increases, this is a strategic advantage as firms handle larger volumes of data at faster speeds. Therefore, lower data latency is key.

intraday markets. This creates an adaptation of Moore's Law[2] where, once performance levels are seen in one domain, the demand expands almost virally to other functions, which are not so speed driven. So the knowledge of what is being made possible for the front office equities and FX organisations, means that others in the front office will start to exert performance demands on aging systems and processes.

The result is that Direct Market Access (DMA)[3] and the emergence of new execution venues is transforming the trade data environment. For example, even though MiFID does not actually legislate that 'Best Execution' requires cross venue price searching, the very presence of a possible better execution venue means that firms are looking for the ability to demonstrate that a 'satisfactory best' price was in fact achieved. The proliferation of trading venues and feeds therefore can only grow in the short term, before market forces consolidate, which is asking data processing functions not currently required to suddenly become hugely responsive.

Overall, one can therefore see a number of new forces including speed, cross border and inter-firm trading, and a democratic access to market prices, which will place massive new demands on software, hardware, network and overall system reliability.

The fascinating aspect is that when faced with new processes in the past, the market has responded by adaptation of what is already out there: the tried and tested. A few million dollars invested in incremental processing power however, does not seem to resonate in today's market of cost control and commodity systems.

Meantime, the sell side front office has long been the focus of innovation in optimised processes and systems, with the buy side some way behind but hedge fund cultures, DMA, open access to execution venues, and the promise of carving a trading edge, have to put pressure on this environment. Bear in mind that this is an environment which frequently sees 'e' and the internet age as an innovation too far, and awaits an only marginally more proactive OMS vendor to become FIX-enabled.

---

[2] Editor's note: Gordon E. Moore, a co-founder of Intel, made an observation in the 1960's that the power of an integrated computer circuit doubles, whilst the cost halves, every two years.

[3] Editor's note: DMA is the ability for buy-side firms – institutional investors, fund managers and asset managers – to invest directly in the markets via automated systems without a requirement to use sell-side brokers for advice or, more importantly and increasingly, execution.

This has to change, although old habits, cultures and necessities die hard.

Automated data throughput in the buy side front office will accelerate. Will the traditional software vendors in this space be able to respond with effective approaches based on their development cost model today? Will the vendor market in its current shape be able to move on effectively and quickly from where it is today? We wait and watch.

19.2   MIDDLE OFFICE

The middle office is where data comes to life, or at least it should. Capture data in the front office, settle it in the back office, but analyse and leverage data in the middle office.

In a post-MiFID world, we will be seeing an environment which has exponentially enhanced access to data, transforming that data into information to be used for reporting to clients, to regulators, and most importantly to the internal sales organisation, in order to present and promote a differentiated, enhanced, value adding profitable service.

If any market trend drives better information availability then it has to be a positive movement, but there lies the challenge. Systems today are structured to operate by instrument and set up to manage a sequential flow from front to back office. The challenge will be to access data cross-asset class, and to make this highly consumable by sales, risk managers and counterparties at myriad points across the trade life cycle.

Trade processes today compensate by translating, consolidating and massaging data between systems, due to the lack of appropriate design of the legacy services which are in common usage. In future, we will see increasing levels of technology-enabled direct access to information, by-passing much of today's mainstream technology middleware which is installed purely to bridge the gaps in information generation.

19.3   BACK OFFICE

Although DMA is one of the key drivers in the front office, the same pipes set up for trade execution should see similar high levels of information flowing in the reverse direction. In other words, the front office should not just be feeding the back office, it should work both ways. At present, this is not a high priority in the scheme of things but will become more important in future as systems adapt to these new structures.

This is because the back office is the data engine room: the data factory.

Whereas, the middle office is where data becomes information, the back office is where the strain is taken for record keeping, storage, retention and audit trails. Extrapolating the numbers gives monumental statistics in terms of the bytes of storage required. If we look at the landscape of inputs and signals driving trades and advice the depth of implied data is almost infinite. A 'Google Earth'[4] approach has to be taken to this engine room such that it is managing massive amounts of data as a norm, as opposed to storing transaction details purely for resolving reconciliation errors during settlement or later dispute.

Clearly we are at the frontiers of data processing here.

19.4 MARKET INTERCHANGE AND INTEROPERABILITY

If the buy- and sell-side firms have to look at the effect on strategy and internal processes, the players which manage the market, manufacture the data and provide the infrastructure are starting completely new businesses. If the late 1990's boom saw dot.com Exchanges, the ramp of liquidity and the growth of ECN's, we see a new regulation and competition generated evolution in the late 2000's with the same market landscape.

We have seen horizontal and vertical consolidation of exchange businesses via the big plays.[5] Equally, there have been a number of new commercial propositions emerging, enabled by the availability of low cost technology and a proportional reduction in barriers to entry.

---

[4] Editor's note: Google Earth combines satellite imagery, maps and the Google Search engine to allow internet users to search the world's geographic information online. http://earth.google.com/.

[5] Editor's note: a good example are the two major US transactions during 2006 with the $9 billion merger of the New York Stock Exchange (NYSE) and Archipelago Holdings followed by the merger of the Chicago Mercantile Exchange and CBOT.

Project Boat,[6] Project Turquoise,[7] the LiquidityHub[8] and so forth, all indicate that the market is on the move.

These movements will bring a revolution in market data. You only have to cast your mind back to the early 1990's and the emergence of ETC, along with the debacle over interoperability back then, and this is why we should expect seamless processing. We should accept nothing less than complete interoperation across the market, via standards-based messaging, operating across the trade life cycle.

Latency, intelligent networks, and standards all come into play. You then add the fact that the Internet has commoditised technologies into the home, and these same technologies will enable new marketplaces to arrive at very low costs, unheard of until recent times.

We are truly at a turning point for the markets.

The paradigm of large, dominant domestic Exchanges is coming to an end, as liquidity becomes electronically data driven. Services, value-add and efficiency of execution become the differentiation with data, and its underlying manageability, the critical enabler.

Taking data at this market level, we only need to look at the debate on reference data. The debate rages as to whether reference data should be centrally administered, commercially managed, and/or a firm's individual prerogative. Whether I am naïve or a dreamer, it must surely be logical to centralise and standardise reference data.[9]

While the markets offer the most efficient form of achieving price and liquidity they seem, conversely, totally unable to cooperate in a common logical cause of standardisation of post-trade, non-differentiating functions that would make life easier for all. Why? Perhaps it is just not the focus in a competitive world to worry about the downstream once the trading job has been done, and we hence

---

[6] Editor's note: Project Boat was formed in October 2006 by a group of leading investments banks including ABN AMRO, Citigroup, Credit Suisse, Deutsche Bank, Goldman Sachs, HSBC, Merrill Lynch, Morgan Stanley and UBS, to aggregate European trade data and market data in competition with the traditional Exchanges.

[7] Editor's note: In November 2006, Citigroup, Credit Suisse, Deutsche Bank, Goldman Sachs, Merrill Lynch, Morgan Stanley and UBS announced plans to create their own exchange, code-named Project Turquoise.

[8] Editor's Note: In July 2006, Bank of America, BNP Paribas, Citigroup, Deutsche Bank, Goldman Sachs, Lehman Brothers, Merrill Lynch, Morgan Stanley, Royal Bank of Scotland and UBS announced their plans to launch LiquidityHub, an aggregation service for fixed income pricing. The initial focus was for dealer-to-client prices on euro and dollar interest rate swaps and USA Treasury bills on the basis of increasing automation in the swaps market.

[9] Editor's note: see Chapter 3 for more on this debate.

will continue to tumble through levels of inefficiency for some time to come.

With the luxury of detached commentary, I have to express the view that we will never achieve full, post-trade, data-enabled, efficiency. The markets simply are not applying sufficient resources to fix this problem. Hence, we stumble between sub-optimum work-arounds and fixes, each with promise but never realising critical mass and realising their true potential.

19.5   TECHNOLOGY READINESS

By way of example of this dilemma, many people talk around the idea that you could take today's legacy systems and then add the Service Oriented Architecture (SOA),[10] and all will be sorted. Despite the eloquent slides and strategies of the IT vendors, I do not think so.

Technology is both an enabling and disruptive force behind the markets.

In the trading area, it is enabling DMA connectivity and the latency squeeze at every point along the trade cycle, with massive contribution to processing speeds. In the post-trade area, it is making possible different approaches in domains where previously only mainframe computing could have prevailed, at costs which were only sustainable by the largest investment firms.

If you look at the complete technology stack, from processing chip to user interface, there is no other market like financial services where there is such massive choice of options, at every point of the process. But along with other themes in this chapter, the technology market has much to do to achieve efficiency of supply.

In keeping with the observation that a renaissance is with us, the smart way to work with technology today is to embrace innovation and work actively with what is available out of the laboratories. However, for a risk-averse industry, such as financial services, this is not always a natural behaviour. The only area that embraces such an approach is the pre-trade front office.

---

[10] Editor's note: Service Oriented Architecture (SOA) is a computer-based solution to the fact that traditional systems do not work well together due to their proprietary nature. These old systems are referred to as legacy systems. The idea of SOA is that new systems are developed using standardised and open approaches, and will work in any technology operation using today's open systems. This includes complex applications, as well as interfaces.

Nevertheless, positions in the technology stack are evolving and one of the most critical issues for the industry is how to exploit the innovation whilst, at the same time, managing the operational risk of both new technologies and smaller suppliers who have little or no track record. In this area, both buyer and vendor sides of the equation can do a lot better as there is the potential for organisations to gain innovation and differentiation. Perhaps it is at the human, organisational level, where we should look to drive engagement models which enable new approaches, and with them the ability to break today's creaking operational models.

Whilst SOA is not the answer to everything, it is a directional journey which is both intellectually and practically correct. It also enhances the focus on standard functions and services, as opposed to proprietary activities crafted for each point in the system.

In this area, we need to do better on standards. This is not meant to criticise those who work hard for the cause of standards, but we have to do better. The truth is that the commercial imperative to agree and implement these standards has still not reached the point to cause dramatic progress. But there will be a day when there is not a place for those who slow this process. What we are looking for is intra- and extra-SOA. SOA that goes across the markets.

The other must have trading accessory of today is Grid Computing.[11] However, look deeper at where this technology has reached and you find that the computational grids are well established, harnessing unused processing power and spreading the load across the network. These grids will provide power behind arbitrage engines, but it is at the grid frontiers where further MiFID context emerges.

Data grids, semantic web and other information centric technologies have the promise to open up new levels of processing. These technologies will provide the compensation for the stovepipe data management in the back office, and offer seamless information access and manipulation across the middle office.

So in this mode, where is the innovation available to be tapped in the MiFID context?

---

[11] Editor's note: Grid computing, or Grids for short, is a computing model that provides the ability to perform higher throughput computing by networking many individual computers together, usually through the internet, into a virtual supercomputer. By doing this, Grids can use the resources of many separate computers to solve large-scale computation problems. In investment firms, this means handling the highly complex, large-volume, low latency issues of trading across global markets in real-time.

Well, take the latency issue in the front office and then look at the complete technology stack from the network to the hardware to the chip to the systems and operating environment to the applications. As an observable trend, each layer elevates towards its higher neighbour and, in this context, the chip is capable of so much more than simply driving the operating system.

Today, we can build software functions into the silicon chip. In so doing, we can reduce the operational risk and complexity of integrating another layer in the stack and, more importantly, massively increase performance by eliminating a complete interface layer. For example, performance in FIX[12] trade message throughput is improved by a third and FIX FAST Protocol[13] market data exporting is reduced 100 % by using silicon embedded acceleration tools.

19.6   THE LATENCY WORD IN CONTEXT

For many financial instruments the race is on for ever lower latency, with no apparent end in sight. A trading edge is a trading edge. However, as technology and operations become ever more finely tuned, the opportunities for significant contribution towards 'market data' latency are becoming less.

This is why proximity hosting is yet another topic in vogue. Proximity hosting enables organisations to squeeze out milliseconds of processing time for trading by physically shortening the network distance between trading engines and execution venues. This is why some Exchanges are looking at utilising vacant data centre space to offer 'close proximity hosted services'. However, this is not sustainable long-term, as scrutiny will expose the unsuitability of Exchanges running hosting businesses. In addition, there will be issues of democracy emerging within the Exchange itself.

The fact is that we are at a turning point, where the complete trading environment needs some fine-tuning as a whole. A bit like a car. We do not send the car into service by taking out the engine for treatment

---

[12] Editor's note: The Financial Information eXchange ('FIX') Protocol is a series of messaging specifications for the electronic communication of trade-related messages in the pre-trade environment.

[13] Editor's note: FAST, FIX Adapted for Streaming, is a development of FIX that allows compression of the FIX messages by a factor of 80 %–90 %. In trials on various Exchanges during 2006, this allowed much higher volume of FIX messages to be electronically communicated, e.g. the market can send eight to nine times more volume of data using the same networks as today.

with one organisation, the gears at another, whilst taking the chassis to a third. The whole unit is serviced as a whole.

That is what the trading environment requires.

The trading environment needs a complete service to optimise it as a complete working system from price export through import, processing, trade routing and execution. All the way through, we need to reduce interfaces wherever possible, standardising and tuning data handoffs and interfaces at every other point. Undoubtedly, there will be different combinations in different markets and different instruments. As a result, regulatory arbitrage will give way to technology and latency arbitrage, and sooner or later operational risk will arise.

In this context, the path to best technology operations will become a valid discussion, especially as we move from the finely tuned car to the regular annual check-up.

19.7   THE FUTURE

The whole technology procurement environment will see significant change.

The front office will always be an area of outright competitive edge but, as middle and back office systems look to respectively tackle the information explosion and shake off legacy stovepipes of inefficiency, service provision will see yet another renaissance.

Already we are seeing new value proposition coming to market from market data to routing to systematic internaliser hosting offerings, to name a few. This will continue, fuelled by lower barriers to entry as a result of technology-enablement along with a release of energy to experiment and break paradigms. After all, there is no status quo in this as yet uncharted world.

Let's hope however that the innovators win over the protectionists who will be guarding comfort zones, and trying to protect processes not designed for the world we are about to enter.

Glossary

ABI	Association of British Insurers
AFB	Association of Foreign Banks
Algorithmic Trading	Trading using highly complex strategies which are managed in real-time market dealings by automated systems
Alpha	The most actively traded equities based upon the measures of market liquidity; the terms originate from the Exchanges which divided stocks into four categories – alpha, beta, gamma and delta ('the Greeks') – according to the frequency with which they were traded
AMF	Autorité des Marchés Financiers, the French regulator
AML	Anti-Money Laundering
APCIMS	Association of Private Client Investment Managers and Stockbrokers
Arbitrage	Investing in markets or assets, so that you gain by taking advantage of a price differential
ATS	Alternative Trading System
BaFin	Bundesanstalt für Finanzdienstleistungsaufsicht, the German regulator
Basel II	The 'International Convergence of Capital Measurement and Capital Standards – A Revised Framework', known as the second Basel Accord or Basel II for short, is the recommendation by bank supervisors and central bankers from the thirteen countries making up the Basel Committee on Banking Supervision (BCBS) to revise the international standards for measuring the adequacy of a bank's capital. The main aim is to avoid systemic risk in the markets, by ensuring a bank's capital reserves is able to cover their risk exposure.
BBA	British Bankers' Association

The Future of Investing in Europe's Markets after MiFID Edited by C. Skinner
© 2007 John Wiley & Sons, Ltd

BCBS	Basel Committee on Banking Supervision
BCD	Banking Coordination Directive
Benchmarking	Comparing specific processes with best practice; an approach proposed by the UK's FSA to measure 'Best Execution' by building a databank of dealer operations
BESG	'Best Execution' Subject Group, one of several MiFID Joint Working Group specialist groups
'Best Execution'	The principle that demands trading execution firms be able to prove they provided their clients with either the best price, cost or speed of processing for their trades
Beta	The second category of most actively traded equities (see Alpha)
Big Bang	Major changes to the UK Stock Markets implemented on 27 October 1986, when the traditional style of trading was replaced with a model of transparency, based upon the American practices of the time
BIS	Bank for International Settlements
Block order	An order submitted for the sale or purchase of a large quantity of securities
BMA	Bond Market Association
bps	A basis point: a unit of measure to describe the percentage change in the value of a financial instrument. One basis point represents 0.0001, and usually is associated with changes in interest rates and bond yields
BSA	Building Societies Association
Buy-side	Those who make the major investments in the markets, including Institutional Investors, Pension Funds, Hedge Funds and related Fund and Asset Managers
BVLP	Bolsa de Valores de Lisboa e Porto
CAC	Cotation Assistée en Continu, *Continuous Assisted Quotation*, an electronic trading system implemented at the Paris Bourse in 1986 for the handling of less liquid equities
CAC40	The CAC-40 Index is the benchmark tracking index for the Paris Bourse. Started in December of 1987 with a value of 1 000, the index is comprised of the forty largest and most liquid stocks trading on the Exchange.
CBOT	Chicago Board of Trade, merging with the Chicago Mercantile Exchange

CBX	Continuous Block Cross, an ECN platform capability to continuously match and fill block orders
CCP	Central CounterParty
CESR	Committee of European Securities Regulators
CFD	Contract for Difference: a product traded on margin which allows the investor to gain the returns of a share's performance (price, dividends, etc.) without the stamp duty costs
Chi-X	An MTF launched in the UK in 2006 by Instinet, which was then acquired by Nomura holdings
CME	Chicago Mercantile Exchange, recently merged with the Chicago Board of Trade
COB	Conduct Of Business, a set of rules applied to client dealings for investment firms
CPSS	Committee on Payment and Settlement Systems
CRD	Capital Requirements Directive, the European implementation of Basel II
Credit Derivatives	A contract which transfers the risk of a credit asset's returns falling below an agreed level, without transfer the underlying asset itself
CSD	Central Securities Depository
CSFB	Credit Suisse First Boston
CSSF	Commission de Surveillance du Secteur Financier (CSSF), the Luxembourg regulator
Dark Pool	A dark pool is a pool of liquidity which is not visible to the public, for example, orders that are on a broker's book or in a crossing network
Data Latency	See 'Latency'
DAX	Deutsche Aktien Xchange
DAX30	The DAX Index is the most commonly cited benchmark for measuring the returns posted by stocks on the Frankfurt Stock Exchange. Started in 1984 with a value of 1 000, the index is comprised of the thirty largest and most liquid equities traded on the Exchange taking its prices from Xetra
DMA	Direct Market Access, the ability for a buy-side firm to invest directly in financial instruments through automated systems without a requirement to use sell-side brokers for advice or, increasingly, execution
Double Banking	Where EU legislation covers the same ground as domestic legislation, and the two regimes are not fully aligned such that banks have to adhere to both
EASDAQ	The European version of NASDAQ which closed in 2004 to be relaunched as Equiduct

EBBO	European Best Bid Offer, a possibly corollary requirement of MiFID to reflect the USA's National Best Bid Offer under RegNMS
EC	European Commission
ECB	European Central Bank
ECN	Electronic Cross Network
ECU	European Currency Unit
EEA	European Economic Area, entered into force on 1 January 2004 to allow Norway, Iceland and Liechtenstein to participate in the EU while not assuming the full responsibilities of EU membership
EMU	Economic Monetary Union (EMU)
Equiduct	A pan-European trading exchange service for the smaller investment houses of Europe
EMS	Execution Management System, the technology application handling trade execution, usually FIX-enabled
EP	European Parliament
ESC	European union Securities Committee
ETC	Electronic Trade Confirmation
EUREX	Germany's highly successfully European electronic derivatives exchange, the world's largest derivatives exchange based on volume, jointly operated by the Deutsche Börse and Swiss Exchange
Execution	Executing a trade which has historically been performed exclusively by broker-dealers but is increasingly accessible through technology to direct access (see DMA)
FESCO	Forum of European Securities Commissions
FISD	Financial Information Services Division of the Software & Information Industry Association (SIIA)
FIX	Financial Information eXchange, the open system technical protocol for pre-trade technology connections in the investment markets
FIX FAST Protocol	FIX Adapted for STreaming, a development of FIX standards that compresses messages 80 %–90 % allowing existing networks to handle eight to nine times more data
FOA	Futures and Options Association
FSA	Financial Services Authority, the UK regulator
FSAP	Financial Services Action Plan
FTSE	Financial Times Stock Exchange, an independent company owned by The Financial Times and the London Stock Exchange (LSE) launched in 1995 to provide the indices for the LSE markets, although FTSE indices have existed since 1962

FTSE100	The Financial Times 100 Index, the most widely used benchmark for the performance of equities traded on the London Stock Exchange. Started in January 1984 with an initial value of 1 000, the index contains the hundred largest companies traded on the London Stock Exchange, based on market capitalisation
Fungibility	The measure of how easily one good may be exchanged or substituted by other examples of the same good at equal value, for example, gold rings and gold coins
FX	Foreign Exchange
GDP	Gross Domestic Product
Giovannini	The Giovannini Group is a group of financial-market participants, under the chairmanship of Alberto Giovannini, which advises the European Commission on financial market issues
Giovannini Barrier 1	Giovannini Group, as advisors to the European Commission, published a report in 2003 identifying fifteen barriers to creating efficient EU securities markets; Barrier 1 cites national differences in information technology and interfaces used by clearing and settlement providers
Goldplating	Where the domestic implementation of an EU Directive goes beyond the minimum necessary to comply by, for example, using wider legal terms than those in the directive, or extending the scope. Some Member States do this to make markets more attractive whilst others to make enforcement easier and more in line with existing domestic policy
Group of 30	International group of experts who recommend rules for clearing and settlement
Home State	European country of registration for a financial institution's main European office
Host State	European country where a financial institution transacts business in a European country other than in their home state
HSBC	Hongkong and Shanghai Banking Corporation
ICMA	International Capital Market Association
IFRS	International Financial Reporting Standards, a set of accounting standards
IMA	Investment Management Association
IOC	Immediate Or Cancel orders under RegNMS, although better known as the International Olympics Committee
IOI	Indications of Interest, the start of the trading process

IOSCO	International Organisation of Securities Commissions
IPO	Initial Public Offering
ISA	Individual Savings Accounts, a UK savings vehicle
ISD	Investment Services Directive of 1993
ISDA	International Swaps and Derivatives Association
ISE	International Securities Exchange
ISITC	International Securities association for Institutional Trade Communication
ISO	International Organisation for Standardisation, the global standards-setting body; also Inter-market Sweep Order, under RegNMS
KYC	Know Your Client, a key regulatory term relating to suitability and appropriateness within MiFID's conduct of business rules, as well as being critical to other Directives, such as the Third Money Laundering Directive
JPMC	JP Morgan Chase
J.P. Morgan	John Pierpont Morgan, 1837–1913, an American financier, banker, philanthropist, and art collector who dominated corporate finance and industrial consolidation during his time
JWG	Joint Working Group – the MiFID JWG was formed in May 2005 by the key industry associations of the FIX Protocol Ltd, ISITC Europe, the Reference Data User Group (RDUG) and SIIA/FISD
Lamfalussy	Baron Alexandre Lamfalussy who delivered the four-stage process for better regulation to the European Commission
Latency	In the trading world, data latency refers to the time delay of the transfer of data between the moment a trade is initiated to the moment the trade is executed. As volumes of data increases, this is a strategic advantage as firms handle larger volumes of data at faster speeds. Therefore, lower data latency is key
LIBA	London Investment Banking Association
LIFFE	London International Financial Futures and Options Exchange
Liquidity	The more an asset is bought and sold, the more liquid that asset becomes as price moves more rapidly.
Liquid Shares	Defined by EC Regulation 1287/2006 to be equities that have a free float of $> €500$ million, and a daily turnover $> €2$ million or an average 500 transactions a day
LSE	London Stock Exchange
Maastricht	The Treaty that created the Euro and EMU
MDS	Market Data System

MiFID	Markets in Financial Instruments Directive
MiFID Connect	Formed in November 2005 to represent the major UK Financial Market Trade Associations, including the Association of British Insurers (ABI), the Association of Private Client Investment Managers and Stockbrokers (APCIMS), the Association of Foreign Banks (AFB), the Bond Market Association, the British Bankers' Association (BBA), the Building Societies Association (BSA), the Futures and Options Association (FOA), the International Capital Market Association (ICMA), the Investment Management Association (IMA), the International Swaps and Derivatives Association (ISDA) and the London Investment Banking Association (LIBA)
MiFID JWG	See JWG
MTF	Multilateral Trading Facility
MTS	Mercato dei Titoli di Stato, market for government bonds
MTS Group	The European market for the trading of fixed income securities, with over 1 200 participants and an average transaction volumes of up to € 90 billion a day (single-counted)
NASD	National Association of Securities Dealers, a US trade association
NASDAQ	National Association of Securities Dealers Automated Quotations system, an American electronic stock exchange founded in 1971 by the National Association of Securities Dealers (NASD)
NBBO	National Best Bid Offer, a requirement of RegNMS
NMS	National Market System (see RegNMS)
NYSE	New York Stock Exchange
Open Outcry	The traditional form of trading floor, where broker-dealers physically stand together in an open exchange shouting out – open outcry – their bids and offers
Passporting	A MiFID ruling allowing investment firms to be registered under one national regulator in their 'home' state, and transact business anywhere in Europe under that registration
PEACH	Pan-European Automated Clearing House, part of the SEPA implementation
Project Boat	Formed in October 2006 by a group of large pan-European investments banks, to aggregate European trade data and market data

Project Turquoise	Formed in November 2006 by seven large pan-European investments banks to create an alternative exchange to Europe's existing national Exchanges
Proximity Hosting	Proximity hosting aims to squeeze milliseconds of time from the trade processing cycle, by physically placing trading engines next to execution venues
OMS	Order Management System, the technology application which manages order routing and handling, usually FIX-enabled
OTC	Over-the-Counter trading
RDUG	Reference Data User Group
RegNMS	Regulation National Market Systems, USA regulation implemented in 2006 to eradicate the practice of trade-through
Regulatory Creep	Where regulatory burdens are increased by guidance or other non-statutory means
RM	Regulated Markets
SEAQ	Stock Exchange Automated Quotation, the London Stock Exchange's electronic price quotation system for non UK securities
SEC	Securities and Exchange Commission, the USA regulator
Sell-side	Those who provide services to the investors, including the Investment Banks, Boutique Investment Firms, Brokers and Dealers
SEPA	Single Euro Payments Area, the creation of simplified pan-European Automated Clearing House structures for cross-border payments within the European Union and, particularly, the Eurozone
SI	Systematic Internaliser, a new term introduced by MiFID to describe firms that trade in an *'organized, frequent and systematic'* manner from their own book of business
SIIA	Software & Information Industry Association
STP	Straight Through Processing
Swaption	A financial instrument granting the owner an option to enter into an interest rate swap
SWIFT	Society for Worldwide Interbank Financial Telecommunication, the Brussels-based standards body and infrastructure that enables the global processing of high-value payment transactions
SWX	Swiss Exchange

TARGET	Trans-european Automated Real-time Gross settlement Express Transfer system, the real-time gross settlement system of the central banks of Europe for the processing of cross-border transfers throughout the European Union
TARGET2	The second generation development of the TARGET system, implemented by the ECB in 2007
TCA	Transaction Cost Analysis
TCF	Treating Customers Fairly, a term coined by the UK's FSA in relation to client business handling rules
TDM	Trade Data Monitor
Trade-Through	The execution of an order in a market at a price that is inferior to a price displayed in another market; the USA regulation, RegNMS, prohibits such activity
Transparency	The MiFID principle that ensures trades are published, rather than being covered purely internally
TWAP	Time Weighted Average Price
UBS	Union Bank of Switzerland
UCITS	Undertakings for Collective Investments in Transferable Securities, a form of fund management product
virt-x	The company, virt-x Exchange Limited, was founded in 2001 as a cross-border trading platform for pan-European blue chip stocks
VWAP	Volume Weighted Average Price
Xetra	eXchange Electronic TRAding, an electronic securities trading system operated by Deutsche Börse from Frankfurt that supplies pricing to the DAX

Index

Index compiled by Terry Halliday